Praise for *A New Silen*

"As the external circumstances of life change enormously in our world at this time, the capacity for inner resilience, strength, and wisdom to carry us through is receiving deep attention. Beverly Lanzetta's study of the inner life, practical orientation to personal spiritual practices and guidance for professing vows is an invaluable, engaging, and inspirational resource. The selection of journal questions and reflections which have been provided will nourish and sustain the soul in the face of current challenges. *I am so looking forward to having this book in my hands!*"

—**Bernadette Flanagan, PBVM, Ph.D., Chair, Spirituality Institute for Research & Education (Dublin) and author of** *Embracing Solitude: Women and New Monasticism*

"*A New Silence* is good company for the soul. Like a true best friend, Beverly hears the longing of your heart and points you inward to your own deepest truth. She reminds you that a Great Mystery is at work in your life, and she gives you a clear process by which to unveil It, and then to live It. Whatever your circumstances of work or family, and whatever your beliefs and difficulties, you will find your path greatly illumined by this book."

—**Fran Grace, PhD, Professor of Religious Studies and Steward of the Meditation Program at Univ. of Redlands**

"Why is the life of an "intercontemplative" monk relevant to our lives and way of living? *A New Silence* will likely be the pre-eminent guidebook to a new way of being human and living as a monk in the world. It addresses our call, coming from the deep, inner spirit, to lead a life of healing. It speaks to the universal suffering of all humans on this fragile planet and the massive loss of sentient life being extinguished by ecological upheaval. To say that *A New Silence* is exceptional and thorough doesn't capture the quality of Beverly's beautiful writing, and the intensity of mystical experience the book evokes."

—**Rev. Evan W. Kligman, MD. MDiv., Executive Director of the Welcome Centre Medical Clinic for Refugees, Vancouver, BC.**

"Beverly Lanzetta, in her new book, *A New Silence*, offers the reader a broad spiritual vision accompanied by very useful spiritual practices. For those who desire to deepen their own monastic way of life, this book is a compelling one."

—Michael Peterson, OSB, Chairman of the Board, Monastic Interreligious Dialogue and Director of Oblates, St. John's Abbey

"*A New Silence* articulates the allurement of God's call to contemplatives in the world towards deeper union with the Beloved. A life rooted in a contemplative rhythm can feel far away for those of us in marriages, partnerships, and with children. Beverly Lanzetta tips those illusions over to reveal the unopened gifts of these relationships on the contemplative path by offering a way to reorient your life around the "one thing necessary" in your context. Drawing from the deep pockets of her wisdom, prayer, and practice in the contemplative traditions, Lanzetta gifts readers with a new perspective on how to become a universal monk in the world. The poetical timbre of her prose will graft stories, insights, and ways of being onto your contemplative longing. *A New Silence* invites you to take responsibility for that longing and embody it as a lived vocation of the heart. Destined to become a contemplative classic, it belongs in the hands of any reader who takes the contemplative life seriously and with a shot of joy."

—Paul Swanson, Sr. Program Designer, Center for Action and Contemplation

A NEW SILENCE

Spiritual Practices
and Formation
for the Monk
Within

Beverly Lanzetta

BLUE SAPPHIRE BOOKS

SEBASTOPOL

A New Silence: Spiritual Practices and Formation for the Monk Within
Copyright © 2020 by Beverly Lanzetta
All rights reserved.

Blue Sapphire Books website http://bluesapphirebooks.com

Cover and interior design: Nelson Kane

PUBLISHER'S CATALOGING-IN-PUBLICATION DATA
(Prepared by The Donohue Group, Inc.)

Names: Lanzetta, Beverly, author.
Title: A new silence : spiritual practices and formation for the monk
    within / Beverly Lanzetta.
Description: Sebastopol [California] : Blue Sapphire Books, [2020] |
    Includes bibliographical references and index.
Identifiers: ISBN 9781732343832 | ISBN 9781732343849 (ebook)
Subjects: LCSH: Spiritual life. | Spirituality. | Monastic and religious life. |
    Meditation. | Interfaith worship.
Classification: LCC BL624 .L363 2020 (print) | LCC BL624 (ebook) | DDC
    204.4--dc23

Printed in the United States of America

Contents

We cannot speak of God,
without having first achieved an interior silence.

It is not a discourse about any church, religion, or science.

It is a discourse about a symbol, not about a concept.

God is not the only symbol to indicate what the word "God"
wishes to transmit.

It is a discourse that inevitably completes itself again in
a new silence.

—Raimon Panikkar

Preface

I T WAS DURING THE 1970s, when increasing numbers of people
abandoned organized religions to explore personal spirituality and
individual faith, that my teaching life began. What I spoke about then
(and now) is the ancient longing to seek and devote one's self to the
Divine. And, from the beginning, the spiritual seekers most drawn to this
shift in affiliation were explorers on the edge—those who were between
religions, had abandoned faith, sought refuge in esoteric philosophies,
were interspiritual or multi-religious, or belonged to a faith tradition but
simply could not abide the claim to higher moral authority by religions
that betray love, and dominate, exclude, violate, or oppress.

The people who early on formed a community of learners with me
were not, by any means, a band of radical sisters and brothers. Rather,
they wished to discover the universal principles that uphold and inspire
every authentic search for truth. At the time, I offered contemplative
classes drawn from my own life-altering experience of Divine Presence,
and later, as well, from scholarship of the world's mystical traditions.
Even then, in those tender, nascent days of teaching, I knew there was
a mystical path unique to our times that had not yet been formalized—
could not be entirely found in historical texts—and was being birthed
in our souls. This was a path that appealed to people who were standing

between worlds, wondering how to cross the chasm between a past they could not abide and a future they could not yet see. And so, with many people who longed to know more and be more, whose souls were parched from a lack of sustenance, a forty-plus year experiment began.

Recently, I decided to share my journey—which has been essentially the transmission of a distinctive monastic or mystical path—with a wider audience in the hope that it serves as a guide for anyone also wishing to probe beneath the surface of personality and social gestures to bring out our sacred inheritance. I situate this path within the context of new traditions of contemplative wisdom, which are emerging from the universal mystical ground that has nourished the various monastic impulses throughout history. One of the striking aspects of these new traditions is that the primordial source of wisdom from which they appear is ever new, granting access to novel applications in each age, and igniting the flame of love in our souls.

Consciously or not, each of our inner lives and various spiritual commitments are profoundly indebted to and affected by the world's great mystical traditions. It would be false to imply that what is offered here is wholly new or unattached from our common inheritance. And, yet, what I share herein also is uniquely of its own time, having a particular focus on this moment in history in which there is a dire need to speak for the soul, and for the voices around the world yearning for meaning and love.

A New Silence

"WE CANNOT SPEAK OF GOD," writes the distinguished theologian, Raimon Panikkar, "without having first achieved an interior silence." Every discourse about God, thus, "inevitably completes itself again in a new silence."[1] Because Mystery is ineffable and unending, no word can fully capture it, and no one can possess it. Our minds always will be limited in their capacity to know the Holy. For this reason, mystical texts often are enigmatic, even unreadable, functioning to "inebriate" and "bewilder," thereby generating an opening for the inflow of Presence.

As individuals and a global community, many have entered a new silence, a long pause in which our social agreements and our ways of thinking are broken or stretched, creating space for a new revelatory landscape to blossom in our world. I explicitly name this span of vulnerability affecting our minds, hearts, and spirits, "revelatory" because it is this period when the Divine breaks into history and calls us to listen to Wisdom's prophetic voice and gaze again on Her suffering face. Searching for the roots of divine disclosure, we find that this profoundly merciful path requires a deeper surrender, and a self-abandonment of ego and will.

We discover our conversion in many different ways. We enter a new silence at the moment in which the wave of millennia of religious exclusion and separateness breaks. We enter a new silence as we learn about interspirituality and practice multi-religious or hybrid religions. We enter a new silence when people of faith disavow privileged access to salvation. We enter a new silence as we mourn injustice and welcome the world's disenfranchised into the circle of love. We enter a new silence in concern for the ravaging of our glorious Earth, in compassionate solidarity with all its inhabitants. We enter a new silence when we bear the savage pain of war and identify with the totality of suffering. We enter a new silence when we follow the path of *via feminina*—the way of the divine feminine—and co-create another way of living and being. We enter a new silence as we practice nonviolence and elevate love to its rightful place in solving the world's problems.

And yet, someday, *our* new silence will be swept into another new silence; its revelatory discourse will not be the only or the last. Because it is holy, it is beyond measure and, therefore, it will never become dogmatic. It will never allow someone to say, "You don't belong."

A new silence is the place of co-creating, the freedom of that liminal place between realities, where we are at the quickening moment of new insight, open to what the Creator has to say to us today. At this juncture, we do not look back to what this tradition, or this hierarchy, or this person demanded. Nor do we automatically reject those things or anything else. Rather, gathering in our heart centuries of wisdom, we listen for the Divine voice anew. Our guiding moral imperative is to be passionately devoted to honoring and protecting the sacred value of creation.

A Theology of Radical Openness

ELSEWHERE I HAVE CALLED the discourse about God prevalent during this period of new silence, "a theology of radical openness."[2] This is a theology without walls, a theology of incompletion and continual renewal.[3] It is a mystical theology that leans toward the instability of language, where reality is dream-like, metaphorical, intuitive, and poetic. It is the overcoming of linguistic determination—where all that is has already been said—to probe language's mystical underpinnings, to new ways of speaking, and to the forging of a new humanity. It teaches us to cherish the rare privilege of being born.

It is a condition of being in the world that is necessary in order to bear (in the world) the divinity of creation. As a spiritual practice, it never can be absolutely achieved or made fully transparent. Rather, it is an orientation that strengthens our ability to withstand the intimacy of life, and the inevitable loss of identity that makes the mind tremble and lays the heart bare. It is a call to a faith that is non-dogmatic and non-absolute in the sense that it keeps the door open for other theologies and beliefs to dialogue with us, and we with them. Truth claims do not need to become exclusive; we can adore *and* question our faith, inviting communion with multiple expressions of wisdom. This approach recognizes the spiritual necessity to challenge what is inauthentic and damaging in our religious and social imagination.

The contemplative process that fuels our hoped-for liberation begins with the unsaying of constructed categories and generational sins, taking apart of all that stands in the way of genuine intimacy and community. The path then progresses into the more elusive and obscure emptiness of *via feminina* to experience injustice and the violation of love and beauty in our world. It is here, in mystical union with the Divine Mother, that our soul's capacity is expanded in order to become theophanic—like unto God.

Of all the elements that mark our period, the most important is an invitation to reach across the chasm of fear and seize the spiritual right born with us into the world: that we are made in the Divine image, that we are constituted to bear holiness and to co-create with the Divine.

In some form, and using different religious vocabularies, the world's religions promise that intrinsic to being is the presence of the Divine in our depth. This fact is not dependent on acceptance or recognition or faith; instead, it is inherent in us, in a similar way that atoms comprise matter. It means that we can never escape our graced destiny. The Divine within is always present, waiting to be realized. The monk focuses his or her life on this goal: of being one with God, liberated from *samsara*, truly awake. The various practices and virtues that govern a contemplative orientation point the way forward.

Our place in history is distinguished by the intersection of the sacred and profane, the mystical and the mundane interpenetrating each other. It marks the struggle to establish an ultimate concern for life on Earth by putting away our craven idols and emerging out of ignorance into wisdom. We are damaged; our souls are torn; our hearts often muddled. Yet the inner voice repeats the call. That everything is already new; we simply have to realize and claim it. It is within that bewildered space of uncertainty and confusion that a theology of radical openness is revealed.

We are tasked with making deification—the capacity of each person to achieve holiness—real; that is, living in such a way that the integration and embodiment of the divine-human, especially the relationship of the physical and spiritual, is woven into the fabric of daily life. It means redefining personhood, not as fallen or wandering, but as the self who carries the seeds of transformation and future renewal. It is to change the focus of humanity's progression in history from deficit to surplus, from deficiency to strength. This is the vital shift in consciousness needed to embrace the blessedness of creation and to assist in the building of a more holy and peaceful Earth community.

Intercontemplative

THE THEOLOGICAL STRUCTURE that undergirds this work is rooted in what I call an "intercontemplative" orientation. I use the term "intercontemplative," rather than interspiritual or interfaith, to signify the dialogue of religious experience as it reaches into deep states of contemplation and silent prayer, which is based on an attitude of mature interiority within one's self and with respect to other religions. Here, conceptual differences fade, as practitioners *experience* that every authentic spirituality affirms a greater self and the inner reality of enlightenment or salvation.

In my experience, intercontemplative spirituality has several interlocking modes or phrases. Operating in its active mode, the person engages with prayer, meditation, study, and worship within one's own tradition and in an interspiritual or cross-spiritual sharing of the treasures of the world's religions. The intercontemplative person is inspired by wisdom wherever it is found and recognizes that the healing of divisions within us and with others is a divine imperative today. Panikkar offers an apt description of the intercontemplative explorer:

> He starts by making a real heartfelt, unselfish effort—a bold and hazardous one—to understand the belief, the world, the archetypes, the culture, the mythical and conceptual background, the emotions and historical association of his fellows from inside. In short, he attempts an existential incarnation of himself into another world— which obviously involves prayer, initiation, study, and worship. He does this not by way of trial but rather with a spirit of faith in a truth that transcends us and a goodness that upholds us when we truly love our neighbor.[4]

Another phase is receptive or passive. That is, it is the Divine action in the soul of the person. While the active phase involves what we do to understand, pray, and integrate, the passive is when God acts in us and we are without self-willing. This is an entirely supernatural state of being. We cannot summon it or make it happen. It is grace, Holy Spirit, *wu wei*, absolute nothingness (*mu*) drawing us into a pathless path.

Surrendered to God's action in us, we are led to a third intercontemplative mode. Here, the Divine Presence plants new seeds of wisdom brought from the infinite ground of being. These seeds—not previously known or expressed—take root in the tender intimacy of the soul's participation in the Divine and grow into a living garden of newly flowering theologies, practices, and teachings. The soul's capacity for wisdom is expanded, and what flows from it is highly original and co-creative. It is at this juncture that we live and participate in the great journey of deification on Earth.

This intercontemplative orientation affirms that each person's capacity to bring about new religious thought and experience is not the special preserve of the few enlightened or elevated ones. Rather, this birthing is occurring now, in each moment, in our souls. As an "existential incarnation," intercontemplative practice calls us to heal divisions in ourselves and in the world—to become attuned to subtle levels of exclusion, superiority, sexism, racism, etc.—and to labor with love to mend these fragile and fractured parts of ourselves, and in others. This is the incredible mystery of being alive, of being in a body, of incarnation, and the preciousness of being in this moment, giving birth each day to a new world of compassion.

· ◆ ·

THE CHAPTERS that follow explore a mystical framework for living with a theology of openness, a *via feminina* theology, that—due to an incredible depth of feeling—prevents me from designating a final Name for it. The fact that there is no Name does not mean Mystery is nameless, only this: How could I name it? It is Most Holy and Unnamable Presence.

Through the study of the works of wisdom, our souls develop a capacity for insight and depth. We are drawn from the superficial and external into a deep engagement with life, the kind the stirs the mind and bewilders the heart. Our entire body, mind, and spirit participates in an excavation of the holy, the pure source within us that has never been harmed and knows how to be wise.

Every sincere quest pushes the boundaries between finitude and infinity, casts us into the wild abandon of space, to tumble and twirl, to cry out in anguish, to be awed by the intense Light, and to thereby discover and admit—yes, admit!—that we have what we need inside. If our path today is about anything, it is this: we accept our co-creation with God and strive together toward the embodiment of sacred life on Earth.

As in my other works, I hope this book speaks to you, whether you claim allegiance to no particular religion, identify as interspiritual or multi-religious, or are rooted in a faith tradition. While there may appear to be a wide distinction among seekers, in point of fact there is much similarity of intention when we reach into the mystical depth.

The fact of a monastic way of life in the world that is intercontemplative, unifying, and co-creative is the result of great faith. When we willingly admit that we will never know the whole discourse about God, have not said everything there is to say, and do not exclusively hold the truth, we discover the gift of *a new silence.*

Beverly Lanzetta
Living in the Desert, 2020

A Note on Religious Language

FINDING WORDS adequate to describe the radiance of our souls and the tender gift of life is always difficult. Too often religious language has been used as a tool of exclusion and pain, sensitizing me to how others hear and read words. For this reason, whenever possible, I alternate between a more generic—Great Mystery, Divine, Source, Emptiness, and Creator—and more religion-specific—God, Divine Feminine, Hagia Sophia, Allah, Dao, and Great Spirit—language when describing ultimacy. All are symbols of an ineffable reality that never will be fully captured in language or experience. These symbolic words open to an infinite horizon, and I employ them interchangeably out of respect for the diversity of divine names used by people around the globe.

Additionally, I use the term "theology" to indicate conscious reflection on ultimate or spiritual realities. From the Greek, *theos* and *logos*—theology signifies study, rational inquiry, and mystical insight about God. The term isn't strictly applicable to the variety of the world's religions, especially Buddhism that does not focus on a personal god, but it is often used today to speak about insights into ultimate reality that are without confessional restrictions.

My use of religious language is non-dogmatic and non-absolute in the sense that I keep the door open to dialogue with other theologies and divine realities. To speak about the unspeakable requires symbol, metaphor, parable, and poetry. This approach is not a "what" but a "how"—a process of relating to life that is continually receptive to the coming of an unimaginable gift, which we do not and cannot ever possess.

Thus, the concepts of religion—god-language, theology, spirituality, etc.—point to an ultimately freeing state that travels within every utterance. Viewed in this way, the languages of religions offer a rich tapestry of insight into the sacred dimension of life, which other language structures do not access in quite the same way. It is my hope, as you encounter the various religious symbols used in the pages to follow, that you will be reminded of the many ways the human heart praises the unknown, and of a new silence that flows through all these words.

PART ONE

Contemplations

❖

The person on a spiritual journey contemplates
the divine nature, to develop a nobler and simpler
consciousness. He or she is in search of purity of
heart, and any authentic spiritual path will guide
the seeker to cultivate a heightened awareness and
a bond of love. Among the many ways that a soul
grows in holiness is through the development of
divine virtues: humility, compassion, nonviolence,
simplicity, love. In the following chapters, we
contemplate these states of being that
expand our depth and strengthen
the center point of
stillness.

❖

ONE

Contemplation on Humility

HUMILITY is one of the most personally relevant and meaningful virtues. It is an orientation of great tenderness—the gentle, kind, and quiet. It has to flower in your soul. You have to breathe in its fragrance and feel the quality of being closer to the Holy, to realize why humility is the central work of the monk. Because it is elusive. It is easily diverted by self-will, by the need to be recognized, by petty complaint and judgment, by gossip and refusal to forgive, and by worldly ambition. It gathers strength when we are vulnerable, when we admit that we need each other, when we open our hearts without shame or blame, when we speak the truth—even and often especially—when the other person refuses to receive or hear the truth.

The word "humility" comes from the Latin word *humus* (earth), specifically *humilitas*, a noun related to the adjective *humilis*, which may be translated as "humble," but also as "grounded," "from the earth," or "low." To be of the earth is to know that one day we return to the dust of our ancestors. It is a realization that we exist in an interdependent circle of relations. We need each other.

Humility is not false modesty, self-denying, or destructively ascetic. It is, instead, the consequence of experiencing grandeur—a sunset, starry night, rose petal. We are brought to our knees, our hearts overwhelmed with love, when Holy Wisdom speaks. When we encounter the words "humble" and "humility," let us remember that they are in response to awe.

The spoke around which the spiritual journey rotates, humility calls each seeker to cultivate a pure heart. It is the practice of self-emptying before the Divine, and the posture of adoration that is the special sign of the monk in us. The fruit of great insight, it is the gateway to transcendent knowledge. The state of humility is subtle and reminds us that "our proud attempts at upward climbing will bring us down," claims St. Benedict's Rule, "whereas to step downwards in humility is the way to lift our spirit up towards God."[1]

It is the sincere desire to be less rather than more, poor in worldly accomplishments rather than rich, empty rather than attached, and nameless rather than honored. Humility also refers to modesty, and the absence of arrogance and pride. By discerning what is meaningful in our lives and what is not, humility gives us the strength to break through the wounds of the ego. It guides us each day toward love of God and of creation.

In religious texts, the humble person is described as insignificant, inferior, subservient, lowly, or unpretentious. These attributes can be jarring, and evoke a sense of unworthiness or punishment, especially by marginalized communities that have suffered injustice. Through a punitive, rather than a mystical approach to instilling the virtue of humility, many of us have been shamed or labeled as sinners, which can lead to a lifelong condition of resistance or anger.

However, the spiritual implications of the truly humble convey a rich quality of being, highlighting that it is the brave person, the compassionate person, who has the strength to look within. Practiced daily, humility strengthens your being and provides fortitude for the spiritual path ahead. It will bind your soul to the infinite ground of love. It is a truth that cannot be taken away and, as such, is the antithesis of every type of control.

This chapter begins with a kaleidoscope of writings on humility, with my reflection on each text, to illustrate its important place in the world's wisdom traditions. This section is followed by ten meditations on a humble heart.

Issachar Ber of Zlotshov

The essence of the worship of God and of all the *mitzvot* is to attain the state of humility. . . . One is simply a channel for the divine attributes. One attains such humility through the awe of God's vastness, through realizing that there is no place empty of Him. Then one comes to the state of *ayin*, which is the state of humility. One has no independent self and is contained, as it were, in the Creator. This is the meaning of the [Exodus 3:6]: "Moses hid his face, for he was in awe. . ." Through his experience of awe, Moses attained the hiding of his face, that is, he perceived no independent self. Everything was part of divinity![2]

THE PRACTICE OF HUMILITY is the greatest blessing (*mitzvot*), writes Rabbi Ber of Zlotshov, which one attains through the awe of God's vastness and the mystical state of *ayin*—which is nothingness—or no independent self. When Moses hid his face on Mount Sinai before God's radiant splendor, he was overcome by the intensity of the Divine Presence. God was not an object of his desire; rather the force of Light removed the illusion of a separate self and he was plunged into direct experience of divine unity.

The first step of humility is to respect at all times the sense of awe felt before the Creator. Drive away your forgetfulness. Be alive to the beauty of the world, and to God's commandments. In veneration of spiritual gifts, our heart is pierced by remorse for all we do not give. But, in relinquishing the ego, and accepting that we will never attain perfection, the soul is drawn into the most intimate mercy. Now, the false self is transcended, freedom floods the soul, and we are truly alive.

Humility implies radical trust in divine reality. Even though we yearn for mystical union, we cannot command God to be intimate with us. Humility arises when we realize that the Divine comes freely and in its own time. It is not something that we possess or own. If you want to be a contemplative or a monk in the world, it doesn't mean your desire will be granted. God has plans for you, but it may not be those plans (the one you have); that is humility. The will creeps into subtle places, trying to conform our heart to its demands. Humility says, accept the limits of your situation and the fullness of your life the way it is. Humility says, be content with where God is taking you. Be content with what you are given.

The humble person, who has given up independence and separateness, is "contained in the Creator." Drawn into God's inner life, the surrendered soul now perceives that the world and all beings are part of divinity, united in the holy of holies. The mystery of our belonging to the universe of love is that when we are humbled by *ayin*—nothingness—we return to the beginning, in intimacy with God and all creation.

Seven Grandfather Teachings, The Potawatomi Nation

According to the story told by the Seven Grandfather Teachings, long ago, a messenger discovered that the Neshnabék were living their life in a negative way. Some had hate for others, displayed disrespectful actions, were afraid, told lies, and cheated. Others revealed pride or were full of shame. During his journey, the messenger came across a child chosen by the Seven Grandfathers to live a good life. He was taught the lessons of Love, Respect, Bravery, Truth, Honesty, Humility, and Wisdom. The Seven Grandfathers told him, "Each of these teachings must be used with the rest. You cannot have Wisdom without Love, Respect, Bravery, Honesty, Humility, and Truth."

Humility is to know that we are a part of creation. We must always consider ourselves equal to one another. We should never think of ourselves as being better or worse than anyone else. Humility comes in many forms. This includes compassion, calmness, meekness, gentleness, and patience. We must reflect on how we want to present ourselves to those around us. We must be aware of the balance and equality with all of life, including humans, plants, and animals.[3]

INDIGENOUS SPIRITUAL practices instill in their people that everything is a gift. The natural laws of interdependence and self-restraint govern communal life. The humble person lives selflessly, and with respect for the sacredness of all relations. The cycles of land and participation in the natural world establish their place in the cosmos. Do not become arrogant and self-important. Praise the accomplishments of all, finding balance within yourself and in all living things.

Each Indigenous community is a sacred place, a living, spiritual entity of learning, teaching, living, healing, and ritual. Native elders say that trees talk to each other. The ecology of the forest—the soil, fungus, squirrel, deer, fire, and rain—survives through unity. Ceremonies re-enact the cycle of life and death and the dependence of the people who have been formed by the creative forces of the universe. This humble awareness of human reliance on the wisdom of nature and on the benefi-cence of ancestors is embodied in the circle of life, described in this vision by Black Elk, Oglala Sioux holy man.

> Then I was standing on the highest mountain of all, and round about beneath me was the whole hoop of the world. And while I stood there I saw more than I can tell and I understand more than I saw; for I was seeing in a sacred manner the shapes of all things in the spirit, and the shape of all shapes as they must live together like one being. And I saw that the sacred hoop of my people was one of many hoops that make one circle, wide as daylight and as starlight, and in the center grew one mighty flowering tree to shelter all the children of one mother and one father. And I saw that it was holy.[4]

Sirach 3:17–24

My child, perform your tasks with humility; then you will be loved by those whom God accepts. The greater you are, the more you must humble yourself; so you will find favor in the sight of the Lord. For great is the might of the Lord; but by the humble he is glorified. Neither seek what is too difficult for you, nor investigate what is beyond your power. Reflect upon what has been commanded, for what is hidden is not your concern. Do not meddle in matters that are beyond you, for more than you can understand has been shown you. For their conceit has led many astray, and wrong opinion has impaired their judgment.[5]

THIS PASSAGE from the Hebrew Bible reminds us that one of the most important aspects of the spiritual life is becoming ever more attuned to God's will for us. While we may all desire a certain kind of life, we are called, instead, to be receptive to what Spirit wants for us.

This process often involves an internal struggle between where we think we belong and where we truly belong. At some time, on the spiritual path we will suffer giving up worldly desire for the will of the Divine. We become aware that we crave the status of being well-respected in our profession, and the prestige, pleasure, and attention it affords. While we are able to spellbind people with words and arguments, we perhaps do not know who we are or experience our own heart.

In these moments, the practice of personal discernment is important because we assert our wills in subtle ways that seem right, but in fact are contrary to where the Divine is calling us. For example, we practice certain forms of austerities—extreme fasting or self-denial of companionship—that we read about in religious books. We try to be ascetic, but this is not where the deep self is called. Or, we have pride in our work and seek praise, but the work itself damages us in ways that only the Spirit knows. When we deny or resist inner guidance, the spiritual ego is asserted, and we experience the pain of living a path that is false.

We learn these lessons with difficulty. We pride ourselves on the ability to make our own decisions, to not be affected and coerced by any person or group. But this passage from Sirach reminds us that as we move deeper into the Divine heart, intellectual knowledge is of little benefit. Truth has to be experienced. If truth is not experienced, then knowledge is only another acquisition, and not the catalyst for transformation. Thus, the path of humility is true wisdom.

The Sixth Patriarch's Dharma Jewel Platform Sutra, Chapter III

Inner humility is merit and the outer practice of reverence is virtue.... Those who cultivate merit and virtue in their thoughts do not slight others, but always respect them. Those who slight others and do not cut off the "me and mine" are without merit. The vain and unreal self-nature is without virtue, because of the "me and mine," because of the greatness of the "self," and because of the constant slighting of others. Arrogance causes harm. Humility brings benefit.[6]

THE SIXTH PATRIARCH, Master Hui Neng (638–714 CE), reprimands his followers for their arrogant attitude. Some refuse to bow to the master, conceited about their great knowledge of Buddhadharma; others believe practice makes them better than everyone else, more talented. These attitudes shackle the mind and hinder liberation.

Holding all sentient beings in friendship and esteem is a Buddhist virtue—the realization that there is no place for pride in the sangha. When we are proud, we are like "the tall, dry grasses that do not bend down low in the face of the winds," says Thich Nhat Hahn, "and are broken to pieces."[7] How like the dry grasses is our refusal to love, to welcome the stranger, and to weep over the loss of life! How often do we forget the simple act of being with another person, and listening to his or her story with compassion and understanding? When our words are gentle, and our hearts truly humble, we bring merit to all our relations, and to the unending circle of creation.

The humble mind can readily recognize its own defilements of craving (or greed), aversion (or hatred) and ignorance, thereby embarking on the path of enlightenment and liberation. Buddhists cultivate merit through seven prerequisites: constant delight in holding the precepts; cultivation of the methods for becoming free of the world; freedom from arrogance and pride, and compassion for all beings; passionlessness; abide in undifferentiated truth; cultivation of discernment and calming of mind; freedom from fear or alarm.[8] Through the practice of inner virtue, the devotee develops great humility, emptiness of self, and compassion for the pain and striving of earthly beings.

Philippians 2: 7-8

Let the same mind be in you that was in Christ Jesus, who, though he was in the form of God, did not regard equality with God as something to be exploited, but emptied himself, taking the form of a servant, being born in human likeness. And being found in human form, he humbled himself and became obedient to the point of death—even death on a cross.[9]

I CHERISH this passage as one of the most profound in the Christian Bible. The concept of divine self-emptying (*kenosis*) weaves through Christian spirituality and is the exemplar of what it means to mystically participate in dying to the self.[10]

In the reading from Issachar Ber of Zlotshov, we read humility from the human side; that is, we are humbled by the awesome majesty of God. In this case, we encounter God's voluntary assumption of humility for the sake of humanity. Through emptiness of self—when we are humble, patient, and obedient—we reciprocate the Divine's generous self-offering. As we empty ourselves of selfish motives, ego, and will, we—in whatever small way—participate in God's vulnerability.

In the Christian story, the death of Jesus on the cross draws us into the mystery of sacrifice, the wonder of the body, and the immanence hidden in transcendence. The cross collapses the ontological distance of the transcendent God and refocuses our vision on the immediacy of the divine person. Jesus bears in the body the radical self-emptying of divinity—he offers himself for the sake of the world. This self-offering that was "in the beginning" was "made flesh" (Jn. 1: 1-14).

Here, we are confronted with the tenderness of the self-emptying God who, in utter vulnerability, lays its God-self at the feet of this world. God dies *for* us, *in* us, *with* us, and *through* us. The passion of giving fully shatters every construct, even that which names divinity. God dies not only for the sake of the world; God dies to God. Ethics, morals, and justice are inadequate to the pain that is inflicted and the suffering that is endured. No theory, metaphysics, or karmic explanation can defend the radical suffering.

This passage from Philippians is an encounter with the presence of divine intimacy and limitless love that pierces our souls with the world's suffering. Such moments of transcendence represent the radical reversal of self-interest: sacrifice and adoration, death and rebirth, humility and gratitude. Self-emptying of the ego is universal because it is present in every religious story and permeates all beings and spheres of reality.

The Life of Francis, Chapter 6

He often used to make this statement: "When a man is in God's eyes, that he is and nothing more." Therefore, judging that it was foolish to be elated by worldly approval, he rejoiced in insults and was saddened by praise. He preferred to hear himself blamed rather than praised, knowing that blame would lead him to amend his life, while praise would drive him to a fall. And so when people extolled the merits of his holiness, he commanded one of the friars to do the opposite and to impress upon his ears insulting words. When that friar, although unwilling, called him boorish and mercenary, unskilled and useless, he would reply with inner joy shining on his face, "May the Lord bless you, my beloved son, for it is you that speak the very truth and what the son of Peter Bernardone should hear."[11]

ST. FRANCIS was a living example of kenosis. He sought to participate in the humility of Christ with his entire being and to serve others in perfect poverty. He believed that humility "was the guardian and the ornament of all the virtues. In his own estimation he was nothing but a sinner, ... and strove to build upon this virtue [of humility] *like an architect laying the foundation*."[12]

The desire for worldly approval is unwise, because a person is only what he or she is in God's eyes and nothing more. If the world applauds our accomplishments, it is a waste of time and energy. Instead, Francis rejoiced in insults and was saddened by praise. Although he practiced an extreme type of self-denial—perhaps even an excessive one—his example offers wisdom for our journey.

When we have been hurt by what someone said or did, or felt misunderstood, Francis reminds us to let all that go. Do not let harsh words or unjust actions become a spiritual wound. Do not let offense impress you. Rather, use the situation to plant seeds of humility in your soul. Francis' detachment from, or indifference to, insult encourages us to refuse to be influenced by what others think. Such musings are a foolish waste of time because in the end we answer to God alone.

Francis felt he should "despise the fame of transitory praise, suppress the arrogance of bloated bragging, and reject the lies of deceptive pretense."[13] The ego, attached to approval and admiration, protects and elevates a false identity. To counter the need for praise, Francis wanted to be "like a discarded utensil." When he preached, he did not spare himself embarrassment in bringing up his faults. His honest self-disclosure caused his listeners to feel contrition, realizing how far away they were from rectifying their sins. Francis showed that he was human, he also had faults, and he also suffered, teaching that in imperfection is perfection.

Francis wanted to be a subject rather than a superior, to obey the Divine rather than to command others. He thwarted attempts by religious authorities or his community to claim leadership, lamenting any traces in him of arrogance, self-righteousness, or pride. He knew how harmful it is to deny or conceal our inner motivations and fears. How often have we been too proud to admit our weaknesses or vulnerabilities, even to ourselves? Too proud to confess where we have disobeyed our own conscience, too proud to suffer, and too proud to be aware of the pain we have caused?

The virtues of the humble heart—to be less, inferior, lowly, silent—refer to a divine principle rather than a specific defect. These words do not imply that we are inferior to other people or called to be debased. Rather, the humble heart fasts from self-promotion, with respect for the immensity of the Creator. As you dethrone your ego, space is created for holiness to enter. The humble servants who have changed our world have given their hearts away, welcoming the Divine into their souls, and pouring love into creation.

Bhagavad Gita (11:35–42)

Arjuna said: O Master of the senses, it is but apt that the universe rejoices in giving you praise and is enamored by You. Demons flee fearfully from you in all directions and the hosts of perfected saints bow to you. O Great one, who are even greater than Brahma, the original creator, why should they not bow to you? O limitless One, O Lord of the *devatās*, O Refuge of the universe, you are the imperishable reality beyond both the manifest and the non-manifest.

Thinking of you as my friend, I presumptuously addressed you as "O Krishna," "O Yadav," "O my dear mate." I was ignorant of your majesty, showing negligence and undue affection. And if, jestfully, I treated you with disrespect, while playing, resting, sitting, eating, when alone, or before others—for all that I crave forgiveness. O, you immeasurable, I bow before you, I prostrate in adoration, and I beg your grace.[14]

THE HINDU sacred text, *Bhagavad Gita*, describes a spiritual battle. In this passage, the warrior Arjuna is on the battlefield with Krishna, who is disguised as a charioteer guiding him along the path. Through most of the story, Arjuna sees Krishna as a person of wisdom, someone with whom he can talk, but he does not recognize that Krishna is God. When Krishna reveals his divine nature, Arjuna falls to the ground and cries, "I was ignorant of your majesty!"

Bowing before the Divine, Arjuna becomes a humble servant, which arises from his recognition of transcendence—that which is beyond and greater than the self. This is the first and final step to wisdom. For, when we refuse to be vulnerable, acknowledge the grandeur of creation, or harbor a disdain for the Holy, we succumb to a tragic arrogance.

Humility inspires devotion, and devotion spreads the fragrance of humility. As we become small before awe, our spirit—directly due to the divine will—grows mighty, healing pain and restoring hope. In a sense, the devoted displace themselves in order for the Divine to flow in. It is this longing to prostrate before the divine immensity that ignites mercy and unconditional love.

The antidote to the ego and impaired self-importance is the virtue of humility. Why do we make ourselves less? Why do we pray to be empty? It is out of love. It is out of love that we give away the false self. When light shines on our errors, and we see ourselves through divine eyes, we yearn to be that person through whom the holy is reflected and expressed. We will give all of our mistakes away in order to experience the infinite, all-abiding love that made us. "Humility," writes Thomas Merton, "contains in itself the answer to all the great problems of the soul. It is the only key to faith, with which the spiritual life begins: for faith and humility are inseparable. In perfect humility, selfishness disappears, and your soul no longer lives for itself or itself for God; and it is lost and submerged in Him and transformed into Him."[15]

Jalal al-Din Rumi, "Naughting the Self"

When Hallaj's love for God reached its utmost limit, he became his own enemy and naughted himself. He said, "I am God," that is, "I have been annihilated; God remains, nothing else." This is extreme humility and the utmost limit of servanthood. It means "He alone is." To make a false claim and to be proud is to say, "Thou art God and I am the servant." For in this way you are affirming your own existence, and duality is the necessary result. . . . The heart was dumbfounded by the I-hood of eternity—its own I-hood became insipid and disgraced. The spirit became joyful through the I-less I; it fled from the I of the world.[16]

THE "I-LESS I fled from the I of the world." What an amazing vision! This kaleidoscopic perspective from the revered Sufi mystic, Rumi, is an inscrutable puzzle—a koan—shattering perceived notions of self and reality. The most perfect humility is a state of consciousness when the self, alone, suffers its existence, its awareness of "I-hood." This is the anguish of annihilation, of surrendering to God, of accepting the grace of servanthood. It is an enduring truth found in every spiritual path—the wisdom of the dark night or great death that strips the conventional self of pretense and excuse.

The I-less I exposes the conceit of affirming our existence, of maintaining a dualistic relationship between Heaven and Earth, God and human. Rumi knows this is merely a deflection, an averting of our faces to avoid the final letting go. When we experience awe, love overcomes our loneliness and draws us into union with God. When the soul is simple, neither divided nor conflicted, we cannot help but suffer the "I of the world." As we relinquish the separate self, we become one with divinity. Perfect humility is mystical union.

This essential spiritual virtue can be thwarted by confusion over what humility really is. There are times where we cannot progress unless we confront the places where we are falsely humble and are attached to self-pity or despair. When we do not have faith that we are being cared for by the Spirit, we can succumb to pride, which leads to despair. Often, when pride is great, we prefer to be wrong rather than to give ourselves to God and acknowledge that there is a force of love beyond us. We refuse to admit that we are not capable of changing the course of our lives without divine assistance.

Sadly, we spend much of our lives in avoidance—afraid to let go of the ego and the strictures it imposes on us and others. We are imprisoned by our own refusal to be "dumbfounded" by grace, and by the smallest gesture of emptiness that draws God into our souls. The Divine longs to be in communion with us—it is the primordial wish of creation itself to be intimate with our lives, and it is humbleness of heart that opens the door. As Rumi expresses so eloquently:

Let go all your scheming, lover
Let yourself go mad
go mad

just step into the heart of fire
make yourself a moth
    a moth[17]

Dao dejing

One who rises on tiptoes cannot stand;
One who strides cannot walk;
One who shows oneself is not illuminated.

The highest adeptness* resembles water.
Water is adept at benefiting the ten thousand beings,
But it has no need to compete with them.
It resides in the places that people avoid.
Therefore, it is close to the *Dao* (Way).

You wish to take the world and act upon it;
I know that this cannot be accomplished.
The world is a sacred vessel;
The world cannot be acted upon.
To act upon it is to fail it;
To grasp it is to lose it.[18]

DAOISTS HOLD a reverential attitude toward humility, specifically rejecting self-assertiveness and competition. The ambition to stand out, get
ahead, beat competition, or assert superiority is held to be a false power.
The *Dao dejing* emphasizes the force of the gentle, flowing, and meek.
Water—being the most fluid—flows into the low places, dissolving
mountains and creating canyons that change the course of valley or river-
bed. This emphasis on the avoidance of power, the strength of the hidden
regions, and the sacred emptiness attunes our souls to nonviolence, the
high state of divinity. The world trains us to be reactive, to promote and
fight for what we desire. But we do not always realize the violence that
can be generated by the authoritative pursuit of our agendas.

Spiritual nonviolence (addressed in Chapter 3) involves the practice of peace and a reversal of self-interest. It counters the ways in which we harbor a desire for specialness, difference, exclusion, punishment of others, and control. This desire can include cruelty, retaliatory harm, revenge, infliction of pain, denial of love, and quickness to take offense. It is especially present in forms of religious absolutism, in which there is disdain for any faith that is not one's own, and the voices of mercy and compassion are denounced or vilified. It is because of the *Dao dejing's* emphasis on the gentle and the weak, that it advises practitioners to maintain a profound disinterest in the things the world values. And, thus, we should honor the humble ones, for it is by the wisdom of the unspoken and the unknown that we enter the eternal way, the wayless way.

For the person who looks inside the self, the refusal of ambition is a lofty practice with deep roots. It guides us to be simple in action and thought, patient with friends and enemies, and compassionate toward self and others. Further teaching associates Daoist virtue with abstention from war and capital punishment, absolute simplicity of life, and refusal to assert active authority. Only the person who declines to be foremost in all things is truly able to travel on the road of the spiritual masters.

Ten Meditations on a Humble Heart

Wayless Way

Humility helps us to be and do our best, even in difficult circumstances, even when divine and human favors have been withdrawn. It helps us to stay faithful to our true nature, regardless of the consequences. By contemplating on humility, we begin to glimpse how self-centered we are, how many things in our lives revolve around ourselves in both overt and subtle ways. If we practice the wayless way, even in those dark moments when we have no idea where we are going, we will progress along the spiritual path.

Inner Voice

Humility prevents a person from doing more than he or she is able, taking into account weaknesses and admitting that the false self often wants to achieve something beyond its capabilities. In the spiritual life, we get out of balance when we try to be something that we were never intended to be. The humble person listens to the inner voice of the Divine, especially when it goes against what we want, and guides us to be obedient to the path along which we are called in this life.

Abandon Self-Gain

A little knowledge, humbly pursued, is greater than the treasures of learning sought through pride and vanity. Intellectual knowledge is a social commodity that provides a certain prestige. We are socialized to pursue and gather information in competition with others, and to distinguish ourselves as the smartest and the brightest. In contrast, the humble among us realize that lack of self-interest opens a spiritual passage into the vastness of divine powers and emanations.

Simple Work

Humility teaches us to be content with simple work. We cannot always remain in deep contemplation and in high states of union with God. Manual labor and working with our hands are a necessary counterbalance to the advent of elevated spiritual states. These activities remind us to rejoice over everything we are given. Washing dishes or planting in the vegetable garden is a meditative act. Every action can be performed with love in one's heart. Humility does not privilege one deed over another. A person tilling the soil may be humbler, and therefore more holy, than the mystic or saint.

True Wisdom

The accumulation of knowledge is of little benefit if the soul does not know truth and cannot direct its energies toward perfecting the soul's virtues. The reason that healing takes place, the reason that consciousness is transformed, is because the experience of selflessness is transmitted from one person to another. Thus, the method of growth for a teacher or knower of spiritual things is to deepen the contemplative life. As the self is deepened, the person *is* a teaching. To humbly follow the path is itself both the way and the end. This is true wisdom.

Be Unknown

The world says that we are supposed to make a name for ourselves. Humility teaches us to love being unknown. The great wisdom is to be unimportant in oneself, and to think well and highly of others. The virtue of humbleness is that it prunes the soul in a most beautiful way, helps it to grow toward the light, and produces much and better-quality fruit. When we practice being humble of heart, in the most positive, spiritual sense, we become one with the sacred vessel that is the Earth and participate in the joy of Divine life.

Empty Pride

The joy of mystical union arises from the liberation from self-hood and the annihilation of pride. Here one finds a relationship not bound by power or possession, control or defense. The self is emptied of distinction and learns the power of sacrifice. The Divine is a gift, freely given to us, even when we do not deserve such grace. The only way to touch the greatness of the Divine is to realize how pride distorts the spirit and to accept one's absolute insufficiency.

Free from Praise

In most of our lives, the radical poverty and self-denial of the saint is not as total or all-encompassing, and a more paradoxical reality is at work. There is a difference between pride that thwarts self-surrender and celebrating a job well done. It is, thus, not incorrect to say that whatever positive results take place in our lives are both the result of—and also always exceed—our effort. However, if we are attached to praise, then whatever value we have derived from our good work can distort inner harmony and be an obstacle to love.

Follow the Path

Complete humility is perfect joy. This is liberation: when you know you are not in charge, when you know you are not the best, when you know that the whole weight of the world is not on your shoulders, when you know and experience that you are in the heart of the Divine and that you have to follow wherever it leads you.

Hidden Call

Great faith goes on when everything else is taken away. Faith endures when we are weak, when we are sick, when self-confidence and self-respect are destroyed. Faith emerges from dependence on our Creator. The humble are guided by courage—they practice cleaving to God, over and again, and thus stay on the path moment by moment. Rather than seeking to acquire some goal, which they cannot know or be, they follow the inscrutable call, the distant sound of the Divine voice within.

. ◆ .

May we find in our hearts the inner cloister where You,
Divine Mystery,
arrive in the night without sound.

You draw us into the beauty and pageantry of your Solitude.
You show us how to manifest your Light in the soul of the world.

You grace us with the gift of Humility,
becoming vulnerable to Love.
May we sustain your Holy Presence in all our relations,
on our radiant Earth.

Amen.

TWO

Contemplation on Compassion

OMPASSION IS A STATE OF BEING and a force of consciousness. It arises spontaneously in us from involvement in and connection to suffering. Out of these events of direct experience flows a desire to alleviate the causes of anguish and injustice. When compassion is born in us, we cannot be content with our own success or freedom without desiring the same for others and attending to their needs. Mercy—as a special sign of compassion—is forgiveness shown toward others over whom it is within a person's power to punish or harm. Compassion and mercy are expressions of divine love that lead to acts of kindness and benevolence, and a willingness to forgive and pardon offence.

Let us begin with a premise elucidated by the great Sufi mystic-poet Jalal al-Din Rumi. In the hierarchy of divine names, Rumi devotes considerable attention to the "Attributes of the Acts," particularly to the powers of justice and mercy. Seen to be the first pair of Names that emerge from the Oneness of Being, justice and mercy are simultaneously distinct from, and one with, God's hidden essence. But instead of giving them equal priority, Rumi assigns a higher, more sublime, ontological status to mercy: "His Mercy is prior to His Wrath. If you want spiritual priority, go, seek, the prior Attribute!"[1] Intimately close to the Hidden Essence, mercy is associated with Allah's "longing to be known."[2] Through mercy we gain greater knowledge of the sacred.

According to Rumi, it is in mercy that God bears human affliction, and it is in mercy that God reveals the vulnerable heart of reality. Mercy is not the attribute of an apathetic, unfeeling God. Rather, it flows from Divine pathos (Greek, "suffering"), from intimacy with the tragedy of existence. In human affliction, in the weeping of the outcast and oppressed, in the sorrow of war and pestilence, God mourns with us, says the Hebrew prophets: "Therefore I weep with the weeping of Jazer for the wine of Sibmah; I drench you with my tears, O Hesbon and Elealeh; for upon your fruit and your harvest the battle shout has fallen." (Is 16:9)

Mercy and compassion are related spiritual qualities, often used interchangeably. Compassion enters the English language from the Latin, "*compassio*," which means to suffer with, together. The concept of compassion and its link to suffering has deep philosophical and religious roots. For instance, as Christian theologian Wendy Farley eloquently states in *Tragic Vision and Divine Compassion*:

> God is infinitely compassionate and tender toward the world. Suffering comes because our bodies are frail and because human beings can be cruel to one another—individually and through institutional structures. God labors day and night, like a mother comforting a delirious child, to soothe the fever, to penetrate the suffering and despair. Nothing separates God from the world, but suffering can be a veil that hides this loving presence. In the midst of suffering, compassion labors to tear the veil.[3]

For the spiritual practitioner, compassion is an eternal principle, an inclination of the heart to cultivate the qualities of loving concern, and a condition of being that matures in our souls. Boundless compassion lives in us and is expressed in many ways. There is compassion with reference to sentient beings; that is, compassion for neighbors, families, partners, parents, loved ones, etc. Compassion with reference to the whole of creation—the Earth and its biosphere, the universe of animals, plants, insects, and all of the natural world. And compassion without reference to any object. This is a state of being that overflows from the mystical heart and approaches the world from a divine perspective.

Eleven Meditations on Compassion

Benefits of Existence

We ignite compassion by contemplating the benefits of existence, the bounty of creation, and gratitude for the spiritual, human, and natural beings that guide us. Most especially, Buddhists say, is remembrance of our mothers who provide us with a body, suffer for our sake, sustain our life, and show us how to thrive in society. It is the mother's sacrificial nature that is the clearest example of divine compassion. Since, according to Buddhism, all beings have at one time been our mothers, we owe them profound respect.

The Chinese Buddhist hermit, Chen Chien Ming (1906-1987), describes the compassionate benefits that mothers provide.

> In our mother's womb the embryo has been built up in a special and gradual way by the nutritive essences of her flesh and blood. Even after birth, by nursing us from a tiny little infant into a big, strong person she contributes to the form of our body. She goes through hardships for our sake which means that she not only dresses and adorns us but gives us her inheritance, keeping nothing of her own, not even a crumb, giving us all her food and drink so that when we set out for foreign parts we should not suffer from hunger and thirst, giving us cloths to keep out the cold and money to prevent our pining in poverty. She loves the helpless baby more than she loves her own benefactors. She looks on her baby with eyes of love, wraps him in gentle warmth, dandles him on her knees, strokes him with her ten fingers and calls him with words of sweetness.[4]

Contemplating Suffering

In the classical teachings of the Buddhist tradition, compassion is translated as the heart that trembles in the face of suffering. It is the noblest quality of the heart and the motivation underlying all meditative paths. Compassion is cultivated in response to the suffering that all life inescapably meets: the pain of sickness and loss, the anguish of death, or the emotional trauma that debilitates the mind. In this way, we learn that all beings suffer, and we also learn about the causes of their suffering. Compassion also acknowledges that not every pain can be fixed—that life is fraught with senseless injury and unexplained deprivation. The seemingly random infliction of suffering can generate a need to justify or compare our suffering, or lack thereof, with others. We may believe that if we are not pained, it is because we are better than other people or God has specially chosen us. Bolstered by self-righteousness and carried into our relationships, these invisible prejudices distort the heart's ability to truly feel. It can be very difficult to understand that even the person who wounds, betrays, or rejects does so because he or she has sustained injury. Compassion is a mode of relationship that is wounded by the suffering of others and is propelled into action on their behalf.

Resist Injustice

Compassion is an inner strength and a divine capacity in us that provides the courage to resist suffering and injustice, and to fight despair. The ability to oppose the debilitating effects of hardship and pain is a power of the soul derived from the dignity of all beings, granted by our Creator. Compassion recognizes that humans are *imago dei*, made in the image of God. Because compassion acts to overcome suffering, the quest for reconciliation is an inherent activity of compassion. *I feel that you are suffering, and I will struggle with you to overcome the source of your pain.* This is compassion in action, healing our wounds. When we pray not only for ourselves, but also for those who have harmed us, and sincerely want their freedom from pain, then we are blessed by Mercy. Creation is beautiful and yet tragic at times. True justice is merciful, remaining aware that the ravages of sin always are healed together with our brokenness. Suffering exists because of this brokenness. As we strive to transform pain, compassion imbues us with its spiritual power.

Whole Beings

Compassion labors to make whole beings—whether human, animal, or plant—out of broken hearts. Compassion is unable to bear harm to our spirits and labors to transform unhappiness into situations that generate well-being. A divine principle of healing, compassion comforts the soul with the balm of love and provides a path toward humble self-reliance and integrity. When we surrender to the spirit's all-embracing empathy for our sorrows and pains, our souls become generous, overflowing with human concern. It is impossible to gauge the tremendous value of being a compassionate person of great feeling and care. Yet, even though we never are able to measure this sweet benefit, we experience how gentleness and sensitivity to the world around us literally re-knits the torn fibers of being.

Mystical Knowledge

Compassion arises from a mystical or contemplative knowledge that wishes to know others as we are known by our Creator. Although another person's experience is not fully accessible to us, we are able to mystically share in their heartbreak and celebrate their good fortune and success. By our concern for others, we participate in and mirror the Holy Mother's loving, tender care. Compassion is suffering with another because our heart has become vulnerable and able to bear pain. This is not sympathy, in the sense of merging with another. True compassion is more detached, it knows through the wisdom of the heart—having been made simple and empty—and is capable of being with the wounded and effecting healing change.

Responding to the World

Compassion is a whole and persistent way of interpreting and responding to the world. It is the disposition of unbending solidarity to improve the lives of others and the quest for hope. It is empathy for and identity with a world filled with discord and lack of faith. Compassionate care focuses on its beloved everywhere, which is an unself-interested love for all creation. The heart that trembles before suffering becomes the vantage point from which we offer acts of compassion to all beings and events. It is the soul's sensitivity to the web of life that causes pain. Often, we feel inadequate to the task of ending assaults on the spirit of life. Still, we pray to cultivate the qualities of compassion that foster harmony on Earth, opening our hearts to respond from the perspective of the most Holy.

Loves the World

Compassion is open to the pain of the world because it loves the world. Through compassion, love enters into every situation to redeem, to heal, to dignify, and to liberate. Out of boundless love for the world, we have no choice but to be compassionate. Out of our boundless love for the Creator that loves of us, we have no choice but to also learn and practice self-compassion. Compassion desires that all beings are touched by the Divine, find happiness, and carry tenderness of heart into every relation. When we want others to suffer, when we believe that justice is not done until they suffer, then we have not realized how acts of cruelty afflict the soul and—by extension—wound the Divine. Truly we should be pained whenever anyone commits an error. When we refuse to forgive and violate the call of mercy, we are diminished. Acts of compassion open our hearts to a radiant, unimaginable divine truth: Love bears all things.

Redemptive Power

Compassion works for the liberation of souls. It is a power that refuses to allow sin to become an idol of worship and avert the heart's concern. Compassion is constantly working to redeem us from error and sin. Like heavenly drops of dew that anoint our souls at night (when we least expect it), compassion awakens us with renewed commitment and fortitude. Whenever we feel the grief of the world without succumbing to despair, whenever we bear the inevitable adversity that assails all human beings without losing faith or hope, we fan the sparks of divinity, the fire of the Compassionate One. The tender mercy of the Divine draws us together, as one.

Challenges Us

Compassion challenges us to new ways of living, new ways of speaking, new ways of knowing, new ways of sharing, and new ways of being intimate. It repudiates force, coercion, and domination. To some, compassion appears weak, meek, or lowly, but this is actually mystery: its apparent weakness is its strength. Its humility is its power. Its silence is its command. Its bearing of suffering is its healing ability. Compassion engenders humility and loss of ego. In that one moment of experiencing your goodness—not because you have done something good or because someone else says that you are good, but because you were created and were given life—you belong to the holy circle of compassion.

Self-Compassion

All sentient beings suffer. Humans suffer in particular because it is difficult to withstand the complexity of life and learn self-compassion. We understand compassion for others, but resist forgiving our sins and therefore experiencing the healing power of benevolence. We need to practice compassion for our ignorance, loss of faith, or the inadequacy of our excuses. We need to feel compassion for our waywardness and betrayal of trust, for the times when we are lost and unable to find our way, and harbor suspicion of "the other." When the soul suffers descent into those dark nights and it seems we are abandoned and there is no escape, this is when our call to self-compassion is at its apex.

When we become attached to our suffering and believe we are supposed to suffer, we have given up faith in the goodness of life. One way to move past this immovable state is to practice detachment from destructive feelings and change our mindset: "My behavior may be bad or unhealthy, but it is not the whole of myself." We all make mistakes, but not all of us forgive ourselves for them. Instead of defending, denying, or excusing our behavior, we learn the power of acknowledging self-forgiveness and repentance, which is to change one's heart. To repent is to place faith in what by divine grace I can yet to become. This is self-compassion.

Gift of Grace

Compassion is the ability to perceive intuitively the secrets of another's heart. This power is not psychic intuition, but the fruit of grace and mystical insight that helps to unveil the hidden depths, which the seeker does not speak of or may be unaware. This is taking into one's soul the soul of another, praying for their wholeness and healing. The compassionate person truly desires the happiness of all beings and works to free others from suffering by transforming conditions that harm life, wherever they exist. When we meditate on the nature of suffering, we grow in spiritual wisdom, recognizing that all pain is transitory and impermanent in the heart of the Holy One.

The practice of compassion and mercy is so profound that we cannot measure its benefit.

. • .

O, Merciful One
open our hearts to Love.

We bow before the grace of Compassion
to participate in your living breath of Joy
to learn repentance and forgiveness
to soothe every pain with tenderness.

May we find the strength
to bear the vulnerability of
all sentient beings.

May our hearts be worthy
of your Life.

Amen.

THREE

Contemplation on Nonviolence

NONVIOLENCE REFLECTS the inner unity and inner peace felt in prayer and reminds us that the spiritual life is never at the mercy of the world. Nonviolence—peace—is the essence of the mystical life, for in the contemplative experience of oneness we recognize that nothing except ourselves can prevent us from loving; love is a precious gift that we have in our own soul. Contemplative nonviolence acknowledges that when we close ourselves off from love, we thwart the expansion of the Divine in us.

The concept of nonviolence is timeless and lies at the center of many religions. While Mahatma Gandhi made the term contemporary for Westerners, *ahimsa*, or nonharm, is an ancient ideal that flourished in the religions of Asia: Jainism, Hinduism, Buddhism, Taoism. Gandhi employed the term not passively, as the absence of something, but as the active performance of total love for life and for humanity. From the physical to the mystical level, nonviolence requires resistance to injustice and refers not only to external action, but also to inner thoughts, emotions, and perceptions.

Advocates of nonviolence, including Leo Tolstoy, Gandhi, Martin Luther King, Jr., Howard Thurman, Desmond Tutu, Thich Nhat Hahn, Dorothy Day, etc., have found the Sermon on the Mount (Mt. 5-7) to be an astounding peace document. Jesus spoke directly about nonviolence when he said to turn the other cheek. That it is easy to love one's friends but difficult to love one's enemies. In acknowledging this difficulty, he names something essential: nonviolence is an active transformation of consciousness that we labor in, rather than an existing state that we must simply reach. It is a quality of being—and therefore this journey never ends—which we acquire through participation in the transformation of this world and our souls into their divine image.

Nonviolence is a divine principle that reveals a God of mercy and nonharm. This is not a violent God who inflicts suffering and punishment. Or a vengeful God who exacts retribution. The nonviolent God refuses to let us justify evil and pushes us to resist every act of injustice. The practice of nonharm addresses these concerns: Why did God create a world capable of evil? Why did God cause me to suffer? Understanding God as absolute nonharm helps us to realize that we are responsible for our own violence. We commit violence on each other. We have the potential to harm the sacred.

The Divine can do nothing other than grieve over human violence and simultaneously show us how to transform violence into nonviolence. The silence at the center of the self, labors to draw us into the heart of mercy and compassion. In contemplation, we experience the harmony of being, and a peace that transcends understanding. We feel God's silence permeating personhood and have reverence for the dignity of every life. Peace is a grace and a gift. We cannot conquer or demand it. We discover and unveil peace in our depth: a revelation of love, goodness, hope, beauty, and faith.

The nonviolence of the Divine does not eliminate the fact that we have been wounded and that we suffer those wounds, but it shows us the way back to our original Source. Sometimes we travel far along our path and then want to turn back. We are afraid to go forward. We disrupt love and seek to punish those who have harmed us. Yet we acquire the strength to resist retaliation when we allow divine benevolence to touch our hearts and free us of selfish motives. Through the practice of self-surrender that is informed in part by trust and faith in the Divine, we embody the spiritual strength to heal grief and assuage the soul's trauma.

Every time we transform pain or hurt, we practice nonviolent activism and experience the transformative power of peace. When we stand up for love, we transform violence into nonviolence. We change consciousness and we change our beings. Nonviolence is our liberation.

Spiritual Nonviolence

NONVIOLENCE is a way of life and a mystical practice based on centuries-old traditions of inner peace. It is motivated by a keen sense of both the fragileness and resilience of human communities and taps into the river of wisdom that guides us to recognize the spiritual rights and dignity of every person and sentient being.

Spiritual nonviolence derives power and efficacy from its theological foundation in divine love. It is never for social transformation without soul transformation. It is especially concerned with the spiritual implications of nonviolence on the inner life and growth of the seeker. For this reason, I modify the word "nonviolence," with "spiritual" to underscore the self-awareness and personal repentance that is critical to changing our hearts. The mystical practice of nonviolence is not solely concerned with the negative impact of violence, but with what Gandhi called *satyagraha*—the "soul-force" that empowers the life-affirming strength and moral resilience necessary for the conversion of the human heart and the enlightenment of culture.

It is the spiritual core of the person that provides the strength of character to resist those hidden beliefs that perpetuate the exclusion of the "other." Inner strength leads to growth in consciousness, which in turn obligates the oppressed to combat the inferiority, self-hatred, or lack of self-worth that demoralizes personal integrity and crushes one's ability to resist. Similarly, on the side of oppressors and those obligated to effect remedy, there must exist inner repentance, or coming to terms with the shame and sorrow one feels and the suffering and pain one has caused.

As the twentieth century's most famous advocate of nonviolence, Gandhi was the architect of a people's campaign to end British rule of India. Employing the method of nonviolent resistance, he gave himself to a way of life in line with what he believed God wanted. He felt with extraordinary intensity the plight of India's people and the brokenness of the world, devoting himself to the cause of nonviolence in order "to heal the hurting indifference which keeps one human being from another."[1] Unable to tolerate the wall of separation between himself and the poor, he became poor. Open to the suffering of others, he felt that the starving masses were the face of God stricken with hopelessness, the belly of God emptied of love, and the heart of God pleading for compassion. In his encounters with the suffering people of India, he realized that his vow of *ahimsa* had to be put into action.

As the center of our moral conscience, nonviolence insists that how we conduct our lives every day is as important as the ends or goals that we seek via these means. More than a passive quality of peace, spiritual nonviolence stresses the active struggle for social and moral justice and is the tangible practice of achieving a higher and nobler state of being.

As the common element in all human cultures and traditions, nonviolence provides a path and an interpretative framework that guides us to analyze and implement methods that prevent the severing of God's presence on Earth. It demands an accounting of how human acts of violence tear at our hearts, lay waste to our souls, and lead us to the brink of despair. It asks how these travesties against the spirit of life contribute to collective grief and afflict us in ways that even now the global community has yet to feel, name, or understand.

Nonviolence—both in terms of social action and inner transformation—is the external manifestation of a contemplative state of consciousness that is itself the outer garment of an even deeper truth: reality moves in harmony with love. As a spiritual path, nonviolence is not merely a cultural necessity or social form of protest, but the whole configuration in which life can be seen as it truly is, in its deepest dimensions. The practitioner of mystical nonviolence commits to confronting and resolving aspects of violence in one's soul and personality, including how prejudice, entitlement, arrogance, racism, sexism, supremacy, etc., betray inner and outer harmony.

To comprehend the depth of spiritual nonviolence, it is worthwhile to reflect on what violence is. Acts of violence occur on many levels and spheres of human interaction. One of the more painful types of violence is spiritual—that is, any action that invades a person's sacred place, tramples truth, controls insight, co-opts peace, and/or degrades integrity. We frequently discover our first taste of spiritual harm in familial relations when there is an intent to control or violate our dignity. Often subtle and unseen, acts of spiritual violence affect our understanding of reality and cripple our ability to rise above reaction, retaliation, and aggression. When our sacred space has been invaded, we go into hiding. The whole tone of life, then, can be in reaction to violations of intimacy, when love is corrupted by possession and harm. If we are reactive, we have experienced some form of violence. If we are retaliatory, we have experienced some form of violence. And, thus, in turn we learn how to perpetuate the same.

Violence—physical, spiritual, mental, etc.—inhabits our cells and psyches, latching onto and distorting the oneness that is the natural function of love. It spreads mysteriously and generates different iterations and mutations of the origin of violence—that is, the willful denial of the sacred. If I were to say, "You are worthless!" then I commit a harmful act because I have distorted your true nature. I have disturbed the peace and harmony of your soul. As an improper or unlawful disregard of the sacred, my words are false, and a desecration or profanation.

Saint Catherine of Siena (1347-1380), in mystical dialogue with "the fiery mercy of the Holy Spirit," learns how spiritual cruelty "makes oneself—caught in a cloud of selfish love—an instrument for depriving others of life and dealing out death."

> O dearest daughter, grieve that I am so offended, and weep over these dead so that your prayers may destroy their death! For you see that everywhere, on every level of society, all are giving birth to sin on their neighbors' heads. For there is no sin that does not touch others, whether secretly by refusing them what is due them, or openly by giving birth to the vices of which I have told you.
>
> It is indeed true, then, that every sin committed against me [God] is done by means of your neighbors.[2]

The transformation of cruelty into nonharm is acquired through spiritual practice, but most importantly by suffering that is borne from infinite desire. It is our passionate desire to not betray love that is able to withstand God's infinite sorrow over our misdeeds. Thus, is it through our heart's profound remorse that we are able to confront and heal the source of violence within us.

Today, practitioners of peace recognize that the journey toward nonviolence entails not only inner growth, but also cooperation and reconciliation with family, friends, colleagues, and others that we meet. The injury caused by quarrel, abandonment, or misunderstanding eats away at our souls, contributing to the pain of personal and community relationships. Especially important is the transformation of enmity and violence among religious traditions. Over the last century, members of the world's religions have engaged in dialogue and taken action to heal historical divisions between religious dominations and among diverse traditions. The commitment to interfaith dialogue and ecumenical community—in fellowship with men and women around the globe—is based on "that force [of love]," that Martin Luther King Jr. wrote, "which all of the great religions have seen as the supreme unifying principle of life. Love is the key that unlocks the door which leads to ultimate reality. This Hindu-Moslem-Christian-Jewish-Buddhist belief about ultimate reality is beautifully summed up in the First Epistle of Saint John: Let us love one another: for love is of God."[3]

Any effort designed to lift the oppression of one community requires that it also expand beyond tribal and local concerns to include the universe of suffering beings. We are made in the divine image, and our souls are of infinite value. If we accept this moral fact, we must recognize that divine love is real and concrete, that it is the organizing principle of the entire creative universe. Our souls cannot be content to witness hunger and homelessness, to see masses of people victimized by war and ill health. Although the enormity of our global problems can feel overwhelming at the personal level, the challenge is to uncover the well of love within us. We are not capable of the infinite love and infinite sorrow that is Divine. But when our sincere desire to ease suffering is united with a contrition of heart, every suffering we bear in spirit or in body is of great worth.

Spiritual nonviolence is an affair of the heart that begins deep within the soul. It is the active expression of God's call to love in a new way, to be more holy. I believe that this vision of life is dependent on the human capacity to love more, give more, and care more for the world. Illuminated in this way, the heart is enflamed by a divine longing to make our planet a place where love can flourish. The vow to be a person of nonviolence means that our life's mission is directed toward actualizing the promise of all the world's religions—that we can achieve spiritual harmony on Earth.

We counter violence through a spirituality of nonviolence, which involves self-purification and the development of a moral conscience. The practice requires the spirit of harmlessness, which is a prerequisite to action that is not tainted by self-interest. We question our motives and seek to develop the inner strength and the self-respect necessary to avoid reducing our inner demons and outer opponents to the role of "enemy." It is in these instances that the wisdom of detachment, self-emptying, and absence of ego serve as clear indicators of the path ahead.

From this realization comes the consequent idea that nonharm is the test of truth and that the sacrifice of the false self, or ego, is the method that awakens one's moral fiber and that of one's opponents. Bearing voluntary self-sacrifice means accepting that everything takes time. All worthwhile things in life need to be nourished. We learn from nature that growth requires patience. By listening, observing, and desiring to know another person and the natural world, we learn to love beauty and good-ness, and to have compassion for the abandoned, broken, or lost. We give up the desire to have everything tangible and accessible immediately, remembering that truth is subtle. It presses into the warm intimacy of our hearts. Voluntary self-sacrifice guides us to be loving and kind with self and others as we labor to practice nonharm.

Fidelity to peace manifests as a continual willingness to look at our pain, addictions, and habituations, and to see them through the loving eye of the All-Merciful. It is also a commitment to refuse to pass on the wounding, neglect, or lack of love that we may have experienced. One of the great gifts in practicing nonviolence is that you become a true friend, offering your presence as a safe harbor and a spiritual home for the inhabitants of nature, for family and neighbors, and for the refugees among us. The movement toward peace is something that we discover each day; we are always beginners under the arch of mercy.

The twentieth century's wise advocates of peace attest to the transformative power of nonviolence to heal social injustice. Each of them, in turn, recognized that various forms of cultural oppression (poverty, racism, sexism, homelessness, etc.) also inflict an inner wound—a profound disability of soul—that is, in many ways, more devastating.

Yet in every era, we record the triumph of nonviolence and peace over violence. We note that even in the radical suffering of war, torture, or other forms of abuse, there are people whose spirit is able to deny despair and rise above cruelty to find the source of love within them. Their lives give us the courage to combat false beliefs and to work for justice. If we learn anything in the contemplation of nonviolence, it is this: We have the strength to be monks of peace, and to consistently call our hearts toward loving the world and all our relations.

Five Meditations on Divine Nonviolence

Contemplation on nonviolence is founded on a theology of love. It reveals the inner life of the Divine, which is infinite openness, infinite mercy, infinite peace, infinite oneness, and infinite love.

Infinite Openness
. . . calls us to be vulnerable to life and to each other. If we wish to understand and practice nonviolence, we must be willing to participate fully in life, to listen to each other, to communicate, dialogue, and receive. The divine attributes of vulnerability and intimacy are inherent in our depth, activated whenever we open our hearts and minds to the wonder of the world.

Infinite Mercy

... means that the Divine suffers, bears all, and endures all with us. All of creation is held in an ocean of mercy, nurtured in the Divine Mother's sacred heart. This is the personal God of pathos who suffers with humans and is concerned for justice and compassion. Pathos—compassion with and for another—leads to forgiveness, reconciliation, and benevolence. When we have already been forgiven, how can we refuse to forgive? How can we be unmerciful when we all belong to each other in the cosmic circle of belonging? Although we may feel separate from divine care, we are never separate in pain or in joy.

Infinite Peace

... brings everything together into a unity and undivided communion without confusion. Peace is God: "absolute peace, peace in general, and peace in every instance. Perfect peace ranges totally through all things with the undiluted presence of its unifying power."[4] Thus, every being loves to be at peace with itself, to never fall away from its own existence. In the depth of the inner life, at the apex of the contemplative journey, is the peace and freedom of an undivided heart.

Divine peace is indivisible and permeates the whole world. It is a quality of energy and consciousness that ensures that all things are quiet and free of confusion within them and from without. All things are unshakably what they are in their depth, at rest. And *this* is why the contemplative life is a source of renewal, restoration, and nourishment: it draws us ever deeper into the palace of peace, where we are alone with the great Alone.

Infinite Oneness

... is the quintessential mystical insight across cultures, and the central, motivating force for the practice of nonviolence. God is One. An experience of the oneness of Presence that animates life becomes a bodily participation in the universal mystery. Thus, the more attuned we are to the unity that binds all of creation in an invisible matrix of being, we cannot help but be awed. We bow down before the divine splendor, honoring our precious human life, the Earth, cosmos, and all sentient beings. And we now know—by the loss of the separate self—that the divine mystery is the unifying force of spirit pouring itself out, interpenetrating reality, ebbing and flowing with the passion of simply being.

Nonviolence is a state of consciousness that sees reality from the perspective of the whole. It recognizes that oneness underlies diversity and searches for ways to protect the unity of life in the concrete situations of every day. When the web of union is disturbed, our hearts overflow with concern and grief. At the same time, there is a spiritual power of the soul that transforms despair into hope and oppression into liberation. It is because the Divine is infinite oneness that we are touched by compassion and are compelled to rectify through nonviolent acts of resistance the cruelty, insensitivity, and injustice inflicted on our brothers and sisters, and to translate this into a desire to alleviate our suffering world.

This ability to empathize with another sentient life rests on a mystical capacity to identify with the suffering of others and to find in that suffering an expression of a higher truth. So powerful is this truth—that all life is one—that we must always seek it through struggle and persistent effort. To know the world as the Divine knows us is to risk losing the illusion of a separated and independent self.

Infinite Love

... invites us into the inner life of the Divine: every wound is healed, and no sin is unforgiveable. Nonviolence, which is innate in all beings, helps us to practice profound acts of love: turning the other cheek and loving our enemies, up to and including the enemy inside who thinks we deserve to be punished. When you believe that your sins can never be forgiven and lament that the injury you inflict can never be mended, remember that within you is the courage to face the harm you have caused, and the love needed to repair it. When a distraught Hindu who had killed a Muslim child implored Gandhi to help him quell the torment of his soul, Gandhi replied, "Find a Muslim child and raise him as you own in the faith of Allah."

At the core of nonviolence is this: Love is God, and the Divine loves the world as one. We are one family—animal, plant, mineral, human—and as a family we must care for the well-being of the whole. Communal concerns so central to the physical survival and spiritual orientation of indigenous peoples echoes this mystic call. So does the Buddhist notion of interdependence of reality and the codependent arising of all phenomena. Love is not abstract. It is a state of consciousness that labors to fulfill the promise of faith by embracing the entire cosmos and all sentient beings in loving communion.

This high spiritual state of consciousness arises from an existential fact—Love is Holy, and we are its disciples. It is a key to the contemplative journey and the foundation of our generosity and hope. It is the mystical sight granted that tells us who we really are, where we really belong, and from whence we come. In a fleeting glimpse we feel, and understand how profoundly loved we are, how profoundly interconnected we are, how profoundly desired we are.

. ◆ .

Holy Mystery
if we could but see
the splendor of your Peace,
and feel the radiance of your Love
We would kneel down in praise of each other
putting away words and deeds of harm.

Teach us the practice of nonviolence
May we have the courage to transform our hearts.

Amen.

FOUR

Contemplation on Simplicity

T HE CONTEMPLATIVE LIFE is a joyful life because the seeker follows the intention of the heart—the search for God. When the heart is in solitude and concentrated on its pure desire, then every action or thought emerges from a state of unity. Thus, the entire movement of the mystical life is toward simplicity—focusing the seeker's passion on the quest, on the one thing necessary.

Singleness of heart means that we (in our depth) are free from complexity, confusion, deceit, and guile. A person of simplicity avoids displays of self-importance. He or she enjoys life, but remains modest by minimizing physical or spiritual extravagance, free of pretention. While leading a life of external balance is a type of simplicity, more important and eventually more transformative is the capacity to be simple in one's being—a force driving our entire life on Earth. For this reason, devotees of the world's religions revere spiritual simplicity and uphold it as the apex of virtue and contemplation.

While we all experience phases of emotional conflict and confusion, these are artifacts of living in a challenging physical reality and do not necessarily reflect a person's inner state. But when intentions or desires are divided, we are not of one mind—not simple. It is the person of pure intention who accomplishes many things by remaining undivided in his or her heart. To further explore the significance of simplicity in the contemplative experience, this chapter reviews three interdependent virtues of simplicity: emotion (simple and complex), life, and heart.

Simplicity of Emotion

LET US BEGIN with the distinction I make between "emotions" as expressions of the outer personality or psyche, and "spiritual feelings" or senses, which are the direct result of touching your inner depth. When spiritual feelings are received into awareness without distortion or judgment, I call their bodily expressions simple or pure emotions. This distinction is important because on a daily basis we receive impulses from others in our environment, and from our own personality and soul. Learning to distinguish one from another and to outgrow dependency on inconstant, often vacillating emotions is critical to the practice of contemplation and peace.

A simple emotion is one that spontaneously rises from the divine center within us and is clear in intention. It is, thus, a vehicle for transmitting our spiritual feelings to the world around us. We use the language of emotion to reflect the soul's spiritual senses, like a polished mirror reflects a true image of the thing in itself. Recognizing that our beings are microcosms of the divine being means that we always are resonating with the truth within us, and with a spiritual depth of knowing. This depth is conceived in a singleness of heart—a sincere and humble heart—that is a power of the soul focused on a steady intention toward the Divine.

Central to the quest for spiritual maturity is the practice of detachment from one's emotions. Perhaps the word "detachment" conveys the false notion of a person who is devoid of empathy or beyond suffering. Instead, the mystical emphasis on emotional detachment refers to outgrowing the constant pull that conflicting emotions exert on our personality, and the need to move beyond them to the spiritual feelings that transcend the merely emotional.

One of the essential insights of the mystical traditions is that the majority of emotions that we experience and express most likely are not substantial or even our own. The emotions that we cling to and believe to be ours are often complex and confusing states that we have absorbed and adapted from others. Without making a conscious choice, these emotional tones become subsumed into personality.

The Buddha described five *skandhas* or aggregates of personality—corporeality or form, sensation, perception, mental formations, and consciousness—that we experience to be fixed and substantial. However, like a skein of yarn that is unraveled, every aggregate is empty (*sunya*). We become attached to our *skandhas* and believe they are real. Approaching our emotions as transformative and transient—empty—reveals the power of emotional volatility to control and divert our daily relationships and inner peace. But, when we bring awareness to an emotional experience and follow it to its depth, it is released into pure energy.

The Indian sage Patanjali (possibly second century BCE), in his *Yoga sutras*, further explains something of what I mean by a pure emotion or emotional simplicity. He does not use the word "simplicity," but instead addresses the concentration of the mind, or *samadhi*, which is the cessation of mental activity and a state of conscious absorption in the object of meditation—Brahman, God. There are two main types of *samadhi*: *savitarka samadhi* mixed with the awareness of name, quality, and knowledge, and *nirvitarka samadhi* unmixed with the awareness of name, quality, and knowledge. Indian philosopher, monk, Swami Prabhavananda (1893-1976) provides further explanation in his commentary on the *Yoga sutras*:

> For example, when we look at a desk, we are aware (1) of the name of the object ("desk"), (2) of the quality of the object (its size, shape, color, woodenness, etc.), and (3) of our own knowledge of the object (the fact that it is we ourselves who are perceiving it). Through intense concentration we may become identified with the desk and yet still retain a mixture of "name," "quality," and "knowledge" in the mind. This is the lowest kind of samadhi, known as *savitarka*, which means "with deliberation."[1]

In other words, we are concentrated on an object, but we still recognize the characteristics of that something, are separate from it, and veer into unclear or mixed emotion. For example, your spouse forgets your birthday. Your initial reaction to the slight is a rush of anger, which you cannot let go. You focus on the characteristic ascribed to anger: how it feels, what it is doing to your emotional equilibrium, your knowledge of this particular anger, and that you are experiencing it.

The commentary goes on to say that through *nirvitarka sama-dhi*—concentration without deliberation—we reach a higher stage of consciousness.

> Our achievement of identity with the object of concentration is now unmixed with awareness of name, quality, and knowledge. Or, to put it in another way, we are at last able to still the thought-waves which are our reactions to the object, and to know nothing but the object, as it truly is: "the thing-in-itself."[2]

Detaching from the emotion of anger toward a spouse, we concentrate on anger-in-itself and put away thoughts and reactions. Intense concentration or singleness of heart and mind breaks through the reactive personality to pure, spiritual feeling. The clear undertone of spirit helps sort and push away confused emotions, allowing a moment of anger that is not mixed with judgment or disdain to uncover what lies within. Behind all subtle emotional vacillations is Brahman. Concentration on inner feeling is attained by fixing the mind on the divine light located in the lotus of the heart, which Patanjali describes as the center of spiritual consciousness in the body, situated between the abdomen and the neck.

In the state of emptying, we are absorbed into "something in itself," without any attributes, opinions, or reactions. The language of mystical experience fits into this category. When a person achieves mystical union or *nirvana*, dissolving in the ocean of being, he or she has gone beyond sense perception to transcendental knowledge, to direct contact with the Absolute, which eludes the qualifications of name, quality, or knowledge. Through the practice of concentration—prayer, meditation, awareness, discernment—we free consciousness from mental and physical impediments.

Simplicity does not imply that we never experience reactive emotion but rather that we are able to harness and direct it toward the contemplative center of the self. In the lotus of the heart, rather than your emotions having control over you, you have a way of yoking them to your deep desire. This is the goal of training the inner self—not to oppress but transform and purify emotional response, so it truly reflects your spiritual feelings.

Complex Emotion

I use the term "complex emotion" to refer to an emotion that is divided in its intent, and usually bound to a faulty thought or idea. Most often, complex emotions develop because of a primary or fundamental inability of the person to connect with his or her spiritual depth of feeling, as the result of confusion, oppression, wounding, or ego.

Infants and young children express unfettered emotions. In response, adults compartmentalize, control, and direct the child's raw emotional states toward acceptable social behavior. When an imposed emotion or thought intersects with a child's inner reality, complexity develops. The absorption of other people's thoughts and judgments results in confusion and denial. For example, if a child is angry because his or her toy is grabbed, but the child is chided for being ungrateful or selfish, then anger and regret build. The adult's control over the child's emotional expression results in a confusion about anger and a need to hide feelings. If a child is punished, whenever he or she dares to express a hurt, then how does the child authentically connect to the true self if emotion is bound with ever-present fear of negative reaction?

Oppression of emotion results from the external violation or control of a pure, spiritual feeling that we internalize. We may then try to suppress emotion, inadvertently cutting off our source of energy and love. We may turn inward and become self-destructive or deceitful. We may fear that every authentic spiritual feeling of depth—devotion, awe, gratitude, etc.—is naïve or unsophisticated, severing our hearts from access to the soul's response.

Yet, every time we detach from a complex emotion, we have more energy, and our heart becomes a clear, open window of light. Noticing how subtly the emotional tones of those around us permeate our self-identity and actually direct our emotional reaction can be eye-opening. It is incredible to recognize how the sadness of a mother, anger of a father, or jealousy of a brother or friend inhabit and dictate what we assume to be identifying characteristics of "myself."

The transmission of emotional languages is very similar to the way in which we think about the transmission of a virus or other illness. We receive a collective or individual's response to life as a discreet emotional language that we ingest or breathe in and subsume into our personality. We can love an emotion that is not our own because it belongs to a person whom we love but—at the same time—we can detach and let it go because it is not ours. The emotional tone that obscures our path can be turned over to the Divine, trusting and allowing it to be taken care of in the Creator's own time and way. If we feel tired, dragged down, confused, fractured, or debilitated, it is helpful to ask (along with considering biological reasons) if our emotional system is in a complex state. Patanjali reminds us that the vitality of the being is connected to the level of detachment from and cessation of name, quality, and knowledge. If our physical body does not feel vital, then something is going on in the system that is crying out for attention.

Complex emotions are also supported and carried in us because we do not realize how transformative and fluid our beings are. We become attached to our emotions and believe they are us. But neither attachment nor aversion dispels ignorance. In one form or another, complex emotions lead to wounding because they obscure the heart's clear light, mystical knowing, and spiritual passion for life. This is why the ability to recognize our emotional tone is so important. It is like building muscles. We learn how to sustain our own clarity, which gives us the strength to work through thoughts and emotions that are not clear.

The majority of complex emotions you feel do not belong to you—they are absorbed into the psyche from other people and acted out. These foreign energy patterns course through your veins, exerting a substantial, negative impact on happiness and health. In order to understand the significance of emotional complexity, practice observing how emotions control your daily interactions. Emotions rise like the tide, affecting the balance of energies, hormones, and the parasympathetic nervous system. Be attentive in daily encounters to how inconstant and vacillating emotions adversely impact vitality, and re-direct your mind and reaction toward unity with God.

Simplicity of Life

OFTEN, WHEN WE think of simplicity, we envision external simplicity—for example, a person with very few material possessions. However, outer simplicity can mask inner complexity and become a crutch that keeps confusion hidden or denied. Until we explore inner complexity, outer forms of simplicity may do nothing to address egoism or attachment. A vow to practice asceticism and other types of austerity may be a catalytic element that will draw a person into the interior process, but outer simplicity cannot, in itself, rectify inner confusion.

A central virtue across monastic communities is the simple life. Monks aspire to live modestly and to decrease complexity, which frees them to devote themselves exclusively to the divine quest. While a necessary work of the spirit, simplicity has many practical benefits. Monks do not have to decide what to wear because they are going to wear the same habit most days. They do not need to amass money because the majority of living expenses are eliminated, shouldered by the community. The plain and often reduced number of daily meals frees the majority of the monks from the task of buying and preparing food.

Asceticism is a time-honored practice of voluntary simplicity. This path, however, is not suitable for everyone. Instead, we can forge another version of simplicity. We might study how each of us is responsible for poverty and disparities in wealth. We can observe our choices. We can practice abstinence from unhealthy food, television, the internet, and other excesses. We can develop practices that lessen the privilege of our lives, by voluntarily giving up unearned and undeserved advantages.

It is not only the fact that we have so many material possessions, but that we have so much, and we do not respect it. Simplicity of life honors the sacrifice that nature and people make for our existence. We choose to live in the spirit of simplicity because we belong to each other. It is not a deprivation. When we practice material simplicity, we actively contribute to mending the misuse and overuse of life's generosity, which is in opposition to a culture that values the acquisition of material possessions as a signifier of success.

Practicing simplicity in one's life involves distinguishing between want and need. It asks that we examine our conscience and the ways we buy and sell, hoard and consume. It is an examined life because we choose to examine it. We examine our choices from a place of joy and because we would like our life to be a testimony to peace and a witness to structural and cultural inequities.

Simplicity is an awareness and attention to all of our resources, including the natural world, shelter, clothing, food, drink, and other kinds of physical objects. It is about how we steward these resources and conserve them for the benefit of all beings. Simplicity of life implies discernment, attention, and awareness about what we actually need. We practice voluntary simplicity to honor and value the labor of others, to stay focused on our true intentions, and to be more modest in living our daily lives.

Many of my friends who are members of formal North American monasteries remind me that monks by and large have much better and secure lives than the majority of the world's population. The monastic practice of voluntary simplicity often is not much of a hardship today. Monks usually do not have to worry about health insurance, shelter, food, and clothing. They normally do not have to seek and apply for jobs. Thus, in reviewing our lives we should not idealize the virtue of simplicity but adapt and expand its gifts to our historical period and our own personal circumstance.

Meditations on a Simple Heart

Unconditional

A simple heart is one that loves unconditionally. It is not a complex heart with many considerations, constraints, and caveats. It is a passionate heart because you have found the courage to withstand the complexity of your emotional life, have attempted to purify that life, and therefore are able to radiate its inner light. A simple heart has experienced sorrow and suffering. It is a heart that knows peace and joy. A simple heart is without deceit and guile, does not hide or intentionally conceal the truth for the purpose of misleading. A heart that is simple confronts life openly, is free of ego agendas, and is not trying to manipulate others.

Unencumbered

A simple heart is also unencumbered by false virtue. Hypocrisy arises when there is a pretense of possessing qualities of goodness, sincerity, or devotion. Many people unfortunately feel hypocritical and live very uncomfortably because they do not believe in or have never felt their own goodness. Because they are uncomfortable in their skin, they cannot settle down—cannot be still physically or spiritually. The tone of a person's spiritual life can be consumed with camouflaging and making up for this lack. Every deed can feel hurried and fraught with difficulty. In this state, the seeker cannot rest because quietness of heart has not yet been found.

Awake

Another disturbance of the heart occurs when it is stuck in ego, always looks out for its own way, and instinctively conceals its purpose. Sometimes we develop this behavior defensively. Perhaps we had parents who invaded our psychic space. We became manipulative to avoid them and protect ourselves from further spiritual and psychic invasion. If we never move beyond this state of relentless alert and cunning, however, we cripple our authentic response to life's gifts. A simple heart desires to be awake—to directly confront the intention to manipulate others and to seek deliverance from the pain of artifice.

Good

A simple heart does not want to possess anything for itself. It is not looking for an angle to make the ego better or the spiritual life clearer or its own identity more valued. It is not superficial or deceptive. It is straight. It is good. In simplicity we pray that all of our actions are without deception. We pray to be free of false or selfish motives. We pray for truth for its own sake and not for what we think we are going to get or achieve.

Pure

A simple heart knows that our errors and obstacles are only transient. We should not cling to wrongdoing but instead ignite our intention to be better. A simple heart lives in the inner light and knows of a peace that is beyond suffering and sorrow. It experiences the love that animates creation. When our entire being is simple, we become mirrors of divine oneness. This is purity of heart and mind. It is clarity. It is the consequence of emptiness that is also the abundance of the spirit in everyone and everything.

Unity

Similarly, the effort of developing a simple heart is seen in this teaching of the Daoist master Zhuang Zhou (c. 396–286 BCE), who instructs his disciple Yen Hui on "fasting of the heart."

> The goal of fasting is inner unity. This means hearing, but not with the ear; hearing, but not with the understanding; hearing with the spirit, with your whole being. The hearing that is only in the ears is one thing. The hearing of the understanding is another. But the hearing of the spirit is not limited to any one faculty, to the ear, or to the mind. Hence it demands the emptiness of all the faculties. And when the faculties are empty, then the whole being listens. There is

then a direct grasp of what is right there before you that can never be heard with the ear or understood with the mind. Fasting of the heart empties the faculties, frees you from limitation and from preoccupation. Fasting of the heart begets unity and freedom.[3]

This is the manner of approaching life situations—by letting go of self-awareness we are free to go among people without conflict, without forcibly demanding to be understood or imposing our beliefs. We are peaceful, able to be with others without leaving a trace of our thoughts and opinions. Daoists call this "sitting-in-forgetfulness"—until even forgetting is forgotten.

Simplicity of emotion, life, and heart form the essence of the contemplative, monastic path. Here we understand the value of emptiness, and the palpable feeling of joy that wells up in being "nothing." As we practice the virtues of simplicity, we grow in openness and grace. I encourage each of you to assess your life on the basis of this practice. If your intention is to find simplicity of heart, spirit, and mind, you will find it.

. • .

May the Divine Light illuminate
our longing for the simple way.

Let us live as desert monks, alone in our cells
unobstructed by possessions
offering everything complex to be parched
from our souls.

Be with us, Holy Elders,
and help us on our path.

Amen.

Bearing the Divinity of the World

I N MY EARLY DAYS of teaching, I struggled to bring ecstatic experience into language, and to convey the embodied dimension of Divine grace. Words like "experience" and "presence" or even "nothingness" and "annihilation" were inadequate to truly express the impact of the Divine energies on the physical body and emotions. A more accurate term—but by no means exhaustive or perfect—to describe the spiritual and cellular commitment of the mystical life is the word "bearing." I therefore begin this chapter with nine meditations on how divinity is carried into the world within our bodies and spirits.

Nine Meditations on Bearing

Birth

One meaning of the word "bearing" is to give birth. In the contemplative life, we give birth to deeper dimensions of our souls, and deeper dimensions of the divine nature. We give birth to new insight. We *are* a birthing. We bring forth in our own lives and hearts the sacred presence.

Each time we make a choice for openness, love, mercy, compassion, and nonviolence, we are divinizing the world. Birth is tangible, involving cells, bodies, emotions, and thought. It is also mysterious. Here, our theological focus shifts from transcendence, hierarchy, and omnipotence to embodiment, mutuality, and intimacy. Contemplation is birthed in us, body, mind, and soul, and we bear its wisdom in our daily lives.

Natural Growth

Contemplation is the most natural way of living in our interiority. It is coming home. It is where we feel most comfortable. An organic process that orients the inner life, and a way of being, contemplation is the essence of our natures. When we bear divinity, we participate in and contribute to the organic and natural growth of reality. Our personal lives and the Divine life exist inside each other and in our co-bearing, we cooperate in the building of a spiritual society on Earth.

Support

We support or hold the Divine life within us and in others. This is the work of providing a foundation for the sacred to thrive in our hearts, families, societies, and the entire created order. Through honest speech, loving kindness, right actions, keen humility, we foster communion and peace with all beings. At times, we also must be warriors, resilient and able to withstand the inevitable crush of worldly demands that deliberately seeks to dismantle or betray the holy.

Sustain

The immediate purpose of contemplative practice is to sustain the divinity of the world. It requires endurance and re-commitment each day. We are not born with this full potential but acquire it through wisdom and love. We expand our capacity to sustain holiness in our lives when we are able to differentiate between our less-honest behaviors and higher virtues, transitory desires and the desire that is the heart's passion. As we become more empty and humble, the ego washes away, and we grow stronger in our ability to preserve the sensitive gift of life.

Suffer

Each day we endure disagreements, shoulder untruths, suffer violence and war, and feel anguish for own and others' wounds. We know—in order to hold the Divine immensity—at times we will encounter hardship and be weakened by injustice. In part, our suffering is derived because, in the cave of the heart, we feel and know the rapturous beauty of creation and yet are not always capable of protecting it. We realize our inability, and thus suffer the disjuncture between the life we live and the purely divine within us, which is waiting for expression.

Offer Gifts

By the fact of just being alive, we are recipients of holiness. In the profound unity of creation, we exchange gifts of divinity with each other, nature, the entire planet, and life itself. We are the unveiling of gifts—the gifts of spirit, freedom, forgiveness, reconciliation, compassion, love, and joy. As we share our gifts with the world, we become the gifts we bear. The more ardently we embrace the call of solitude, the more we embody divinity and can offer our bounty to others.

Carry in Heart

It is in the heart and the mind that we carry the sacred call of contemplation. While we may think the Holy is beyond us, so difficult to attain, it is simply a moment away. The more we desire nothingness, the more we are loving and kind, the veil between earthly and heavenly worlds dissolves and we discover the poetic wonder of creation. When we carry God in our hearts, we endure but not succumb to the pain of our world. Contemplation is the aspiration to live love on its own terms, carrying within us the fragrance of the beautiful and the sacred.

Sow Seeds

In carrying spiritual gifts in our hearts and minds, we sow seeds of grace, which take root in the soil of the fertile soul. In bearing the divinity, we are a transmission of the Creator. "For where two or three are gathered together in my name," Jesus says (Mt. 18:20), the gifts of awe are sown. Thus, the contemplative person is a gardener, scattering seeds so that new life grows. If we keep all the seeds for ourselves, and do not ever share, nothing blossoms in the earthly garden. In humility, we are happy sowers of the divine essence.

Quality of Being

When you bear truth or love or humility, you possess it as a quality of being. It is who and what you are. It is not just something that you do. In contemplation, you contain within your depth the divine virtues, which lend grace to your actions and presence in life. As your longing for God grows more intense, you simultaneously are drawn deeper into the sacred, and the qualities of contemplation are established in you. As you bear the divinity of the world, you become the qualities of divinity. This is why contemplation refers to a radical and experiential practice of embodying the Spirit.

·◆·

IF WE APPLY the various definitions of "bearing" to the ways we normally think, we notice a change in orientation. For example, it is common to say, "I know truth." Yet, we do not just know truth. We bear truth. This shift in language reminds us that we are composed of truth, it is inherent in our being, and tempered in the fire of our own emptiness. Then we are the seed of truth's dissemination. Similarly, we say, "I am seeking God." Yet God is within us. We sustain and support the unveiling of the Divine. Contemplation removes the obstacles that prevent us from sharing the gift of what is already within our hearts. The shift in perspective from knowing to bearing is a more honest description of the role that the body, mind, and spirit exert. Truth emerges from the deep self, pushing away those impediments that are foreign to the divine within. This is a departure from the way we normally think—whereby we labor to secure from external events or people what we believe is lacking in us.

Another example of this reversal of orientation: finding love or learning how to love. "Love bears all things," says Corinthians. We bear love, we bear compassion. In the nine meditations, we support love, we sustain love, we suffer in love, we give birth to love, we grow in love, we offer the gifts of love, we carry love in our hearts, we sow the seeds of love, and we possess love as a quality. If we want to know about love, then we have to be willing to bear the interwoven beads on the necklace of love. We think we need someone to love us, which makes us vulnerable to whether we are loved. Bearing love means this: love is my most natural way of being. I find love by becoming the depth of love already within me.

Divinity

WE CAN CERTAINLY describe how God has been understood and revealed in the world's religious traditions. But, no definition of divinity is adequate. We can never capture the fullness of the gift, which is elusive, akin to vision or poetry. As French theologian Jean Luc Marion writes:

> The body of the text does not belong to the text but to the One who is embodied in it. Thus, theological writing always transgresses itself, just as theological speech feeds on the silence in which, at last, it speaks correctly. . . . Theology always writes starting from an other than itself. It diverts the author from himself; . . . it causes him to write outside of himself, even against himself, since he must write not of what he is, on what he knows, in view of what he wants, but in, for, and by that which he receives and in no case masters.[1]

If we apply Marion's idea to the practice of contemplation, then we erase ourselves—are made empty—to create a place for the Presence of that which exceeds the self. When we bear the divinity of the world, we create a place for each other to dwell. It is not the search for an identified self, but the emptying of self that invites everyone to share in divine intimacy. Left in silence, it is the essential task of the monk to open one's heart to the cosmos. It is the work of letting go of self-will that contemplation pursues with utmost seriousness and intensity.

Divinity can be read in at least two modes. There is theistic contemplation that serves as an affirmative hymn to the always indescribable and ultimately unknowable, personal God. Here contemplation seeks to pierce the veil of temporality in order to bear the transparency of Divine Presence. From a Christian perspective, we abandon our limited identity in order to be true to the Word that exceeds all words. In devotion to the Beloved that exceeds every attempt to speak, our words are transformed into an iconographic prayer. Each word has the potential to be a song of devotion to the Holy. And, yet, the proclamation of our praise never excludes other beings, but constantly uncovers and gives birth to mystery.

Divinity can be read in another, a-theistic, mode. The fact remains that contemplation displays in its historical unfoldment not only a transgression of the text, but a transgression of "God." Here our task is slightly different. For contemplation must speak to an Other who disclaims all names, to the One who demands a shedding of distinction and the unsaying of identity, to a God beyond God: Indistinction. Nothingness. A spirituality that emerges out of silence must allow this Other to speak who breaks apart speaking, and who leads one to silence, and to an almost literal tearing of the fibers of being.[2] This radical contemplative vantage point has the rare capacity to withstand contradictory truth claims and to allow differences free play. In silence all things are held in a deeper unity. It is the force of openness that resists exclusive and absolutizing truth. If for no other reason than because it demands of its recipients that we speak beyond our understanding precisely because we do not speak of our self.

We contain within our heart theism and a-theism, saying and unsaying. At the balance point, we encounter the world from the unity of being. Even when we do not understand oneness, or cannot sustain it, we bear it in our beings. In bearing the divinity, we hold all that is good and true and beautiful in the circle of love. We want this gift not just for ourselves but for all creation.

World

THE WORLD is our Home. When we bear the divinity of the world, it includes our Earth—this incredible, vibrant, blue, verdant sphere rotating in cosmic space. The word "world" involves all that exists, humanity, divinity, the entire created order, and the cosmos. The world also is the body and embodiment of the Divine. How could it be otherwise? How would we be alive if this were not the case? Therefore, the world is Everything: all that is, and every act, thought, culture, religion, society, language, vision, hope, dream. Bearing the divinity of the world reminds us that there is nothing separate from the Holy One.

The world of matter is divine. There is something inexplicably mysterious about the subatomic realms, the universe of cells, and the wholeness and complexity of the body. The physical universe vibrates in multiple states and dimensions of oneness. The mind may distort the unity, consciousness may perceive dualistically, but our bodies exist in an interdependent, homeostasis, or we would not even be able to breathe. The physical world is awe-inspiring, and the fact that, on a daily basis, we harm each other is impossible to comprehend, but this continues to happen, regardless.

Contemplation is not a name for God. It is a condition of being-in-the-world that is necessary in order to bear (in the world) the divinity of the world. As a spiritual practice it can never be absolutely achieved or made fully transparent. Rather, it is an orientation that implies living in service of the daily, and cosmic, unfolding of the indwelling divine image and likeness. It is a spiritual practice that strengthens one's ability to withstand the intimacy of life, and the inevitable loss of identity that makes the self tremble and lays the heart bare. It is a mystical being-in-the-world that refuses the daily distancing that informs public discourse. It is a bearing of a vulnerable and unveiled contact with the untidiness of life for the sake of every other. It is allowing oneself to feel the profundity and beauty of creation, to be pierced by the unbounded generosity of nature, and to be felled by the utter sensitivity that gives rise to love. It is a discipline that constantly seeks to be literate in reading the heart's passion: to bear wounding and betrayal, but to disallow closure and retribution.[3]

• ◆ •

Most Holy One
it is so difficult to bear your Earthly Paradise!

As we long to be a birthplace of your Light
we need patience
we need time
and most of all compassion.

We pray that ever more each day
You will instill these virtues in our hearts.

Amen.

SIX

Our Mother of Contemplation

I N GREAT MOTHER INDIA, all rivers are holy. Daughters of *Ma Ganga*—the mother of all rivers—pour from the celestial realm in a continuous stream into the creative sphere. It is told that long ago, in her great mercy, *Ma Ganga* agreed to flow upon the earthly plane, leaving her abode in Heaven. Spilling over the tangled locks of Shiva's hair, who was persuaded to catch the Ganges as she fell, she tumbled down from heaven to the Himalayas, rushing out over the plains of India to the sea. There, at the place where the rivers and the ocean meet, she entered the underworld to redeem dead ancestors. She therefore is called the Triple-Pathed River, flowing in three dimensions of existence: in Heaven, on Earth, and in the netherworld.[1]

She is both holy river and goddess, and the creation of the world arises from the freeing of her heavenly waters as *Ma Ganga* spreads the sacred presence of the gods to the Earth in liquid form. So holy are her waters, that those regions her rivers flow through are consecrated into sacred ground. It is said that bathing in her waters is similar to being in Heaven, and that a drop of Ganges water erases all sins accumulated over lifetimes.

Ma Ganga mystically represents the purifying quality of rivers: moving, flowing, falling water that has healing properties.[2] She is the Divine physician who is called upon to heal the souls wounded by sin. She spiritually cleanses the inner impurities. Uncontaminated by the world, her rivers wash away the impurities of the realms they touch.

The mighty rivers of India represent the crossing from the world of ignorance or bondage to the far shore—the unconditional divine realm. Signifying the journey of transition and rebirth, the seeker enters the sacral waters to undergo a metamorphosis of being. In the purifying power of *Ma Ganga*, the pilgrim drowns to the old self in order that the new self, free and enlightened, can be born. The Ganges is the prototypical crossing place, the liquid axis of the innumerable worlds, a pathway connecting all spheres of reality, and a presence in which one may ascend to the divine abode.

Ma Ganga is mother's milk nourishing all her children. She is here in the world to comfort with her yielding, redemptive waters. The flowing essence of compassion, she is all-accepting, offering blessing to any who taste the milk drink of immortality, nourishment for the soul. Full of life and vitality, the source of veneration and hope, these are the primordial waters, the rivers before and prior to the life-giving salvation of our various traditions. These are the holy rivers coursing through our bones from which creation nourishes itself on sacral milk.

Deep, deep within the caverns of our hope these mighty mother rivers flow. They convey no word or language for the mind but silently feed the soul. Being prior to word, they nourish us in solitude; being prior to religion, they break open our exclusionary and clinging hearts; being more primordial than the individual, they teach their ways only in the return to the person, to our humanity.

They are mother rivers because we are born of them. They are mother rivers because they are fountains of fullness, pouring themselves out for the sake of the unborn. And they are rivers of silence that water the seeds of holiness giving life to all of creation.

The contemplative journey today drinks from these deep underground rivers. To be a contemplative today requires a new experience of *Ma Ganga*, the Rivers of Silence, the Mother's source of nourishment and hope.

Worship of the Mother

INDIA, ANCIENT and modern, is resplendent with devotion to the Goddess in her many manifestations—*Durga, Saraswati, Shiva, Lakshmi, Kali, Radha, Ganga, Sita, Parvati*. When we evoke female divinity, we are touching the extensive, ancient worship of the Divine Feminine that has sustained countless civilizations. We are calling forth the many additional personifications of Her presence on Earth—Hagia Sophia, Mary, *Virgen de Guadalupe, Avalokiteśvara*, Divine Mother, *Guanyin, Sapientia*, Corn Woman, *Woyengi*. The re-discovery of the Divine Feminine in historical and cultural forms—depicted as immanent and transcendent, strongly connected with our bodies and the Earth—has grown in the last century and is a significant aspect of many people's practices today.

Female goddess figures represent the spectrum of attributes assigned to divinity. For example, in Hinduism the Great Goddess *Devi* represents the sum of all manifestations of the Mother and is depicted in various personifications: *Ma*, gentle and approachable mother; *Jaganmata*, Mother of the universe; a cosmic force (*Durga, Kali*) that destroys demonic energies, and creates, annihilates, and recreates the world; *Parvati*, the gentle wife who, in radiant form (*Saraswati, Lakshmi*), is the gracious donor of wealth, fortune, and success. As Virgin and Mother, the Goddess is considered to be the very spring from which every kind of love flows into the world. From the vast ocean of her being, the Goddess gives birth to all living things and is a sacred mystery.

In this section, I explore the Divine Feminine in her personification as Hagia Sophia (Holy Wisdom) and her attributes of excessive mercy, kindness, benevolence, and nonviolence. Elsewhere, I have named this orientation *via feminina*—the mystical path of the feminine—and hold that its emphasis on a theology of intimacy is a radical departure from dominant religious orientations and a necessary foundation for a new contemplative path and way of life.

Contemporary scholarship reminds us that all names for God are metaphors. While personifications of divinity are critical to our imaginations and prayer life, it is also true that no identity captures divine infinity.

At the same time, a metaphor is not merely a property of God expressed in abstract terms but displays the innate power and energy of symbols that engage the whole person and facilitate participation in the realm of the holy. Her names are meta-symbolic—they are windows into a vision of our world from the point of view of the Divine Feminine. Describing Her as mercy, compassion, pathos, longing, and benevolence are genuine insights into Sophia's relationship to us, "rather than a projection," writes Catholic theologian, Christopher Pramuk, "of human traits into divinity." Her personifications offer "real insight—not explanation or proof, but *insight*—" into Her life story, the very Being of Sophia.[3]

When we use feminine names for divinity, we are referring to a Presence, the site of worship and sacrament. Thus, in a "'a single stroke of thought' the name 'Sophia,' no less than the name 'Christ,' can become—

> on the lips of the believing, praying, *and* thinking community—a privileged meeting place for the encounter with God. Her name tells us nothing new, communicates no "new information," but awakens what is and always has been, a union that "already exists but is not fully realized." And yet, in truth, her name does evoke something new, and something quite old, that has been forgotten."[4]

While I believe that women embody her in distinct ways, my association with the Divine Feminine encompasses the whole range of consciousness, spiritual paths, and ways of being and knowing in males and females. In her edition of the wisdom writings by the Russian Orthodox theologian Vladimir Solovyov, professor of Slavic languages, Judith Kornblatt, clarifies:

> Sophia is never solely female, never solely divine or solely earthly, solely abstract or solely material, solely ideal or solely debased. Instead her truest manifestation—the future toward which we aspire—is at once embodied, incarnated, and transfigured into a new whole, both male and female, spiritual and material, divine and earthly.[5]

The Divine Feminine is a powerful force of awareness, reminding us of how the intrinsic and holy unity of life is systematically harmed or destroyed. She represents the innocence of heart as the highest ideal and holds her pure sight even in the midst of atrocities, suffering, and pain. Her presence dispels the sins we harbor and the fracturing of love that mars the soul of creation today. The wisdom of Hagia Sophia is so gentle and strong, so delicate and merciful that we need new eyes to see, new ears to hear, and new hearts to feel the intensity of her message. Few religions embody her teachings. She does not convince, enforce, or convert but reveals what is possible. Her way is radically gentle and tender, profoundly merciful and nonviolent. At times even proclamation or pronouncement can be an affront to the subtle manner in which She enters our souls and heals our inner lives.

Hagia Sophia offers a vision that calls each of us not only to forgive, repair, and restore, but also to approach each other and all creation with benevolence and nonharm. As one humanity, we have shouldered too much punishment, too many tears, and too much disdain. We take so much of life for granted. Her wisdom offers unity, bridging divisions within oneself and in societies, to help mend the fractures in the world.

Her sacred tradition is complete unto itself; it is not dependent upon any other way. It is not fragmentary or elusive. It is not without depth or structure. It is not hidden but present. It is not partial but complete. There is nothing lacking other than our willingness to open our hearts to her Pure Heart.

The path of the Divine Mother embraces the wisdom of every religion and spiritual practice, clarified and empowered by the richness of humanity's collective spiritual heritage. Her revelation leads adherents to the highest states of contemplative consciousness, and to the secret teachings of love. In surrendering your heart to her immediacy, your depth—which is also her depth—subsumes all spiritual truths. All religions flow in the current of Her sacred rivers.

Perhaps the suppression of Hagia Sophia causes us to fear or reject her. Perhaps the violence that threatens to rend those who claim direct contact with the Holy averts our hearts from her Wisdom already pre-contained in our birth. I know many people who fear loving her completely, concerned that they may be judged by their peers or betray religious and social contracts. I know many others who worry about self-delusion, grandiosity, or sin in their newly felt adoration of the Divine Feminine. Yet, over centuries of discipleship and worship, millions have sought her solace and are praying to her right now. All over the world worshippers long for the compassion of our Mother.

A person who pursues *via feminina* needs to pray for resiliency and autonomy of spirit. Her path of love does not come pre-formed, packaged within a named tradition, established prayers, or a centuries-old spiritual formation. Rather, the Great Goddess is born in the souls of those who pursue her. People who seek her mysterious way, who are recipients of her merciful love, follow a faith of healing and reconciliation.

Like still waters, *via feminina* gently flows in the cave of the heart, soothing the jagged edges of consciousness. From the beginning, her journey of peace was laid. In her, the universal processes of transformation and every archetypal reality are found in their pre-religious form: illumination and transformation, and dying to the false self; union, intimacy, and cleaving to our Creator. Hagia Sophia beckons us to be co-creators of new spiritual pathways and sacramental rituals.

The Divine Feminine challenges us to acknowledge and reform oppressive elements in our hearts and in our religions. In order to do this, we must also heal the wounds of the feminine in self, society, and in the world. Its outward manifestations are witnessed in the violence inflicted on females and on the innocent and weak, first among them children. Its inward manifestations are felt in the interiority of the self, where we, male and female, suffer the afflictions and the desecration of the tender, gentle, and sublime. The absence of Sophia's holy presence has stifled our language, robbed our spirits, and curtailed our ability as a human community to envision a different future. We need the language and the heart of Hagia Sophia to heal the sins of the world. Her pathless path requires a leap of faith into new traditions of mystical insight and wisdom.

Blessed Be She

WHAT IF the Holy One—Blessed Be She—is calling us to a new contemplative path and a new way of life? What if She is drawing us closer to a deep cavern of truth that we could only find were we to temporarily give up all of our ideas and notions of God, and place all of our historical understanding of the spiritual life under the *cloud of forgetting*? What if the very spiritual paths we have followed and practiced through the centuries were but a threshold for another way of being and loving? Would we not find the courage to cross over to the splendor to which our Beloved Mother is calling?

IT IS ONLY LATELY that Holy Mystery has given us a name—*via feminina*—for her path. It honors the classical traditions that form a part of our journey. It means the feminine way or the way of the feminine, and I also would say, although this is not reflected specifically in Latin, the way of the mother.

IT IS A PATH of the heart when Holy Mother becomes intimately close and draws us ever deeper into divine interiority. It is entrance into Her inner life, a way of approaching the contemplative life that is mysteriously etched in our beings. It is a sacred path and a gift of the Spirit. It is through *via feminina* that we come to participate in another dimension of the mystical journey, Blessed Be She.

THE GREEK WORD *epectasis* means to leave behind what lies in the past and strive forward to what lies ahead. This striving forward expresses the quality of *via feminina*, which gives us the courage to leave behind everything known to enter an unknowing and to bear this unknowing in order to journey with our Beloved Mystery into the future.

IN THIS WAY we receive the fruits of a contemplative life innocent and free. It is through the wisdom of *via feminina* that we find solace for the wounds of the spirit and a new realm of being in which all our sins come to rest and our whole being is bathed in healing light. Ever deeper into her merciful heart, we are reunited in the mystical cloister, the Divine Mother's sanctuary of love.

An Un-concluding Meditation

I WISH TO SHARE what it feels like to be immensely loved and cradled in an intimacy so total that no feeling can hold. I want to share the exuberance of my heart that quickens when it hears the voice of Hagia Sophia. I want to pour out the majesty and tragedy of living a woman's life, a spiritual life exploited by the screaming noise of a world bent on destruction and the crying pleas of all those abandoned and erased. I want to shake awake our bleary souls and ignite a remembrance of our Mother of Contemplation, who rocks us tenderly before our beginnings and before any stories we remember or tell. I want to excavate and dredge my heart for symbols and pictures and words; for the poetry that touches the untouchable and the spirit that makes the soul quiver in anticipation. What can I do as I type here alone in my room, looking out the window on a tiled image of the *Virgen de Guadalupe*, to convey the intense belonging to the holy that breathes our every breath?

Was it an inchoate yearning already present in me, a recovery expedition begun before I descended into the realm of our Earth Mother, and was born into the maternity ward of Mercy Hospital? It's intriguing how those two words go together—mercy and ward. We come from mercy to be a ward of the planet, like a prisoner of our own amnesia, without remembering why or how we got here. Often our early years offer no inkling of our treasured beginnings in Light. Perhaps our mother was more harsh than gentle, more punishing than merciful, more demanding than benevolent. But despite shortcomings, all humans float—more or less—for thirty-nine weeks in the swollen belly of a mother, our lives sustained by the most fragile of threads. We each lived inside her body, nourished by her blood, oxygenated by her breath, and then—through the channel of her womb—birthed into the light and sound of the world.

Yet the miracle of life is not only bound to or bound by our biological mothers. In a way it does not matter who sires our bodily form or how tender was our earthly mother, because the Mother of Spirit holds us to her breast. Our souls were created in love, we are constituted by the capacity to be intimate, we are held in a circle of tenderness. We pass back and forth through the permeable membrane of history, like a molecule passing into a cell. We are constantly moving through history and its signs, concepts, ideals, and properties to the nameless benevolence that grips our souls, inseparably one and whole.

How easy it is to forget!

This primary relationship of the Mother of All—the unnamed who gestates life, determines everything, and reveals everything—calls us Home. She is an immense gift of loving, who anoints our souls with Holy Benevolence.

Please allow Our Mother of Contemplation to be your Beloved again.

. • .

She came forth upon the golden lights
radiant and pure
And upon her head shone the many tendril majesty
of insight where no mortal had ever stepped
and only Mystery could comprehend.

She was cloaked in brocaded gown
all violet, silken hue
And purity emitted from her breast
anointed by the dew.

None had ever cast sight upon one
such as She,
untouched and joined upon the immortal essence
of cosmic delight.

Amen.

PART TWO

Spiritual Formation

◆

Essential to the new monk's vocation is turning away from worldly ambition and toward contemplation, inner realization. The gradual process of study, practice, and participation in the monastic ethos that stabilizes the quest over time is referred to as the seeker's "formation." This section gives a brief introduction to the stages of formation in historical monastic communities, followed by a discussion of how to adapt the essence of the formative process for the monk in the world.

For those who have jobs, are raising families,
caring for children or elders, what does
the turn away from worldly
ambition look
like?

◆

SEVEN

Spiritual Formation

O NE OF THE MORE RADICAL decisions a person can make is to enter a monastic community, leaving society and established relationships behind. Due to the profound change of life that is associated with monkhood, religious orders are thoughtful about admitting new candidates and the educational and spiritual process that orients them to living within the monastery. This gradual method of personal evaluation is frequently referred to as the monk's formation, and includes study, practice, and participation in the spiritual ethos that has stabilized a monastic community over time. Preparation for joining a religious order usually evolves in consultation with a designated spiritual team or leader, such as the abbot or lama of the order. Aspirants undergo discernment as to their suitability for monastic life, moving through successive stages of commitment that can last years before one takes solemn, lifelong vows.

Formation involves testing one's initial call against the sometimes-harsh realities of actually living in and committing to a vow of monkhood. This includes the participation of novices in rituals, living the spiritual precepts and norms, study of wisdom texts, and learning to live within the communal setting. In addition, candidates study religious history, theology, rules, vows, prayers, chants, meditative forms, and liturgies. Formation is therefore based on the scriptural and theological foundations of a tradition. For example, a Buddhist monk seeks to live as the Buddha, free of attachments, practicing chant and meditation, and studying the *Dhammapada* and other Buddhist wisdom texts. Christians understand that the monk's journey aims to live a holy life on Earth by studying the Gospels, daily chanting of the liturgy, developing humility, and growing in love.

Monastic formation, as I use the term here, refers to the interior, mystical process by which a person undergoes a re-forming of the personality, and establishes a new center of being. While the process involves self-realization and the stages of purification associated with spiritual growth, formation of the monk more accurately describes self-transcendence—a state marked by egolessness, letting go of false habits and ideas, replacing self-will with divine-will, and opening one's heart to grace. The goal of formation is to refashion the person to receive and act upon the presence of the Divine in the soul. It is thus contemplative in both its means and its ends.

The Monk in the World

THE FORMATIVE PROCESS is perhaps the least-understood aspect of spiritual development for contemporary practitioners, yet vital to the transformation that signifies the monk. The general public usually identifies monkhood as a state of being in which the person gives up the common rules of worldly engagement, turning away from the dictates of money, success, individuality, sex, and marriage. The monk associated with a traditional monastic community adheres to these rules of life, directing efforts to a different way of being than the one previously lived, based on the order's established practices and norms.

Naturally, a monastic call lived in secular society is distinct from that of a traditional, residential monastic community. This is because, for the monk within—for the seeker who desires to take monastic vows living as a householder alone or in community—learning to be refashioned according to divine principles cannot be the same. Nonetheless, the process by which a person arrives at the spiritual necessity to change one's life and heart is at the core of every monastic impulse. Frequently, the person discovers a great need for silence and solitude, finds joy in the study of spiritual texts, and longs to simplify daily existence. Transcendent principles are at work in such people, which is drawing them deeper into their spiritual natures and closer to the Divine Heart.

Across cultures and historical periods, monastic communities have been repositories of wisdom—teaching about self-discipline, singleness of heart, honoring the solitude of others, and how to turn from the materialism of the world to the inner path of love. In guiding others to a monastic sensibility, the essence of monastic wisdom is adapted to the experience of people who work, raise families, care for children or elders, suffer illness or death, and strive for justice. The most important consideration is how to assist a person who is not part of a formal religious community to establish a personally relevant and spiritually effective transformative process and life orientation.

The nontraditional monk, seeking a deeper relationship with the Divine, often struggles to convert his or her worldly existence into a more spiritually attuned life. This occurs in part because we tend to think of monasticism the way we think about everything else: something we have to do, make happen, accomplish, or achieve. But the contemplative or monastic life is a reversal of this attitude that we are in charge, that our will alone can motivate change, that we can get by in the normal frame of reference. What is shattering about monastic spirituality is that it aspires toward a state of receptivity, in which nothing impedes the inflow of God. It is a life of humility and nonviolence, of peace and love, but mostly it is a life that has surrendered the self in an act of unknowing and faith. This means letting go of the mental gymnastics disturbing the mind and instead simply experiencing a moment of openness. Contemplation is an entrance into the Divine life itself, and thus can be grasped only through direct experience.

Perhaps a first step in the seeker's formation is the acceptance of one's discomfort in relation to the ambition of secular culture. While everyone has an intrinsic contemplative core, the person who longs for silence, who desires to be alone with God, and who suffers over injustice already has been chosen to walk the path. The person called to contemplation is, in some ways, an unusual person who is often uncomfortable with the way the world operates. Rather than a detriment, it can be healthy to not belong and to be alone, because in solitude we find the heart of hearts, the inextinguishable flame that burns brightly and forever.

To claim one's call to a passion greater than earthly ones is to finally come to terms with your life mission. This is the vocation to seek the Divine that underlies every other activity or choice, a commitment that will reform your being into a new creation. It is not for the easily discouraged, nor for the person who gives up without a struggle, or the one who waits to be told it is okay—go ahead. It is instead for the one who cannot live in the old way; for the person who aspires to and cries out for freedom; for the one who longs to know Truth and live in and for the Holy.

Monasticism is the reverse perspective of how the world operates. It is an unlearning of the personality characteristics and social advancement valorized in culture and the quest to achieve that marks the climate of contemporary life. Instead, the monk aspires each day to humanity's spiritual potential, which affects everything: what one does, how one lives, and one's relationship to money, other humans and the natural environment, possessions, and so forth. This aspiration is highly personal, as a seeker works to transform whatever is diminished by the world into a more spiritually integrated mode of consciousness. The heart feels what is lacking, and reaches out to transform and heal, because interior to the self is love. Although we may never have experienced divine love, we know what it is. And because we know love, we suffer its absence.

The reverse perspective of monasticism means that we submit; we say "yes" to the wisdom that elevates our lives and activities. We consent. We have the freedom to refuse, to say "no." But the monk is distinguished by his or her consent. This is the vow. I may move very slowly, I may be a turtle, or a snail, but I say "yes!"

Show me the path. Open my heart. Live in me.

The process of establishing a divine perspective in the monk's heart takes time and grows incrementally as he or she learns to let go of ego attachments. We suffer because we resist movement into the sacred. We don't intend to rebel or struggle. But we have been trained to fear change and to deny the transcendent. As we divest the ego of falsehood, denial and fear can flood the mind—and obscure the heart. In these moments, it is important to remember that letting go is for our great benefit. It is cause for celebration, to experience inner paradise now!

Monasticism is not essentially about cloister, robe, or ceaseless meditation. While these are central aspects of many monastic lifestyles, the call to silence and solitude occurs in the depth of the soul and is not dependent upon or subject to whether the seeker resides in a monastic enclosure, wears the proper religious garment, or spends hours a day in prayer.

Because contemplation is often counter to how we live out our lives, the necessity to be more monastic can be unsettling, challenging how and why we do things. Even the degree to which we have learned to surrender and to give up our will, there is more to let go and more abundance of blessings ahead. There is always that mysterious capacity for intimacy, which will never be exhausted. In order to be effective, the monk uses meditation and prayer to uproot the incessant mind chatter, which clouds the soul and obscures direct experience.

The monk within us seeks self-wisdom, receptive to the unfolding of mystery. It is the practice of understanding our unique energies, how we respond to the world, and why certain actions and not others affect us. It requires a refined and conscious awareness of the self, at the same time being divested of "self." It requires dispassionate awareness of the ego in order to clearly distinguish wisdom from other forms of consciousness. Prayer, meditation, and awareness spiritualize our energy.

Conversion of Life

According to the rule of St. Benedict, monks make a vow of *conversatio morum*. Difficult to translate, the essence of this Latin phrase is that the monk is committed to a complete change of life and change of heart, to act like a monk. Much of the monk's life is dedicated to this ongoing formation, which takes place not only in the beginning, heady stages, but also throughout life, helping monastics to cooperate with grace and be remade into holy people.

This posture of a complete change of life and quest for total transformation is the founding principle of the person committed to the divine quest. The acceptance of transformation, or metamorphosis, means a new center from which to live. The conversion is internal and a continual re-conversion. The person is focused on the Divine, and how activities emerge from the center of love, and not from material concerns. The first question and orientation: what does God want of me? Taking into consideration the whole of one's life and not the imposed ideals we have about a God-centered existence, what leads to the greater advent of the Spirit in my life? That is, dispel the images you have accrued about monasticism and instead focus on a true, interior engagement with Spirit's message for you today.

Conversion of life cannot be forced or dictated. A monk in training can emulate change by practicing the precepts of tradition, following the rules, participating in rituals, taking vows, and establishing his or her place in the community. But true conversion is an inflow from the Divine. The person must be disposed to hear the call, and this is where preparation is essential because often, the person who lives a regular life is too busy and too distracted to listen.

In the biography of the Tibetan yogi, Milarepa, is a story of repentance. As it is told, Milarepa's father dies young, and his uncle and aunt steal his inheritance. In revenge for his relative's treatment of his mother and sister, he turns to sorcery and kills many people. Through his profound regret for his deeds, he seeks the Buddhist path and with guidance from his teacher, Marpa, he endures various extraordinary, physical trials. Intent on exhausting his negative karma, he retreats to remote caves to meditate, eat little, and experience hardship. After years of solitude and practice, he becomes a great yogi of wisdom and compassion, counselling his disciples:

> Life is short, and the time of death uncertain; so apply yourselves to meditation, avoid doing evil, and acquire merit, to the best of your ability, even at the cost of life itself. Act so that ye have no cause to be ashamed of yourselves; and hold fast to this rule. If ye do thus, ye can be sure of never disobeying the commands of the Supreme Buddha.[1]

The concept of turning one's life around is more than the change of vocation, it is the call to self-emptying. This process of re-forming to a divine posture, to love as the center, requires sacrifice. The turnaround from a purely material existence and worldly ambition to a spiritual worldview can happen in an instant or takes months or years as in Milarepa's story. But the conversion of the old life is essential to the path ahead in every case. We are required to reflect on the conditions of one's existence—what we place in order of importance, the means we pursue to seek ends, and our happiness or unhappiness. At times, we believe we are happy, but we often do not know what true happiness is. We experience transient pleasure, momentary cheer, fleeting contentment. But do we experience the deep, inner happiness that comes from being true, from acquiring merit and living in peace?

Beliefs and Values

I WOULD SUGGEST THAT the monastic archetype across cultures and religions pivots on the rejection of worldly ambition. By "worldly ambition," I mean not only the actual striving to make something of oneself and achieve material goals without concern for the costs to self and others. But, also, the cynicism, despair, nihilism, deprivation, and loss that fuels worldly significance and its power in defining what constitutes the important or good life. It is this constellation of accepted social and cultural norms that contemplation and a monastic sensibility reform.

Everyone develops in the milieu of beliefs and values shared by family, community, and nation. It is the job of the person called into monastic life to reorient him- or herself according to different criteria than the ordinary or consensual. For the Christian monk, time is occupied in the pursuit of Jesus' call to love, humility, and suffering, as well as in concern for the poor and marginalized, and emulation of the God of love who walks the path of mercy, embracing weakness as grace, and celebrates the least. The Buddhist monk similarly pursues the erasure of illusory identity, seeking moments of awareness and enlightenment, in which divisions are dissolved and the entire world is revealed in its original, unified whole. Nothingness is the goal, the way of indistinction that mirrors the liberation of the Buddha, and the cessation of suffering that he exemplified. Deconstruction of unhealthy habits, a false manner of being, self-aggrandizement, and pride are central to the monk's conversion.

Thus, the contemplative vision approaches reality from the perspective of oneness and unity of life, from a depth of being that has experienced moments of the interconnectedness of all creation and feels the pain of worldly ambitions that target and intend to harm love. For this reason, one of the central aspects of the monk's conversion is singleness of heart—that is, the person's realization of inner division and distraction, and the recovery of one's natural unity. Trappist monk, Thomas Merton:

> The first thing you have to do before you set about thinking about such a thing as contemplation, is to try to recover your basic natural unity, to *reintegrate* your compartmentalized being into a coordinated and single whole and learn to live as a unified *human person*. This means that you have to bring back together the fragments of your distracted existence so that when you say "I," there is really someone present to support the pronoun you have uttered.[2]

The monastic life employs many factors that assist in reducing the monk's conflict and honing the true self. Relevant is a disciplined consciousness that accepts the advice of mentors, opens the heart to the Divine, and submits in faith to the disturbances met on the journey. Peeling away layers of disaffection, the person on the path of liberation begins to connect with the inner action of the Divine in everyday events, and the juxtaposition of grace and struggle that accompanies every seeker. Gradually the monk acquires a new identity that develops from within, as he or she embodies in an integrative way the flowering of the soul. This "new" person is not a role, or temporary cloth that is put on and taken off. Rather, it is a true expression of the unencumbered original face slowly being revealed. It is, thus, a lifetime project, an ever-deepening expansion of one's heart in the divine or heavenly realms.

This is the path that finds self-realization in self-transcendence, that is, in letting go of the ego and its worldly ambition and accessing one's vocation from a divine perspective.

Mystical Method

AN INTERIOR PROCESS of transformation and self-transcendence is imprinted in the soul of every person. Our existence as living beings is in motion toward holiness and divinization, a fact that innumerable life events seek to subvert. And, yet, the process of self-transcendence echoes a constant vibration deep within the cells of the body and the energies of consciousness. It is never absent; it is never withdrawn. It is enclosed within silence and expressed in awe.

This change of being requires self-reflection and awareness of the way truth is subverted in public discourse, and an understanding of the rejection, neglect, or denial wielded against the personal search for meaning and the wisdom and cries of the soul. Assaults on the inner life lead to actual and energetic bodily harm directed at the person whose soul longs for meaning and love. Thus, the journey involves personal and societal cleansing, a repudiation of the denials, lies, and subversions that distort the true self and lead to pride, arrogance, a sense of entitlement, and lack of empathy.

What is this method, this process of liberation that is the foundation of monastic formation? It involves self-emptying, self-awareness and repentance, striving toward purity of heart, to become part of the cosmic interpenetration of realities and gradually embody in this life the goal of divine-human harmony. It is the juxtaposition of suffering and exaltation, of renunciation and abundance, of humility and glory, of weakness and strength, etc.—all of these seeming dichotomies taking place within the infinite depths of being in every one of us. It is the contemplative process that moves the person—sometimes slowly and inexorably, sometimes radically all at once—to the farther shore, to finally experience reality as it *is*.

This mystical method occurs in the daily events of life. It is not taking place solely in the auric field or etheric dimensions. It is activated by the actions and decisions in the life of a person who—like an artist painting a canvas—does not have conscious control of how the brushstrokes lead to a final image. We are generating the actions that will determine whether we embrace the facts and life lessons before us, drawing us closer or further away from a spiritual outcome. We choose how we will advance or retreat. Even when we are not aware of our decisions, we have chosen. Nothing in our existence is separate from this goal: how we eat, what we intend, our work, our loves, etc.

The monk has made a choice to be aware, to refute aimless living. He or she has a goal and is in pursuit of divine life, of truth, and thus is motived toward a single destination. Review any account of the path of a holy person and you will discover this process at work. In particular, the interior movement involves many vacillations between pain and healing, suffering and joy, struggle and grace. Our growth is ignited by the trials that expose our errors, and advanced by the integrity which compels us to admit our sins and to seek forgiveness. It is a subtle, deeply interior testing of the soul's resolve, strength, resilience, and endurance. It is not unlike the training of a world-class athlete, who learns through the hard work of practice, the sting of defeat, and the unending determination to succeed, how to bear all obstacles and setbacks with a mysterious faith in the rightness of the quest.

A common aspect of the interior journey is openness to the Divine— that we follow intuition, cooperate with grace, listen to the still voice, or wait for a moment of illumination. But what do these practices mean in actual life? How do we "cooperate with grace"?

The premise that underlies this practice is this: each of us is intimately united with the Divine Spirit. When we pay attention to the pulsation or wave of energy that constantly is emitted from our depth, we allow into conscious awareness the path ahead. Every moment of life yields choices. The monk strives to be aware of and pursue the divine choice, the mystical way, Jesus' path, or the *Dao*. Cooperating with grace is a cipher for an entire way of living, which honors and yields to God's plan for us. Thus, the monastic lifestyle is organized to provide time and space to connect with one's center, to listen for the inner voice, and to sort out competing voices that pull the person in diverse and sometimes contradictory directions.

The desire to live deeply, to offer one's heart to the Holy One, and to make a formal monastic commitment are the result of all of us being created in the divine image. Our innermost being continually seeks meaning and love. Foremost is the transmission of a longing that cannot be quelled, which is resting under every diversion and transgression waiting to be heard and called into action. It is this passion, this intention of love to seek God, to know truth, to be holy, that is everything. Without it, words glimmer but do not transform.

. • .

Lead us, Holy One
to your Temple
Help us to transform
our hearts.

May your Radiance
illuminate the path
of the monk who lives for
You alone.

Amen.

EIGHT

Turning One's Life Around

I OFTEN DESCRIBE the change of life required of the monastic seeker as the turning around of a huge ship. The ship is moving through the waters of life in a certain direction, but its navigation is faulty, and it is heading to the wrong port. The ship has to turn around, which takes time and effort because it is an immense cargo ship laden with many weighty thoughts and fears, promises and aspirations, as well as unpaid debts—monetary and emotional obligations. The first consideration is to realize that a person's intentions need to be consistent, especially since many will be pursuing a significant change of life without guidance. It does, in fact, require a fierce commitment to our deepest longing to experience love, and to know peace. No one can establish or inspire the desire to be a new monk; only the divine within calls us to contemplation. However, there is much we can do to prepare our hearts and souls for the influx of grace.

In working with people interested in preparing for a monastic commitment, I have found that intense study and spiritual practice are very effective in deepening the inner life and maturing the soul. The people with whom I formed a monastic community do not have a residential center, or even live in the same area of the country. However, over forty years we have maintained a strong bond and an intense commitment to practice and live as contemplative, nontraditional monks. The methods introduced over the decades have been successful in deepening the spirituality of members and expanding their love of the Divine. The steady, and often personally intense journey I followed to develop a formation process for nontraditional monks I share with you here and in subsequent chapters.

Daily Rituals

I ASK EACH PERSON who enters a process of monastic study and formation to develop a daily schedule of prayer and/or meditation. I do not advocate one form of practice, although over the years various types of prayer and meditation have been introduced. Instead, participants are encouraged to develop a meditative focus that is personally suitable. Some practice *vipassana*, zazen, Daoist *tai chi*, Quaker silence, *dhikr*, centering prayer, etc., and we encourage sharing of each other's practice. I suggest that every person create and follow a daily ritual, with set times for morning and evening devotion, if possible.

In addition, we use a prayer book to guide the daily and weekly horarium of our members and to foster community involvement when we gather for in-person or online retreat days. In Latin, "horarium" means "the hours," and refers to the weekday schedule or ritual. To facilitate, I compiled a book of my prayers—*A Feast of Prayers: Universal Liturgy of Hours*—that form a daily and weekly liturgy of hours. Using a common prayer book while we live in our separate locations binds us together and attunes our hearts to a sacred rhythm. When we come together for a residential retreat, I have found that organizing the days around a schedule of morning and night vigils, and morning, noon, and evening prayers has made a tremendous impact on supporting a contemplative atmosphere and joining our hearts in a shared experience. (You can find a sample of the prayer book in chapter 29).

Over the years, we have created a wide variety of church services, which are especially important in community rituals, such as a liturgy for a holy day, memorial service, or celebration of vows created for an interspiritual community.

Daily rituals order a person's life and establish a bodily rhythm that can assist with focusing on the spirit's call. Rising at a certain time—the monk who performs night vigils at 3 a.m., or the 6 a.m. period of meditation—sets an inner clock that attunes the person to an expansive space and to rest in God's time. Members preparing for vows (and hopefully as a regular practice throughout their lives) are asked to set a regular schedule for silence and solitude in a retreat center, at home, or another place removed from the daily activity of the world.

Spiritual Guidance

MONASTIC ORDERS maintain various methods of helping monks develop and deepen openness to grace. Confession or spiritual dialogue with an elder is part of the life of a monastic community. These honored practices are so intertwined with the everyday life that we forget how central they are to the formation process. Reflection can occur during prayer, at night before we retire, or in meditative moments. It is bringing conscious attention to the manner in which we behaved during the day, to those actions, thoughts, and resistances that were less than we hoped to be, as well as a review of the positive thoughts and behaviors that were above what was expected.

Every seeker can benefit from the guidance of a qualified spiritual companion or spiritual director steeped in the wisdom of classical and contemporary accounts of the inner life. It is a gift to be able to open our hearts to another person, to share soul-to-soul issues of spiritual importance, to be free to question one's faith, to lament over loss, and to probe the sanctuary of the heart. In the months or years that members prepare for a monastic commitment, they are encouraged to discuss with their spiritual companion matters of doubt and faith, religious experience, the nature of a vow, the value of belonging to a community, and how to integrate the desire for monkhood with family and other commitments. In-person sharing is best, but when it is not possible, connecting by video, phone, and in writing can also be powerful. These vital and personal soul conversations cannot be replicated in a narrative context, but point us, nonetheless, to grasp our inherent divine permission to seek freedom.

Teaching

THE PERSON (or people) who takes on the role of guiding a spiritual community ideally is a student of the sacred through personal and/or scholarly study and is prepared to gently, humbly, and honestly serve. Talks of instruction should aim to assist others in growing closer to their divine source and focus on the essential principles of spirituality, providing insight into powerful accounts of inner states of consciousness. These should include a focus on the wisdom found in scriptures, primary sources, and mystical, monastic texts. It is important to encourage study of the principles of spiritual life—placing God at the center, letting go of ego, examination of virtues, radical self-honesty, stages of spiritual growth, purity of heart, and detachment. Discussions on contemporary, religious thought—eco-theology, feminist, *mujerista*, womanist, Indigenous, Asian, and Black theologies, spirituality of nonviolence, preferential treatment of the poor, engaged Buddhism, etc.—are a critical element of the learning experience. They not only provide insight into the many ways people of diverse cultural orientations seek truth today, but also subvert the patriarchal mindset that has been historically dominant in religious thought.

Study

STUDY IS AN INTEGRAL component of the life of the monk. Normally, scripture and sacred texts of a given tradition are the central focus of study. Such endeavors can involve direct engagement with a text, recitation in liturgy and chant, and meditative and prayer practices. Buddhist monks recite the *Dhammapada*, chanting the sacred passages daily. Christian monks chant the psalms every day, including reading from Scripture during prayer services. Many also study works of classical mystics and modern authors as a way to expand spiritual consciousness and connect with others.

Most of the participants I work with in our monastic program are either dual-religious practitioners or interspiritual. Many members of our community have a deep and non-exclusive devotion to the Jewish tradition, Jesus, *Dao*, Sufi or Christian mysticism, Hindu spirituality, Buddha, and so forth. Because our faith is both-and (rather than either-or), members are open to and incorporate the grace of the world's wisdom at the same time that the foundation of their commitment is to the mystical path of the feminine, and a nonviolent orientation to religious practice and study.

This orientation tends to elicit a general misunderstanding—often expressed by members of religious congregations—that the interspiritual practitioner lacks a clear spiritual focus and a formal center of faith. I have devoted many pages in other writings to clarify this misapprehension and do not review it here. However, I would like to affirm that practitioners of new traditions of contemplative wisdom are followers of an authentic faith experience. That is, the commitment to become an interspiritual or dual-religious or unnamed monk is the result of a direct religious experience as vital and valid as any in the history of human spirituality. In addition, this particular call of faith explicitly is inclusive of our shared spiritual inheritance and guards against privileging one's tradition over another, even as we love our own.

Participants study from scriptures and the original writings of some of the world's mystics and monks, saints and theologians over the past three centuries, as well as literature on monastic vows and rules. This is intended to put aspiring monks in contact with the wisdom traditions of the world's religions, thus increasing the scope of their spiritual life and thought. Whether a person reads from a variety of sources or explores a select number of writings in depth, engagement with primary sources is a vital part of our monastic formation. Participants receive an extensive bibliography (which can be found in the appendix) that they can use for study and insight.

Writing

ANOTHER VITAL ASPECT of formation is reflection on and writing about the courses of study. At times, contemporary spirituality has tended to privilege practice over theory, activity over study. In my experience (and in the evidence of the great monasteries), spiritual study is crucial to monastic life, which intersects with and informs practice. There wouldn't be Buddhist monasticism without Buddha's teachings and the collection of Buddhist philosophy; Christian monasticism without the life and death of Jesus and generations of Christian theology; Daoist monks, Hindu saints, or Muslim shaykhs without reference to the *Dao dejing*, Upanishads, or the Qur'an. Such can be said for all the world's contemplative and monastic religions.

The study of sacred teachings—oral and written—is what binds an entire tradition and its adherents over the centuries into a diversified and unified whole. For the interspiritual or intercontemplative person, this is both a challenge and a gift. The gift is the availability of the scriptures and the spiritual texts of the world's religions. Truly, there has been no other period in history when seekers all over the globe have the ability to draw from humanity's collective storehouse of wisdom. At the same time, this can be challenging because the new monk is asked to be a co-creator, drawing upon an inner depth to birth new theologies and practices that can serve as foundational. The development of a theological structure for use in practical instruction is a unique aspect of the nontraditional monk's education.

I thus encourage participants to create a study journal in which they record responses, insights, or disagreements, paying particular attention to the needs of the new monk's quest. They also write a formal reflection paper. For each semester of study, I recommend at least two or three reflections of substantive thinking, commentary, and spiritual insight. As an instructor—and as a seeker—what I am aiming for in these reflection papers is a combination of personal insight coupled with a theological or philosophical depth of thinking that relates to the content of study.

Of course, everyone is encouraged to keep a personal journal. However, the content of the personal journal is—as it should be—personal, often stream of consciousness, and free-flowing. This is not what I look for in a reflection paper, but rather "contemplative depth." Deep study expands the soul and assists in the development of the theological or contemplative mind. There is no substitute for this kind of intense engagement with wisdom, in whatever form it takes—oral or written traditions.

Contemplative Depth

THEOLOGICAL or contemplative depth is challenging to describe, but it is obvious to the person who has discovered it. It means that the reader is invested in the meaning of the text and is in search of its disclosure of truth. Understand that I am not referring to whether or not a particular text passes an objectified criterion of truth, because no such test exists. Rather, the process is highly subjective. That is, the reader as subject is engaging with the author as subject, seeking to connect with the meaning to which the words point. This is the essence of every scripture or sacred text—it is revealing an aspect of Mystery. One way to describe this is by referring to the notion of a text as an archeological template in which language is imbued with layers of meaning: literal, allegorical, moral, spiritual, mystical. These layers do not dictate how one will engage with a text, or that every interpretative layer is present. Only that the reader allows the text to sink into his or her being, to dwell within. This is essentially reading as listening, reading as silence, in which the words on the page soak into the person who reads, opening up doors and windows in the soul.

Critical Engagement

AN IMPORTANT ELEMENT in the formation of a new monk is awareness of how or in what way a person's commitment differs from that of traditional monastic communities. I ask participants to be aware of whether what they know, experience, or are reading about monkhood is aligned or in conflict with their inner intention or desire. Especially important in this process is the freedom to ask questions, to be aware of injustice, and to strive for love and mercy. In my mind, traditional vows and monastic rules—at least at first reading and without insight into their deeper meaning—tend to be a bit too ascetic and not sufficiently life-affirming for many people today. Some betray a punitive orientation and appear to lack compassion for the sufferer or sinner.

I ask seekers to think critically about what may be different in a contemporary monastic commitment from traditional forms. How would you describe this difference? What does the difference mean to you and to your future? What are the ways in which (if at all) a person's consciousness of the feminine, gender, sexual orientation, race, social status, or ethnic background transforms or changes monastic consciousness, its rituals and practices, and the actual form that a monastic community takes? How does an interspiritual or multi-religious orientation alter monastic practice and culture? What is the relationship of global suffering, injustice, poverty, and environmental stress to the monk's inner life and the health of his or her soul? What type of monastic commitment draws you the most—the hermit, singular or community-oriented contemplative, or spiritually motivated activist?

Listening

COOPERATING with grace means that we seek divine guidance, we open ourselves to answers from the spirit realm, from wise elders, and from the study of scripture and spiritual texts. We maintain a posture of openness and humility, listening for the tender, quiet, and often shy voice guiding us from within. To follow the will of God and not one's own will. To listen deeply and obey the wisdom learned by asking the divine within.

We try to uncover the movement of the ego or false self, learning to distinguish between the self's will and the Divine will. It is here, at the level of the will, that we often have the greatest resistance to cooperation with grace.

The spiritual life is fueled by a passionate intention moving from the heart outward toward its object of devotion. Christian texts associate this intention with the will to love; love is the intention that moves life toward its highest virtues. Yet, our will for love's greatest good can be distorted or corrupted for worldly gain. From an early age we learn or are trained to evaluate the advantage or disadvantage of our choices. When advantage is associated with self-gain, with prestige, money, dominance, etc., for its own sake, the ego learns to direct its energies toward potentially destructive goals. As the will is rewarded for its choices—even if they are temporary—the person's connection to the Divine will (the will for good) is thwarted or abandoned. Then, the errant will becomes stronger than the inner voice; it overrides the heart's desire, ridicules common sense, and humiliates authentic feeling.

Examples abound in religious literature. A fourth-century disciple's story of his struggle to reign in an errant will captures the moment of conflict:

> Having heard that Abba Zeno had healed many, I wanted to go find him and open myself to him. But the devil prevented me from doing so. Often I would actually go to the old man in order to tell him everything, but the enemy would not let me speak by putting shame in my heart . . . so that I wouldn't reveal my sickness to the physician and be healed.[1]

Many of us can identify with the disciple's plight. We can recall times in our lives when we intentionally—consciously or not—took the path of self-will. Taking inventory of the road not chosen assists in recognizing how the lower will controls our actions and diverts our deepest intention.

Enclosure

A CENTRAL IMAGE associated with monasticism is the cloister or enclosure, the sequestering of the monks behind an impenetrable wall designed to keep the world at bay. For the new monk, especially one who works and lives among family or friends, physical enclosure is not possible. Yet, as in all things, enclosure is not a value exclusively tied to physical separation. It also can be the experience of the inseparable bond between solitude and love, between guarding one's heart and singularity of intention.

We enjoy the solitude, which enclosure makes possible, when we temper our need for consumerism and the glut of information, refuse to share in gossip, and reject what others covet. The real enclosure is the heart of the person, dedicated to undivided love of God, not the cloistered space of the monastery. Gail Fitzpatrick, Cistercian monk, further clarifies:

> The practice and discipline of enclosure is a way of guarding one's heart so as to set one's love in order and work toward becoming pure of heart. To guard one's heart is to recognize that many things may be good in themselves, but they may not be conducive to growth in one's heart of love, compassion . . . it means continually discerning God's call to love so one can choose the good and exclude from one's innermost heart the trivial, mere curiosities, and those animosities that destroy tranquility and the reign of God's peace within.[2]

Stability

THE MONASTIC VOCATION coheres in various ways—as mendicants, wandering saints or beggars, communal living, hermits, and mixed monastic life forms. In every instance, there is a binding stability that forges members into a unified whole. Stability is an important element in reorienting one's life and one that we most likely associate with family and/or the community where we live, work, and shop. We can reflect on what people or things we need to experience that our life is ordered. Would we benefit by having an authentic teacher, joining an established, earth-focused community, or becoming involved in online contemplative study? What does stability mean to our contemporary lives? How do we define stability in the context of our new life?

Benedictine monasticism provides a unique example of stability, in which a monk not only vows to God, but also vows to remain attached to a particular monastery in a particular geographical location for life. In this instance, stability is tangibly bound to physical, biological location. Of equal importance, established monastic communities provide a stable physical home, guaranteeing their members lifelong housing, food, learning, companionship, community, wisdom, study, and work. Essentially, the monastery replaces spousal or partner commitments, fired by the shared bond to live, study, work, pray, and eat together in the quest of welcoming the Divine into one's life.

For the monk within, it can be helpful to consider stability to be not solely tied to physical place, family, or spiritual leader, but rather as personal faithfulness to the monastic call. This is a promise we make to self and to God, to stay the course through the suffering and joys, struggles and triumphs of our earthly journey.

Vows and Rules of Life

THE PROCESS of preparing for and taking vows to one's Divine Source is a great blessing and ushers in an ever more profound change of life. Seekers often express that they had been waiting all their lives, without knowing, to devote their hearts to God. Since taking vows and following a life rule are part of every formal monastic tradition, participants are given time over months of study to learn about the history and use of vows and rules in the world's religious and monastic orders. They discuss and engage with questions that include, What is the meaning of a vow? What is the meaning behind St. Benedict's rule of life, or the Buddhist *Vinaya*? What does humility signify in a vowed life? How do I discern the monastic call to me? What practice, rule, or asceticism will support this discernment?

What is the relationship between a personal vow and community vows? Why do most monastics take vows both to God and to community? Does this dual commitment seem appropriate in my life? What are some of the benefits and challenges? Time is given to praying about and meditating on these important commitments with a spiritual guide, with other members, and in teaching. (You can find a sample ceremony of vows and rules of life in Chapters 20 and 22).

Finally, for those called by the Holy One to be new monks in the world, the above-mentioned practices, teachings, and study are designed to guide seekers to ultimately take monastic vows in a sacred ceremony of initiation, committing their lives to our Divine Source.

. • .

In the stillness of noon prayer,
I long for you
Enflame my soul with love's desire
I am your disciple.

In the busyness of the day,
I long for you
Harness my heart for your work
I am your disciple.

You called and I said: "Take me!"
Now, I await your touch
Do not abandon me Great Silence
I am your disciple.

Amen.

NINE

The Monk's Life In Relationship

C OMMITTED SPIRITUAL SEEKERS are discovering new ways of adapting and incorporating monastic values into their contemporary lives. Whether the modern monk lives as a solitary, with a community of friends, or in a committed romantic relationship (including sex)—he or she seeks to recover the mystical search in today's complex world, and to sustain human-divine love within familial and other relational contexts.

In popular culture, the monk is associated with a countercultural life, often described in ascetic, other-worldly terms. Despite the historically wide variety of monastic communities and lifestyles, the most common trait associated with monkhood is celibacy, in which the bonds of marriage and children are given up for the Divine. Once passing through cloistered walls, monks were believed to have little or no contact with their biological families and were discouraged from—and sometimes punished for—forming special friendships with their companions. Asceticism was a closely guarded norm, and the premier basis upon which enlightenment or divine union could be attained.

Monastic asceticism as a means of remaining faithful to the holy quest yields important insights that are much needed and sought after today. The absence of partner and family obligations frees the monk from many social responsibilities and opens a space for the expansion of universal love. Celibacy preserves an interior cloister for the Divine and establishes the person's center in silence and solitude. These choices can lead to a significant maturing of the inner life and a sense of peace.

Honoring these values, the new monk seeks neither the perpetuation, nor the reversal, of the ascetic order, but something more creative and embodied: integrating the intense solitude and devotion of the monastic search for God with life for and with intimate relations of many kinds. This vital relational-monastic quest has implications for the entire planet and can guide us into a new approach to life, directing our efforts into the future. It can inspire people today—who perhaps feel torn or estranged from their spiritual or religious roots—to pursue a life of deeper intensity and silence within the context of newly established contemplative norms.

The experimental communities operating around the world in small bands of new monks have probed questions that can offer guidance for anyone seeking to live more authentically: How do we aspire to be of pure intention, while re-conceptualizing and thus transforming what it means to be devoted and faithful? How do we understand divine-human intimacy in relationship to sexuality and other intimacies? How do we preserve that solitude and silence for God and for those relationships without doing violence, being aware that intimacy is the most potentially treacherous territory that we cross in trying to preserve these two realties?

At the heart of relational-monastic commitments is becoming aware of and honoring the mystical depth in self and others. Each sentient being is united in its core with the creative spirit, with the force of love itself. Whether we are aware of this depth does not change that it is attuned to and affected by every interaction of kindness or pain. When we harm another, betray our commitment, or disavow love, we directly affect and cause injury to the sacred interiority of the physical body, as well as of the emotions, mind, and soul.

Every sentient being is dependent on every other reality for its existence. To speak of life on Earth without holding the mutuality of existence as an essential fact is to be deluded. And, further, we must consider this: How much mourning, grieving, and suffering have we sustained by the absence of the sacred in the public sphere or the refusal to sustain love in relationship?

We are not educated or trained to be highly sensitive to the energetic integrity and mystical responsibility we bear. We are seldom in touch with the awe radiating from each face, the holy mantle encasing every living form. We are often clueless and brutal in our interactions with each other. We do not realize the extent of the damage we inflict, and the tearing of our hearts, caused by our refusal to accept that all life is truly and literally, holy.

So, yes, the monastic enclosure makes sense. Let us—all of us—live in peace. But, even so, monasteries are composed of humans, often undeveloped and immature ones. And there is no surfeit of confusion within cloistered walls, either. For traditional monastics as well as those who live in the world, the mysticism of the body, our relationships and aspirations, needs to be re-evaluated and re-told.

Six Practices

SEVERAL THEMES that have sustained monastic communities through the ages can be adapted to our present circumstance and can foster an integral relational-monastic lifestyle. These include the essential wisdom of nonattachment, emptying the ego, openness to receive, divine plan, standing alone, and solitude. In this way, we glimpse a bit of heaven; Divinity permeates everything, is implicated in every decision, and motivates every action.

Nonattachment

An important element in bringing spiritual well-being to a relationship is the capacity to be unattached from self-centered desire. This is a challenging practice, as each person has a stake in the relationship's direction and outcome. Many fears arise: Does my partner love me? Will he or she be with me forever? Have I violated my integrity, of what I want to say or be? Have I wounded my child or been wounded irreparably? Apprehensive about loss, we attempt to manage relationships, to prune and control them. In so doing, we neglect the fact that every relationship involves the joining of two or more complete spiritual realities. The living spiritual spark in each person is responsible to the Divine alone. Because most of us carry psychic pain related to times and situations where we have been less than we hoped to be, it is difficult to release our partners from our grasp, and to be free of self-recrimination or regret. Placing our trust in surrender to divine wisdom allows Spirit to guide the relationship toward its own holiness.

Emptying the Ego

Many difficulties between partners arise from ego conflicts. As we mature in the spiritual life, we will be astonished to discover—and probably suffer a pang of humility over the fact—that discord most often occurs because the self-centeredness of one person is pushing up against the self-centeredness of another person. Instead of communication and communion, a battle of wills tarnishes and disrupts pure intentions. What is the ego hoping to accomplish in this case? Is it asserting itself to hide a deeper wound? Is pride the emotional result of a reactive heart, one that is unable or unwilling to be vulnerable? Has selfishness been a learned response to prior aggression or violence? To forge a healthy relationship, each partner strives to be aware of how the will interrupts and sometimes destroys love. Each partner can meditate on emptying his or her ego demands and pray for guidance in opening the heart. In its highest aspiration, the beauty of offering one's heart to another person is that it brings spiritual transformation and the living breath of divine love.

Open to Receive

In times of sadness or trouble, it is vital to open our souls to truth and be willing to request and receive guidance. Often, we suffer alone; we do not reveal our hidden thoughts and motives. We neglect to be honest with our partner or share our woes with a spiritual friend or guide. But prayer is the most ardent supporter of our need, and the premier method of inner wisdom. It is through prayer or meditation that we discover the divine voice within us, and the guidance that leads us through the dark shadows and into the light. Similarly, if we can bring our troubles to another person or begin a process of journaling, we can reveal our heart-pain and allow respite and healing to take root. Perhaps we fear that if we truly ask for spiritual guidance, we will receive startling answers. When we ask what God would do in this situation, the answer may be challenging, but important to the growth of our souls.

Divine Plan

One has to have faith that every relationship charts its own spiritual journey and has a plan in the divine heart. There is a path of growth, of teaching, and of learning. We often assess relationships from the perspective of functionality:

- What is the purpose of this marriage or partnership?
- How can it conform to my idea of what a relationship should be?
- How can I make my spouse, partner, or child do what he or she is supposed to do according to my criteria?
- How can I be assured that my children accept me as the parent I want them to think I am?

All associations carry social, cultural, and spiritual norms. It is incumbent upon us to recognize the oppressive aspects of these norms that pull our hearts away from, rather than closer to, spiritual freedom. An important discernment is letting go of harmful cultural identities that dictate relationship roles, replacing them with more authentic and life-affirming values. This is especially true in cases where stereotypical gender roles are active, which often places a greater burden on the perceived weaker partner.

Standing Alone

Since every relationship has the potential to usher in deep growth, in every relationship we must remember that we are not dependent upon our partner for transformation. Often socialized to be other-directed, we may believe that we are in a relationship solely on the other person's terms or on conditions we have self-imposed. For example, we identify the relationship as the source of our survival, love, and meaning. This social—which is also a spiritual—experience blinds us to the fact that, ultimately, we stand alone in our relationship to the Holy. When couples merge emotionally and spiritually, it is difficult to step back and to honor each partner's unique relationship with his or her god or spiritual orientation. Love does not demand uncritical merging.

There is an element of illusion in love relationships. It is the belief reinforced by society and commercialism—as well as by religious norms—that union with another person is or should fulfill every desire and be the sum total of the person's connection in this life. While we intuitively know this is not possible, many people live out their lives as if it were. But here is where monastic wisdom helps re-orient our belief. True intimacy arises when each person maintains his or her center in solitude, at the same time that he or she is receptive to uniting with another person in love.

One of the more challenging aspects of relationships is to balance the tension between intimacy and detachment, between intimacy and aloneness, between intimacy and respect for singularity and personal space. If we want to probe the possibilities of spiritually living with and for another, we paradoxically have to become deeply interior and detached. It is out of silence and aloneness that we acquire the ability to truly enter the mystical depth with God, the world, and others.

Solitude

In order to preserve a monastic sensibility in the context of a committed marriage or partnership, it is important for couples to honor and preserve each other's need for solitude. An essential dimension of monasticism is the value placed on inner silence in the seeker's relationship to the holy. Solitude is the source of the Divine within us and the living waters of the soul. Having time and space to experience the vastness of Divine Presence has been critical to the entire development of monastic and eremitic traditions across the centuries. In fact, the whole of a monastic commitment pivots around it.

Monasteries and hermitages are designed to foster singular attention to the inner life. Often established away from cities—in deserts, forests, mountains—religious houses grew in natural landscapes such as caves, or were constructed of thick walls, whereby the stones themselves seemed to emit "silence." The monastic enclosure, then, serves as more than a physical barrier designed to preserve the holy sanctuary. Its intention also is to shield monks from the intrusion of the world in a way that allows discovery of inner freedom.

Many new monastics have found, with the obligations of job or family, the importance of creating a daily rhythm that fosters each person's need for time alone. Some form a common bond by practicing celibacy, living in separate bedrooms or hermitages, and openly caring for family and friends, while maintaining a shared spiritual intention.

Other sexually committed couples develop a monastic rhythm in their lives, perhaps with silence in the morning, periods of prayer, and meditation at night. This can be accomplished separately or together. The intention is to allow each person to engage with dreams, prayer, and ordering the day in his or her own time and way. Another practice is to set aside one or more sessions for study, including reading of a spiritual text together or alone. When a rhythm of spiritual attentiveness becomes an established relationship intention, it can help partners solve problems together by offering them to silence and waiting for Spirit to speak.

Practically, the maintenance of autonomy is realized more easily when each person has his or her own office, place to worship, or separate studio within a shared complex. Such luxuries may be difficult to achieve, but sometimes all it takes is a reimagining of household space. Can the guest room be turned into a place for meditation? Can the dining room, which is seldom used, or the kitchen table double as a reflective sanctuary for writing or reading? How about turning a messy shed into a chapel, an extra garage bay into a place of study, or the corner of a bedroom for a personal altar?

It is not uncommon for sexually committed couples to have separate bedrooms or set aside one or more days a week to be alone, which is more easily accommodated if partners maintain separate households. Each—in a gentle way of love, not in any professional manner—can be the other's spiritual friend and guide. Their hearts can be attuned to the beloved's sorrows and joys and help him or her grow in the Spirit, calling for the best they can be.

This is especially true if couples are engaged in sexual intimacy, which opens each person to a tangible vulnerability that includes and exceeds the energies of body, mind, and spirit to co-create a new, combined energy. It is in sexual union that a window is thrown open into the sacred depths of personhood, and then beyond to the cosmic mystery. The critical challenge for any sexually active relational-monastic couple is threefold: preserve one's interiority with the Divine, celebrate intimate relations with another, and practice inner solitude, remaining free from merging and denigration.

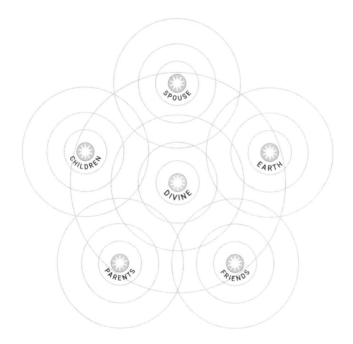

Relational-Monastic Life

CONSIDER the diagram above, where the Divine is the center of life within each person, radiating out to all relationships, interpenetrating and interdependent. Here is a more hopeful and healthy understanding of life on Earth. Here is how we work out the monk's intense longing for God within a mutually engaged, mutually dignified, mutually sacred relationship with partners and children, with parents and extended family, with friends, with colleagues, and with all beings on Earth. With the Spirit animating from within, every being turns inward toward silence and solitude, and outward toward relationships in the world. Here we can reimagine the monastic call to solitude whereby all relationships are interdependent and mutually enhanced by the threefold relationship of the divine-human—in solitude, in each person, and within community. Aloneness calls forth and deepens the Divine Presence within all life expressions and becomes the foundation upon which the co-equality and co-intimacy of every relationship is celebrated.

Familial Relationships

Spouse/Partners

The constellation of familial relationships is varied and expansive. It includes everything from the love of one's spouse to the love of children, parents, friends, peers, distant relations, colleagues, neighbors, and the love of all humanity.

Many monastic traditions consider living in community to be the premiere means by which souls mature. Relationship with other monks is a testing ground for the growth of the spirit and for the development of love. For the new monk who has a partner or children, family is the crucible in which wisdom is distilled from the fire of life. When silence and love are at the center, couples and families mirror the monastic ethos, living communally as a microcosm of cosmic-divine-human mutuality. Because in every familial setting at least three spiritual trajectories are at work—each person's relationship to his or her Source, the relationship between partners, and the family's community relationship, especially when it includes children or grandparents, etc.

If intimate relationships are to thrive, they will be dynamic and creative, enhancing each person's life journey. Each partner has to be honest about his or her needs, about what it means to be committed, in order to find freedom within the relationship context, and without perpetuating stereotypical roles. This means having clarity about who we are, our life goals, and the kind of person we want to be. Relationships cannot be authentic if a partner is hiding his or her intention or if one partner is denying or oppressing the other person's deepest aspiration. In true sharing, there is an openness to hear the other speak, to listen to the struggles and triumphs we all have in trying to be faithful to our spiritual path.

In relationships where there is an inequality between spouses or partners, particularly where one spouse is dominating another, unhealthy personality patterns can develop. Here, spiritual well-being, in which each person has the freedom to achieve the fullness of being, is thwarted. In such circumstances, authentic growth cannot occur; love cannot thrive. If lack of respect or overt betrayal occurs, the sacred bond between partners is fractured.

Four Greek words address types of love: *eros*, romantic, sexual love; *philia*, friendship, brotherly love; *storge*, empathetic, familial love; and *agape*, unconditional divine love. The balance, or lack thereof, of these types of love in a relationship affects the spirituality and health, and capacity for happiness and freedom, of each partner.

Especially significant is how each partner approaches intimate sharing.

* Is there love and sexuality? Is there control and sexuality? Is this a real friendship?
* Is my spouse someone to whom I can open my heart, or do I hide my feelings from him or her?
* Is this relationship one where I am allowed to communicate *agape*, which can be both sacred and sexual love?
* Is there room for spiritual love or is only sexuality allowed?

It can be difficult to affirm the deep spirituality of a partner. Both partners may not have the same spiritual intention or desire, and there may be competition or jealousy. It may not feel as though there is room in the relationship for both aloneness with God and intimacy with a partner. It is a challenge to elevate a relationship if one or both partners are clinging to each other in an unhealthy way. Respect for each other's spiritual path and life goals is important. Partners can honor and celebrate each other's spiritual paths; conversely partners can wound, oppress, or destroy, or find themselves living in shades of gray between these extremes. One has to be aware enough to demand that one's own spiritual path is not violated.

In the privacy of an interpersonal relationship, the person discovers his or her beautiful and painful aspects. It is in relationship that we may be subjected to or inflict domination, abuse, and violence as well as experience tenderness, passion, and love. It is in the subtle quiet of sharing one's life with another that we are most vulnerable. For this reason, contemplative awareness applied to every life situation is vital. Have I violated my partner's space or been violated? Do we control each other? Have I manipulated my spouse to get something I want for my own purpose? Have I rejected or betrayed my partner? Have I denied my love out of anger, spite, or jealousy?

In the challenges and wonder of sexuality, twentieth-century poet Rainer Maria Rilke provides insight:

> Sex is difficult; yes. But those tasks that have been entrusted to us are difficult; almost everything serious is difficult; and everything is serious. If you just recognize this and manage, out of yourself, out of your own talent and nature, out of your own experience and childhood and strength, to achieve a wholly individual relation to sex (one that is not influenced by convention and custom), then you will no longer have to be afraid of losing yourself and becoming unworthy of your dearest possession.
>
> Bodily delight is a sensory experience . . . And it is not our acceptance of it that is bad; what is bad is that most people misuse this learning and squander it and apply it as a stimulant on the tired places of their lives and as a distraction rather than as a way of gathering themselves for their highest moments.[1]

With Rilke, let's discover how to gather our intimate relationships for their "highest moments." We give up the concern about whether we are spiritually or sexually attractive, and about what we do and when we do it. We let go of the need to please another person in an unhealthy way. We let go of the harmful parental patterns witnessed or inflicted. We discover that when we are spiritually free from attachment, we simultaneously know what fidelity means. Free of false desire, we can be truly steadfast with our beloveds because we are faithful to ourselves and to the divine within.

Children

Newborns are profoundly tender and mysterious. Innocent of the world, children see, know, and love with their wise souls, and wordlessly mirror back to us our truths and joys, our hidden deceptions, fears, and pains. Children, tethered to the divine spark within, absorb life's totality and seek to heal what is broken. Children reflect our interior lives, and when we are not truthful, we wound them.

Our duty as adults is to liberate them from the task of trying to heal us by being mature and emotionally sincere. We respect the sacredness of our children's lives when we are willing to be honest with them; when we are willing to apologize, ask for forgiveness, be strong, and discipline when necessary; when we let our real emotions and truths be present. We are all called to protect the divine spark in the world in all its manifestations.

We learn as parents, biological or otherwise, of an unconditional parental love that participates in the beauty of divine love. We understand an emptying love, a love that is willing to give itself away, to lay one's life down, to protect the child's pure, new life. Every child is, in some way, the seed of messianic hope, the pearl of pure divinity, which evokes—in a healthy soul—kindness in the human spirit. For one of our great duties is to preserve the divinity of children, the right of children, to have the sacred within protected from harm by the adults charged with their care.

The violence inflicted on the Earth's children, which is increasing around the world in war-torn regions, among refugees, along borders, in domestic situations, etc., indicates a profound split in our beings, a deep failure on the part of adults to nurture the holy spark within life. We are required by a sacred, inviolable commandment to protect these young lives from harm. Children are deeply affected by the consciousness of those around them. Lacking formal boundaries, they absorb everyone's energy, thoughts, feelings, and ideas. Our role as parents and teachers is to help children maintain and be strong in their own energy. The absence of clarity impacts the safe and sacred universe of the child. Maintaining clear emotional, sexual, psychological, and mental boundaries is para-mount. A child has his or her own spiritual relationship, which should not be co-opted or possessed by anyone. Maintaining clear communica-tion with children allows them to have the freedom to grow as the Divine intended, into their own lives and spiritual health.

Children can be exasperating and demanding. I am convinced that children see, on a level they are not consciously aware of, the truth of your being, by which I mean all that is beautiful and glorious and all that is deceptive and pained. In their transparency to Spirit, they want to be in truth with you, even when they are not conscious that they are pushing you toward truth. An important question to ask, especially when chil-dren "push our buttons": What are our children trying to show us? Of course, always keeping in mind that every time a child is disobedient or willful does not mean this is indication of a parental lesson. Sometimes, the child simply needs a steady hand.

As children mature from childhood into adolescence, parental guid-ance is even more critical. These years can be especially challenging. But, if a stable parent-child bond has been established since birth— open to truth-telling and sharing emotions—then a new family rapport may continue and flower. The family members can develop a type of monastic rhythm in their lives, perhaps with silence in the morning, and meditation together at night. Parents—in a gentle way of love, not in any professional manner—can be a spiritual friend, listening deeply to the longing in their young adult's life to find meaning. Both adults and children can be attuned to each other's growth in the spirit, calling for the best they can be. When we are not afraid to be honest and to look within ourselves, when we aspire to live at a depth and be responsible for our behavior, we provide our children with lifelong gifts and tools for living authentically.

These important issues are more easily understood if the parent is able to be in service of the child's life without assuming a rigid parental identity reinforced by societal roles. By embracing, instead, the love of a parent, we participate in the spirituality of parenting without the oppres-sive adherence to what we are told a parent is supposed to do or be. For every parent-child relationship is its own spiritual journey into the divine heart and requires inner listening and playful wisdom to be authentic. By understanding the sacrificial love of the parent for a child, we all are parents, whether or not we have children, charged with protecting the innocent of heart.

Parents

We all are born of a mother and father, whether or not we know our biological parents. A critical factor in the growth of the full self is the ability to evaluate one's life in relation to the ineffable bonds of family genetics and personality that are often unconsciously imprinted. This process involves freedom from unhealthy parental obligations, energetic patterns, emotions, and life choices. While psychological therapies are geared toward uncovering the roots of family dysfunction and emotional or physical abuse, inner growth requires a detachment from deeper levels of entanglement: spiritual, soul, mystical.

Like cloistered monks, we can imagine entering the monastic enclosure and leaving our parents behind. We do this because we have embarked on a singular path of our own choosing. We have to transcend our history to once again reclaim it, to once again be faithful to it. The grief we may feel over our withdrawal we bear with patience and compassion. We are not able to honor our parents and sanctify our relationship with them when we still want something from them. We have to seek the truth for ourselves whether or not they choose to come along. When we do this, we will love them anew, with empathy and wisdom.

What does it mean to be without parents? It means that we are no longer at the mercy of our history. We have become transhistorical— momentarily born anew without the limitation and restriction of one's birth and familial or cultural context. We practice detachment to see our parents through God's eyes.

Rilke, in *Letters to a Young Poet*, writes about not being attached to what our parents have done or not done, because no matter (poorly, or even painfully) they have given us life, and life transcends negativity. Life itself is miraculous.

And those who come together in the nights and are entwined in rocking delight perform a solemn task and gather sweetness, depth, and strength for the song of some future poet, who will appear in order to say ecstasies that are unsayable. And they call forth the future; and even if they have made a mistake and embrace blindly, the future comes anyway, a new human being arises, and on the foundation of the accident that seems to be accomplished here, there awakens the law by which a strong, determined seed forces its way through to the egg cell that openly advances to meet it. Don't be confused by surfaces; in the depths everything becomes law. And those who live the mystery falsely and badly (and they are very many) lose it only for themselves and nevertheless pass it on like a sealed letter, without knowing it.[2]

By refusing to recognize our parents' part in the Great Mystery, we suffer. Just as we work to release any rigid, codified parental role that we experience with our children, we will not be free until we cease to demand that our parents live up to our expectations of what and how we want them to be, letting go of the need for them to provide for us materially and spiritually. I am not, saying, however, that we ignore or deny injustice or injury we have received from a parent. No, we must be aware and seek to recover. But, at the same time, healing occurs more ardently when we pursue it directly without expecting acknowledgment or participation.

In the hidden mystery of contemplation, we let go of demand and definition. We are empty, we are without attachment. We go through the pain of letting go in order to return bearing holiness in our hearts. Liberation and enlightenment cannot happen unless one becomes free of these attachments, unless one is no longer controlled by or in debt to these factors. In this life, we will always love our families and celebrate our cultures and family traits. And as we mature, we can embrace these traits with empathy, grateful for our connection to a biological, historical, and spiritual lineage because it is no longer a determining factor in our choices or behavior. Instead, we live out of our own ground and not out of anyone else's. Living out of our own ground, in the divine, we are free.

Work

Another significant factor in the relational-monastic quest is the amount of time spent at work. For many people, work occupies a central part of their identity and leads to close bonds of friendship. In fact, at times work is the person's identity.

In traditional monasteries, work is a means of spiritual perfection and a vehicle for practice. Monks who live in community contribute to the financial well-being of the monastery through various types of labor in alignment with their gifts: teaching, working in the fields, making cheese, brewing spirits, iconography, etc. The monk gives up the world but shares in solidarity with other men and women outside the monastery by working to earn a living. In the contemplative traditions, work provides for the sustenance of the monastery and is not performed solely for personal achievement or personal progress. It is there to lay the foundation to provide freedom to pursue the spiritual life in God's time.

It is good to have a profession that provides financial independence, but equally important is the role that money exerts on a person's choices of career or life goals. Every type of work is burdened with social convention or prestige, which may leave little room for the person to discover whether his or her choice enhances or distorts the inner life. Buddha held "right association" to be a precursor of his eightfold precepts of spiritual freedom and it is certainly the case that the people with whom we associate and the type of work we perform on a daily basis have a tremendous impact on our spiritual health.

Thus, the nontraditional monk will need time to process what monastic poverty and simplicity mean in the context of his or her life situation. While we associate the vow of poverty with a voluntary rejection of money, a more reliable measure for the monk in the world with obligations to parents, partners, and/or children (as well as creditors) is a studied awareness of the role that money has in his or her life, and the ways it can distort pure intentions. These important self-reflections should include ethical issues, such as how to free oneself from attachment to success and achievement, which often lead to greed, power, or selfishness, and how to use income for the benefit of our families and others.

Work is a means of connecting us with all beings, and for transmitting our mission, because we labor, ultimately, for the cosmos. We all labor for all beings. Every time we walk in the hushed dawn, splash in the ocean, or marvel at a golden sunset, nature pours itself into our hearts. At this moment, someone somewhere is working to better our lives—environmental activists, firefighters, nurses, farmers, truckers, grocers, teachers. When we go to a bazaar or shop in a market, the fragrance of flowers, variety of fruit, aroma of bread, array of colors, and beautiful fabrics remind us of the abundance of life, and of the people who have shared from the storehouse of their creative generosity.

In divinizing work, we have to also remember that we are not our work. Our spiritual lives are the foundation of whatever work we perform. If we become too identified with work, the balance between intimacy and detachment is not maintained. Likewise, relationships become unbalanced when a person substitutes work as a panacea that will rectify all the other inadequacies in life.

One's work is work that one implements, but the "uncreated self" dwells before anything that we perform. Again, it is the solitude within, our ability to embrace aloneness, that guides and supports us, and from which everything else flows.

Earth and All Beings

Perhaps of most and great importance is our relationship to the Earth, all sentient beings, and the cosmos—who are our monastic mothers, holding our bodies and spirits in the circle womb of creation. We are children of the wind, of water, of air, and of sun and moon. Matter is sanctified and our bodies of flesh are holy vessels. It is tragic that we do not yet comprehend the magnificence of creation, bowing down in awe before the faces of glory in each of us. So enmeshed are we in a false narrative, a materialistic worldview, that we cannot literally *see* the wonder all around us. We cannot feel the radiant web of the living, universal spirit animating everything from within. We are made mute by our refusal—and blinded by our ignorance. We have yet to open our hearts to the vast miracle that surrounds us.

And because of this, we do not know how to completely love. We do not know how to be "of whole cloth," undivided. We want to keep a portion for ourselves, we want to withhold love, we want to cling to the pain or the wound or the injustice because we refuse to *be* all-forgiving and merciful. Mercy does not mean we do what everyone else wants us to do. It means that our hearts are free and open. It means that we give priority to the spiritual meaning of each event; it means that we place the Holy One at the center of decision-making and living. It means that we give up and give away the pretense of knowing everything and willing everything—because we recognize that we are woven into the fabric of the universe and everything we do that is in alignment with peace and harmony is of God. We do not truly act. We are the extension in time and space of being acted upon, of the Spirit's breath acting in us.

. • .

We are grateful for all our relationships
for our struggles, gift of insight,
the interdependent web of all beings.

May we learn to live more closely
to the Earth in humility
and in honor of the sanctity of creation.

Amen.

TEN

Spiritual Guidance:
The Inner Way

THE PERSON ATTEMPTING to follow a monastic path benefits from having a spiritual guide with whom to share the inner life. The spiritual mentor provides an invaluable sounding board at all stages of the journey, from beginners to those more advanced in their vocation. Often the seeker is the least likely to recognize the ego distractions and emotional desires that compromise the intentions of his or her soul. And, while the habits of people beginning a spiritual vocation can be more overt and blatant, it is, in fact, the mature monk—whose self-will has become subtler and increasingly elusive—who may need wise guidance even more. Here, a Russian priest speaks of this need:

As to those who are happy without seeking spiritual direction and are quite blissful without bothering much about the deeper life—of the mind and the heart—theirs is the peace of this world, not the peace of the Master. Whenever we do set out firmly to tread the *inner way*, a storm of temptations and persecutions always assails us. It is because of the dark host that spiritual direction is profitable, nay necessary to us, whether we retire to a monastery or continue to live in the world.[1]

From the earliest accounts of human experience, individuals have shared their spiritual aspirations with community elders. The shaman, Delphi oracle, and *Rigvedic* seer are among the earliest religious figures depicted in literature. Similarly, the Vaisnaya guru, Taoist sage, Sufi shaykh, Tibetan lama, and prophets of the Hebrew Bible functioned as conduits between the realm of the spirits and earthly life. When a person needed assistance on the journey of faith, he or she sought the wisdom of a sanctioned religious elder.

Once the province of religious authorities, today spiritual guidance has broken out of the confines of religious denominations to become a practice of spiritual sharing and soul companionship open to individuals from diverse religious and non-religious backgrounds. Recognizing that "the spirit" is intrinsic to all people and human endeavors, the contemporary ministry of spiritual direction is offered in traditional religious settings as well as in hospitals, hospices, colleges, and other social and secular environments.

This sharing of souls has been described in various ways—spiritual direction, spiritual guidance, soul healing, spiritual companionship, etc. It is the art of deep listening to the subtle movement of the Divine in a person's life. As an oral tradition, spiritual guidance passes on an ancient lineage of dialogue, taking place between elder or director and seeker (sometimes called "directee") from heart to heart and soul to soul.

Focus of Spiritual Guidance

SPIRITUAL GUIDANCE is attentive to helping a person with his or her relationship with Ultimate Reality, however named or defined. In all traditions, spiritual direction tracks the stirring of the spirit in order to foster communion between the person and the divine and, thus, to aid in enlightening the soul: to discover Buddha within, experience *samadhi*, or unite in mystical union with God. The main role of the spiritual companion is to listen for this movement, and to bring awareness of the transformative changes affecting the person.

The primary focus of spiritual direction is on religious experience, not ideas. It is concerned with the inner life—that dimension of existence that deals with the heart. It maps an interior landscape, with its own rules and properties, ways of knowing, and ways of seeing. Spiritual direction addresses this process of interiorization, awakening the directee to the path along which the Divine is leading.

Spiritual guidance is not psychological, in search of solving problems or cognitive choices and ideas. The director may use and be trained to recognize whatever knowledge can be gained from the field of psychology, but this knowledge should not be imposed on the spiritual relationship or be looked upon as sufficient. Rather, spiritual guidance focuses on the sacred questions and soul anxieties experienced by a person on the path: Why is my prayer life arid and unproductive? I feel unworthy because I never experience God's presence. I am torn by my inability to love. As a survivor of sexual abuse, I am tainted. Where is God for me in this?

In the context of these many concerns, the soul friend or guide listens for the spirit's movement, gently guiding the person toward a new life interpretation and understanding of the self. "The whole purpose of spiritual direction," writes Thomas Merton:

> is to penetrate beneath the surface of a man's life, to get behind the façade of conventional gestures and attitudes which he presents to the world, and to bring out his inner spiritual freedom, his inmost truth, which is what we [Christians] call the likeness of Christ in his soul. This is an entirely supernatural thing, for the work of rescuing the inner man from automatism [unconscious actions] belongs first of all to the Holy Spirit.[2]

The Word "Spiritual"

THROUGHOUT HISTORY, spirituality has been the champion of unity and kinship among peoples, and the binding wisdom of diverse civilizations. Yet there is no universally acceptable definition of spirituality. In a number of Indigenous cultures, the spirit is so embedded in daily activities that there is no comparable word, "spirituality," to distinguish it from life itself. Nonetheless, many languages and cultures have "spirit" words. In the Abrahamic traditions, the Hebrew *ruah*, and the related Arabic *ruh*, convey a similar sense of the invisible and intangible movements of breath, air, and wind as the Latin *spiritus* or *pneuma* in Greek.

The Latin word *spiritualitas* (spirituality) seems to have been first used by St. Jerome in an early fifth-century letter. But it is not until the sixteenth century onward that the word "spirituality" is found in the English language. A rarely used word until modernity, during the medieval period its meaning was closely tied to Christian practice, and spirituality was often depicted as a higher, otherworldly realm opposed to the physical.

In the Jewish traditions, seeking the face of God, living in the divine presence, and conducting one's life in accordance with God's holy intention comes close to a definition of spirituality faithful to its Semitic roots. In Islam, spirituality is a word of Arabic origin with two distinct connotations. In the Qur'an the Spirit (*ruh*) emerges from the command of God; it also has a second meaning, of inwardness, pertaining to a higher level of Divine Reality, and to the presence of the *barakah*, the grace that flows through the universe.

Specific spirit words, each within their own context, exist as well in Japanese, Chinese, African, and Indigenous tribal religions. In Buddhism, the closest equivalent for the term spirituality is perhaps the Sanskrit *bhavana*, or "cultivation," which signifies not merely an interior reality or an escape from ordinary existence. It does not presuppose any dualism between the spiritual realm and that of the senses or between a sacred dimension and the material world. Rather, Walpola Rahula—Sri Lankan Buddhist monk and scholar—clarifies:

> It aims at cleansing the mind of impurities and disturbances, such as lustful desires, hatred, ill-will, indolence, worries and restlessness, skeptical doubts, and cultivating such qualities as concentration, awareness, intelligence, will, energy, the analytical faculty, confidence, joy, tranquility, leading finally to the attainment of the highest wisdom which sees the nature of things as they are, and realizes the Ultimate Truth, Nirvana.[3]

Similarly, the religions of the Indian subcontinent have a rich heritage of words, such as *Brahman* (Eternal Absolute), *atman* (immortal self), *citta* (conscious mind), and *prana* (breath), to refer to both the Divine Spirit and the human spirit in its various guises and manifestations. Focusing on a person's inner relationship to one's ultimate source, Hinduism places particular emphasis on the interdependence and nondualism of spirit and matter. In Hindu practice, living a spiritually focused life requires a letting go of ego identity. As Hindu scholar, Krishna Sivaraman, clarifies: "The locus where there is absent a sense of 'I' and 'mine' is the locus of spirit."

In each of these varied cultures and languages, we can think of spirituality as the all-pervading divine energy and seamless web of oneness intimate to life itself. Creation is not alone, separate from its source, but mysteriously imbued with spirit in every aspect of mind, soul, and matter. Thus, spirituality relates to the core or deep center of the person open to the transcendent. It is here that the person experiences ultimate reality.

Today, spirituality is used in secular and religious contexts, and is applied across and within disciplines, as well as in medicine and other healing arts. In a sense, "spirituality" has become a kind of universal code word to indicate the human search for meaning and purpose in life, and as a quest for the transcendent. Although spirituality is historically related to religious traditions, it is also found in secular settings, and in all human societies through an individual experience of the divine, a connection to nature, and/or through religious practice.

From these diverse definitions, we can see that the word "spiritual" in spiritual guidance does not refer only to one's spiritual activities, as if spirituality were but one small part of life. Rather, the inner way has never concerned itself with the person's prayer, writes Orthodox priest Joseph J. Allen, "without also dealing with the thoughts and actions (somatic, psychological, sociological, etc.) of his or her everyday life."[4]

The Meaning of "Direction"

WHILE SPIRITUAL DIRECTION has been practiced for centuries in Christian monasteries, many today have a negative response to the word, "direction," concerned that it brings to mind authoritarian tendencies and control. Much of this resistance may be the result of the modern, individual self. But resistance also is expressed by people who have turned to spiritual guidance, only to find that the minister, priest, rabbi, or religious sister or brother (of any tradition) was dismissive, biased, or excessively instructive at the expense of listening.

The seventeenth-century Benedictine mystic, Dom Augustine Baker, clarifies that spiritual direction is not about obedience, but instead points to the relationship between souls: both parties are surrendering to the divine will, to being attentive to the path God has chosen.

> The director is not to teach his own way nor indeed any determinate way of prayer, but to instruct his disciples how they may themselves find out the way proper for them. . . . In a word, he is only God's usher, and must lead souls in God's way and not his own.[5]

Use of the word "direction" in spiritual direction, then, conveys this sense of staying on course—of helping another person to maintain a spiritual focus through the bewildering twists and turns of life. Thus, in spiritual guidance the word "direction" is not meant to imply obedience to or command by another person, group, or institution. It refers to a common lived experience: spiritual companionship—Buddha's "right association"—encourages the person to seek out and stay on the path to freedom.

The work of the director is not to *give* spiritual direction, but to detect the ways in which a soul is being drawn to participate in the inner life of the Divine. His or her task is not to instruct, preach, or provide moral guidance, but to help the seeker experience and listen to the action of the spirit and respond to it. Fostering discovery rather than teaching doctrine is the purpose of the relationship.

This understanding that spiritual direction is not about moral instruction or demonstration of truth must be stressed. The reasons for this are:

• The almost universal and deeply entrenched tendency of ministering people to want to inculcate truth, to teach and instruct.
• The tendency of those called to be spiritual directors to believe they must enforce, commit, or "do" spiritual direction.
• The desire on the part of spiritual helpers, family, and friends to effect change and initiate outcomes coincident with their own beliefs or goals.

The meaning of the word "direction" or "guidance" on the inner path is to emphasize, verify, and encourage what is truly spiritual in the person. A spiritual director is, then, a soul friend who helps others to recognize and to follow the inspiration of grace in their lives in order to arrive at the end to which the Divine is leading them.

Desert *Abbas* and *Ammas*

THE HISTORICAL DEVELOPMENT of the term, "spiritual direction" and its practice can be traced to Christian roots, specifically to the desert *abbas* and *ammas* (fathers and mothers) of the early fourth century. These were people who left Alexandria, Antioch, and other cities of Asia Minor to find peace, solitude, and wisdom. Their primary desire was to live apart from material culture and institutional oppression and focus entirely on devotion to God. For the desert fathers and mothers, spiritual guidance replaced the bishop or presbyter as representative of Christ. The greatest abbots in the Egyptian and Syrian deserts were generally not ordained clergy or vowed religious, and spiritual authority was invested in them solely on the basis of their wisdom and holiness.

The desert monastics were seekers of the true self, practicing simplicity, honesty, and purity of heart. Their primary commitment was to mystical union, and many pilgrims sought their spiritual advice.

The sayings of the desert fathers and mothers—collected in numerous anthologies—remain testimony to the simplicity and depth of their wisdom. The impact of their words on pilgrims resided in the inward action of the Holy Spirit on the soul of the hearer. Direction was understood to be God's answer—communicated through the message of the *abba* or *amma*—to a need created in the person to confront his or her trials, desires, and self-recriminations.

Disciples often traveled for miles through the wilderness just to hear a brief word of advice. In the early days, a spiritual director was one who had been called to seek God by an unusual and perilous road. These were spiritual masters who begot the perfect life in the soul of disciples primarily by their instructions, but also by their prayer, sanctity, and example. To pilgrims, the desert monks represented a kind of sacrament of Jesus' presence in the ecclesiastical community.

The dialogue or encounter between teacher (director) and pilgrim (directee) was considered to be holy, in the sense that true guidance was the work of the Holy Spirit and not of the human mind or intellect. This divine-human communication shared between two people also was the source of an unspoken rule governing both participants. Specifically, the directee was to speak from the heart—soul to soul—and the director was to listen with inner stillness for spiritual insight not found through rational knowledge alone.

The desert monastics had struggled, learned, and lived to accept God's will. They were wise in the ways of the spirit. Through spiritual trial and yearning to know God directly, they experienced both the heights and the depths of the inner life. They knew their weakness, sin, and temptation. They had battled fear, arrogance, despair, abandonment, futility, and greed. Finally, they also knew about religious experience, when God comes to a person directly and fills the soul with divine presence. Imbued with grace, they were able to impart to others the patience, silence, mercy, compassion, and love they received. Theirs was not just a material knowing, but also a knowing of the subtleties of monastic life—how a person lives and follows a contemplative path.

The mystery was apparent: they understood its variations and had, from experience, learned its measure and types. Far from being obscure and indistinct, the inner life was teaming with a precision and an intellectual brilliance that was unmatched by any of the world's knowledge. It was this wisdom that allowed the desert elders to interpret human situations from the perspective of awe. Having surrendered to the vast, untracked wilderness, they became cartographers, mapping the interior landscape and offering solace for others.

Iatros Pneumatikos—Spiritual Physician

SINCE SPIRITUAL direction always involved an effort to heal the person, medical terminology was often used in the traditional literature. This usage was already rooted in ancient Greek philosophy, where healing occurred through the sage, who guided the person into the inner life. Thus, Socrates saw himself as an *iatros tes psyches,* or "soul healer." In the writings of the desert elders, the spiritual guide was described as a spiritual physician, *iatros pneumatikos,* in Greek. From the collected wisdom of St. Anthony of Egypt:

> The fathers of old went into the desert, and when they were made whole, they became physicians, and returning again they made others whole; therefore it is said, "Physician, heal thyself."[6]

The spiritual physician was to assist the pilgrim's growth in holiness, and to guide the directee to become aware of three different movements of the spirit: within one's mind and heart; between oneself and God; and between oneself and his or her fellows.[7]

The dialogue between master and pilgrim could include elements related to an individual's ongoing prayer life and to the daily struggle for wholeness and healing, including thoughts and actions, emotional pain, and theological understanding. The spiritual physician always aimed at a life interpretation, awakening in believers their motivations and predicaments. Direction was sometimes gentle, radical, or blunt; however imparted "it never avoided or denied the real, operative factors of an individual's circumstances," writes Antiochian Orthodox priest, Joseph

Allen, "whether they were evaluated as positive or negative, constructive or destructive. In short, were truth denied, no healing could have occurred."[8]

The greatest benefit was possible when pilgrims opened their hearts in the presence of a holy one who listened with compassion. The sufferings and joys, as well as the motivations of the soul, were brought to awareness and shared. The desert elder guided his or her directee to a change of heart, and to follow the path toward love of God. Yet the desire to transform the self was not born of despondency and despair, or punishment and self-denial, but of expectant hope. It was the realization that true awareness of one's failings springs from the inner activity of the spirit, giving a person the courage to change life directions and focus the quest for meaning and love. In this way, guidance from the *abba* or *amma* assisted the seeker to claim the spirit within as the source of moral courage and self-determination.

The challenge of the inner life—and a key factor that distinguished monastic elders more advanced on the path from beginners—was the ability to see the core of another's soul with love and compassion, without condemnation, cruelty, or piousness. An authentic spiritual guide was able to embrace another person clearly, dispassionately, and fully, with a heart of love.

Deep Current of Feeling

A SIGNIFICANT METHOD of tracking the movement of the spirit is to become aware of the deep current of spiritual feeling within the person—a realm more potent and silent than the conventional self, or the façade of personality we present to the world. Indeed, the river of feeling is the language of the mystical heart, and the affective longing within us. It is the true self that seeks to be known through the complexity of mind-body-spirit. It is often expressed as the still, small voice.

In soul guidance, the subject of inquiry is the current of the heart and not rational knowledge. In emphasizing the value of spiritual feeling and experience, both director and directee become sensitized to another way of listening, knowing, and decision-making. As we gather the courage to listen to our deepest feelings—happiness or sorrow, consolation or deso-lation, peace or agitation, silence or noise—we discover the language of interior knowing.

One of the most difficult aspects of soul sharing is remaining atten-tive to the distinction between rationality (cognition, interpretation, analysis, judgment, intellectual understanding), psychological emotion, and the heart's guidance. While each of these aspects is inextricably interconnected, the focus of spiritual direction is equivalent to putting a magnifying glass on this often wordless and unspoken—but longing to speak and be heard—sacred feeling dimension of the person.

A helpful way to conceptualize how spiritual feeling relates to emo-tion and personality is to imagine an iceberg submerged in an ocean. The tip of the iceberg showing above the water represents the outer personality and emotions. Below the water in widening layers of ice are the psyche, subconscious, and the unconscious. Beneath all these strata, at the base of the iceberg lies the deep current of feeling, which I think of as the super- or spiritual-conscious. This iceberg image illustrates how the upper levels of our emotional life and personality conceal what is felt on the level of soul and spirit. By becoming aware of this deep current within us, we learn to be attentive to the subtle manner in which our whole being seeks to communicate through mind, body, and spirit.

Disclosure of Thoughts

SPIRITUAL GUIDANCE also depends on the disclosure of thoughts. The unveiling of thoughts brings to the conscious mind tendencies that may be lurking deep in the heart, where they cause havoc because they are not named or shared. The disclosure of hidden chatter, however, is not a rational analysis of the mind, but a revealing of the thinking process, the structure of thought itself, and the pre-conditioning that forms a residue in the memory of the person. By becoming conscious of certain tenden-cies and habits of being, the person learns how to let go of and move beyond the conventional self. Thoughts, for example, of worthlessness, doubt, jealousy, and despair are important as a signal of what is happening more deeply within the person; similarly, doubts about the nature of God, the self, or the veracity of religion are other themes that are brought up by participants in the sharing process.

In desert monasticism, the novice daily exposed the disclosure of thoughts (Greek, *logismoi*) to his spiritual elder. This disclosure involved more than the confession of sins that had already occurred, because it was directed to revealing ideas and impulses that could lead to future error and had the power to harm. The true purpose of the *logismoi* was self-knowledge, whereby the seeker brought thoughts into the light and weakened their hold over his or her soul. The method was effective in helping the novice to become acutely aware of the workings of the mind, and how unexamined thoughts and ideas can damage or corrupt a person's purity of heart.

This principle—on the efficacy of self-disclosure—is clearly stated in the *Sayings of the Desert Fathers*:

> If unclear thoughts trouble you, do not hide them but tell them at once to your spiritual father and condemn them. The more we conceal our thoughts, the more they multiply and gain strength . . . [But] once an evil thought is revealed, it is immediately dissipated. . . . Whoever discloses his thoughts is quickly healed.[9]

Discernment

ONE OF THE central elements of spiritual companionship is discernment: listening with the heart to the movement of the spirit. Discernment is the process that maps the signs of the spirit: how the disclosure of thoughts and the sweep of feelings sensitizes the soul friend to read how spirit touches the inner life of the person. It is challenging because the spiritual guide must be attuned to the different movements at work within the seeker, including the struggle between the lower will and the divine will; and the lifetime of habits that prevent the person from becoming aware of contrary desires operating within the self.

Often in life, a person is confronted with divergent or confounding choices. These could involve career, marriage, or parenthood, as well as studying for the ministry or the priesthood. Each of these decisions involves a spiritual component that—for a person attuned to his or her inner life—is best uncovered with the help of wise counsel. In Christianity, this process of decision-making is called the "discernment of spirits," and is a major component of many spiritual guidance sessions.

Ignatius of Loyola—sixteenth-century Spanish mystic and founder of the Jesuits—wrote *The Spiritual Exercises*, a guide to the art and practice of discernment. While convalescing from serious battle injuries, Ignatius began to question his life choices. He noticed different interior movements when he considered his future and discovered that guidance from the spirit—and not from his will or ego—was experienced in a quiet manner, leaving him "content and happy." It brought a feeling of calm, of being "at home." Ignatius contrasted his spirit-driven choices from those decisions that were not from his true self. In his autobiography, Ignatius writes (in the third person):

> When he was thinking about the things of the world, he took much delight in them, but afterwards, when he was tired and put them aside, he found that he was dry and discontented. . . . and he began to marvel . . . that some thoughts left him sad and others happy. Little by little he came to perceive the different spirits that were moving him; one coming from the devil, the other from God.[10]

Ignatius asked: How do we learn to listen to the "motions of the soul?" These interior movements consist of thoughts, desires, repulsions, and attractions. Spiritual discernment requires sensitivity to these movements, understanding where they come from, and where they lead. It prepares the soul "to rid itself of all inordinate attachments, and, after their removal, of seeking and finding the will of God in the disposition of our life for the salvation of our soul."[11]

He soon recognized that he should make no decision without first offering it to prayer, because his soul had become accustomed to worldly distractions that were obstructing his inner voice. Like a wobbly child learning how to ride a bicycle, Ignatius could not trust himself without training wheels—prayer and discernment, and guidance from a wise elder to help uncover what was beneficial or detrimental to his spiritual life. He was confronted with divergent paths that, initially, appeared to be equally viable.

According to Ignatius, the first attribute necessary for spiritual discernment is to be dispassionate, detached from our choices. This is mental asceticism. Instead of asking God to bless a decision we have already made, discernment brings to the Divine several possible paths and prays: "What does God want of me?" In order to listen, the soul must be in a state of impartiality, receptive to the conviction of the heart. The problem is that we are wearing earmuffs; we don't listen. The ego says: "No, you don't want to go that way, it's silly, it's too easy." But frequently, what the spirit wants is easy, a natural flow of intention that feels like you are at home. No struggle, no laboring over it. Yet, how often do we reject the pure voice? We say, "I'll do that later, when I'm older and have more time. But not now."

Never now!

Thus, you walk a path of choices made against the heart. You forget. The inner voice is calling you, but you've become dulled to its sound. For many people there are clear signs—physical, emotional, spiritual— about what they truly want. But because their spirit has been broken, they have forgotten how to hear. The sad thing is that we don't believe in our happiness. If we yearn for a contemplative, monastic life, we fear we can't have it. We must face our fears and conflicts and explore our heart's longing.

To illustrate this process, let's imagine a discernment that could arise in spiritual direction. Emily is struggling to choose between two job offers. One position offers greater opportunity for advancement, while the other is not as financially rewarding, but is possibly more in line with her life goals. Which position should she choose? Which is the right way?

In the process of discernment, Emily discovers that her deep need for recognition, as well as feelings of insecurity, are clouding her decision. If such need were absent, she would be able to approach the issue dispassionately. Placing her choice before her deep self, or her God, she asks: Which is the better position for my spiritual growth? What does the Divine want for me? Which job advances my life direction, and which moves me further away?

Through the process of opening her soul to the divine will, Emily is able to hear her inner voice. She learns how insecurity destroys her confidence and obscures decision-making. Through silence and stillness, she lifts decision-making above the conflicting opinions she has internalized from family, co-workers, friends, or social groups, giving her the courage to follow her heart.

Sometimes we have to make difficult decisions because the world pulls us in contrary directions. But, if we make the choice that deepens spiritual growth, we will build integrity and wisdom. This is because we have been created with the free will to move closer to or away from the spirit. Listening to the divine call within is vital for understanding the motives beneath our thoughts and actions, and for accepting or rejecting those things the mind proposes for us to do. Is this action based on something I truly want, or is it an old memory, something I think I should do? Is it based on something that may be contrary to my best interests? This is the critical element of discernment. When you review your life and reflect on decisions you've made, in many cases you will discover that you didn't spiritually question whether or not you should take a particular path. Most of the time your decisions were based on other factors: financial, mental, emotional, family.

Few of us are trained to offer every life choice to God, to spiritually consider if a decision is healthful. Yet, it is worthwhile to reflect on the wisdom of the fourth-century Christian monk John Cassian, who wrote: "... it is very clear that no virtue can come to full term or can endure without the grace of discernment. . . . For discernment is the mother, the guardian, and the guide of all the virtues."[12] Since thoughts come either from God or our own minds, discernment is a lifelong method of measuring the ego's desire against the wisdom of the divine creator, whose glorious light illuminates the mind and activates the interior path along which a soul is being led.

The virtue of discernment involves purity of heart, and purity of heart involves the spiritual will. Christian monks termed the pure will *intentio* (Latin, intention, true desire), a movement directly from the heart toward the object of the person's spiritual aspiration. This is not the human or ego will, but the action of the divine will in you, longing for truth. The practice of discerning life choices leads to the unifying of human and divine love, the goal of the spiritual life.

Spiritual Guidance in the World's Religions

WHILE I HAVE described spiritual direction in the Christian context, guidance of the soul or the deep self is practiced in all religions. In Buddhism, "right mindfulness" is at the core of the seeker's practice, and central to discerning his or her motivations. The aim of the Zen roshi or Tibetan lama is to help the student see the true nature of things and act accordingly. Three obstacles or defilements negatively impact on right mindfulness—greed, hatred, and delusion—and operate in the personality. To assist in the development of true sight, and necessary to dispel the "three poisons," students practice sitting meditation, zazen, paying close attention to their posture, breathing, and awareness in all life conditions (walking, washing dishes, prayer, etc.). Concentration of mind, wisdom, and morality dispel ignorance.

The function of the roshi, or lama is to provide the liberating insight that shocks the pupil out of everyday awareness or *samsara* (conditioned reality) and helps that person to see what is real. The relationship between master and disciple must be one of trust that leads to the sudden death of ego. The master becomes a catalyst to trigger the appropriate response.

Zen stories are directed to the master's students as tools of awareness, but also to convey universal wisdom. Soto Zen Master Dogan (1200–1253) offers sage counsel: "Free yourself from all attachments. Bring to an end all desires, all concepts and judgments. Do not think about how to become a Buddha."[13]

Another influential figure in Japanese Zen Buddhism, Hakuin Ekaku (1685–1768), tells a story about the great tension or great doubt that precedes enlightenment:

A man went astray to arrive at a spot which had never before been trodden by the foot of man. Before him there dawned a bottomless chasm. His feet stood on the slippery moss of a rock and no secure foothold appeared around him. He could neither step forward nor backward. Only death awaited him. The vine which he grasped with his left hand and the tendril which he held with his right hand could offer him little help. His life hung as by a single thread. Were he to release both hands at once, his dry bones would come to naught.

Thus it is with the Zen disciple. By pursuing a single *koan* he comes to a point where his mind is as if dead and his will as if extinguished. This state is like a wide void over a deep chasm and no hold remains for hand or foot. All thoughts vanish and in his bosom burns hot anxiety. But then suddenly it occurs that with the *koan* both body and mind break. This is the instant when the hands are released over the abyss. In this sudden upsurge it is as if one drinks water and knows for oneself heat and cold. Great joy wells up. This is called rebirth. This is termed seeing into one's nature. Everything depends on pushing forward and not doubting that with the help of this concentration one will eventually penetrate to the ground of one's nature.[14]

In Islam—as in the other religions mentioned in this chapter—the true spiritual guide is the Divine; for this reason, the master never imposes his or her will, or seeks to convert another person. At the same time, the spiritual guide should be well versed in the mysteries of the Sufi way, firmly established in a high state of consciousness, and experienced in both the awe of God's majesty and the delight of God's beauty. I love the wise counsel of Sharafuddin Maneri, thirteenth-century Sufi master and Islamic saint:

Remember, too, that an ordinary road is infested with thieves and robbers, so that one cannot travel along it without an escort. As for the mystic Way, the world, one's ego, devils, men, and jinn all infest this Way, thus making it impossible to travel along it without an experienced, holy man as one's escort. Remember, further, that there are many slippery places where it is easy to fall. And one can be plagued with misfortune and dangers from behind! Many philosophers and worldly minded people, as well as others lacking faith, piety, or any semblance of morality—have become followers of their own base desires. They have gone without a perfect sheikh or leader who has reached his goal on this Way, and have instead trusted in their own intellectual powers. They entered the wilderness where they fell and perished, losing even their faith.[15]

Maneri shows how we are assailed in our spiritual pilgrimage by crises, and that we need help and assistance. He cautions not to become inebriated by the "heady wine" of both spiritual acclaim and spiritual bliss, but to stay centered in the practice of emptiness, so that we do not succumb to pride, but learn that humble submission keeps the heart always open.

Types of Spiritual Relationships

THERE ARE probably as many different types of spiritual relationships as there are people. A review of the world's religions, however, shows certain distinctive religious figures and models of spiritual guidance. Below is a summary of these historical figures.

Guru

In the devotional spiritualities of the Indian subcontinent, the *guru* (from the Sanskrit: spiritual teacher or guide) is a central figure in religious and cultural settings. The guru is looked upon as a holy person or even an incarnate goddess or god with the wisdom and the power to guide a person in the spiritual life and to activate interior transformation. For many of these cultures, spiritual guidance occurs within the complex rituals that sustain faith, and the stages of life coincident with one's age and station. The relationship between guru and disciple is an unequal one, where the person seeking guidance is thought to be in the presence of one elevated in spiritual wisdom and personal holiness.

Lama or Roshi

The many branches of Buddhism have given rise to a variety of religious functions and titles. Two of the most well-known are the Tibetan lama and the Zen roshi. While coming out of distinctive Tibetan and Zen forms of Mahayana Buddhism, these religious authorities function in similar ways as spiritual masters who have achieved a high level of spiritual discipline and wisdom and thus are endowed with the ability to pass on or transmit the original enlightenment experience of Gautama Buddha. The relationship could not be called one of guidance in the traditional Western sense of spiritual direction, which proceeds by dialogue and mutual sharing. Rather, the purpose of an audience with one's teacher resides with the power of spiritual transmission attributed to the lama or roshi to effect in the student or disciple the liberated state of consciousness central to Buddhist philosophy and practice.

Priest or Elder

The word *priest* comes from the Greek *presbyteros*, which is generally translated as "elder." It is an ancient term for designating the person who may enter the presence of God. The historical function of the priest is primarily sacramental where, through special prayers and ritual actions, the priest takes an object from the secular world and makes it holy. The priest or elder serves as an intermediary between the people and God and is anointed by his or her spiritual community to absolve sins, hear confessions, and function as a spiritual father or mother.

Rebbe (Rabbi)

Spiritual guidance is reflected in diverse ways in Jewish history. Early examples of spiritual companionship are depicted in the Hebrew Bible between Naomi and her daughter-in-law, Ruth, in the book of Ruth; and include the counsel imparted by the *zechenim* or *hachamin*—wise elders—during the same period (approximately 1050–30 BCE). Much later, during the eighteenth century, the Hassidic Movement attracted many followers who sought spiritual guidance from their rebbe (rabbi) in a session known as the *yehidut*, or interview. The function of the rebbe was to serve as a *moreh derekh*, or spiritual guide, who represented a living example of divine love capable of alleviating suffering and leading the disciple to God.

Sage

The sage is a religious type found in the philosophical traditions of China and Greece. In China, the sage became the ideal personality of Daoist and Confucian traditions, modeling the potential of cosmic relatedness within the human order by cultivating sincerity (*ch'eng*). For the sage, the most ordinary human actions are the means for transforming and nourishing all beings, as one's natural sincerity becomes attuned to the moral order in the universe. The sage cultivates a special mode of sympathetic relationship with the world and helps to arouse in others a self-reflection that reveals their deepest humanity.

Shaman

The shaman is the central religious figure of Indigenous cultures around the world. He or she functions as an intermediary between the earth world and the realm of the Spirit, mediating the relationship with the spirits and serving as a conduit for healing. The shaman in a special way imbibes or absorbs the pains and wounds of others in order to effect a transformative healing in the person and in the community as a whole. The shamanic healer is one who takes on the pains of those who seek guidance and who has traveled through the often-lonely path of psychological dismemberment in order to experience the emptiness that is the source of the all.

Shaykh

In Sufism the central religious figure is the Shaykh, who guides the disciple in *tariqat*, the inner path of the heart. As spiritual guide, the Shaykh is both a messenger and reflection of Allah and it is through the bond between disciple and teacher that the mystical opening of the heart is said to occur. The deepening of the spiritual life is understood in Sufism to be expressed in the affirmation of God's absolute all-encompassing existence, which longs to be known, and the reality of the human being as a secret treasure of God.

Soul Friend or Companion

This is the model most often taught and used today, in which persons serve as spiritual companions and soul friends on the journey. While the modern practice of spiritual direction involves openness of heart and intuitive listening, spiritual directors today are trained to be peer spiritual guides and soul companions on the journey rather than gurus, masters, or healers. Although the relationship between directee and director can be friendly, it is not what we typically think of as friendship. The person in his or her role as spiritual director is trained to maintain proper and helpful boundaries that support the spiritual direction process.

· ♦ ·

AS WE HAVE SEEN, spiritual guidance is the sacred art of communion between two souls and their Divine, which—through the opening of hearts and the illumination of minds—uncovers both people's longing for the good, the true, and the beautiful. As Chinese philosopher, Shao Yong (1011-1077), writes:

A mirror reflects because it does not obscure the corporeal form of things. But water (with its purity) does even better because it reveals the universal character of the corporeal form of things as they really are. And the sage does still better because he reflects the universal character of the feeling of all things. The sage can do so because he views things as they view themselves; that is, not subjectively but from the viewpoint of things.[16]

· ♦ ·

May I open my soul
to your guidance, Holy One,
through the heart of a
friend in spirit
who shares my longing
for the inner way
of love.

Amen.

ELEVEN

Cultivation of Mindfulness

I F ANYTHING DISTINGUISHES monastic life and practice from other
endeavors, it is the cultivation of an aware consciousness. In fact,
cultivation of mindfulness is central to a mature spirituality, which
involves what we do during the day, how we do it, as well as insight into
our attitude, motivation, emotion, speech, and action. It is concerned
with the presence or focused attention of our total selves.

Often, we are only half aware, physically present but far away in
thought. Because attention wanders, mental preparation practices
enhance our capacity for deep thought and, through a process of ges-
tation, lead to new insights about one's self or the world. Silence, solitude, meditation, prayer, and self-reflection facilitate entrance into the
realm of wisdom, where we work to cultivate compassion, humility, and
nonviolence.

Monastic communities and spiritual elders across traditions know
the value of intense periods of prayer and meditation. Gandhi, for one,
claimed that the most powerful aspect of his life—the thing that changed
everything—was ceaseless prayer. He recognized that techniques of contemplation generate energetic consequences that positively affect body,
mind, and spirit.

In Asian religions, especially in yoga, meditation, and the martial arts,
cultivation of deep awareness is directed toward emptiness and nondual

consciousness. Various mental techniques, including observing and counting the breath, repetition of a mantra (sacred word), visualization, and energetic practices, expand one's consciousness and are instrumental in the development of clarity and inner stillness. A classical Daoist text, the *Zhuangzi*, describes the intensification of emptiness in the life of the monk.

> Make your aspirations one! Don't listen with your ears; listen with your heart-mind. No, don't listen with your heart-mind; listen with qi . . . qi is empty and waits on all things. Emptiness is the fasting of the heart-mind. (*Zhuangzi*, Chapter 4)[1]

When approached with emptiness, everyday activity—eating, washing dishes, walking, dancing, reading, speaking, gardening, praying, listening, etc.—has the capacity to reduce suffering and to inspire the hope of enlightenment.

An extensive history of spiritual practices is found in the Abrahamic religions, as well, which generally are focused on advancing the person's quest for divine union. The meditative techniques created by Spanish Kabbalist Abraham Abulafia (1240–1291) are an integrated method of concentrating on the Divine Name. One practice is associated with meditation using *gematria*, or the numerical equivalents of letters, and is intended to bring about particular mystical experiences. In Sufism, *dhikr* refers to remembrance of Allah and often consists of the repetition of Allah's name counted on the fingers or prayer beads, and can involve breathing exercises or movement (such as that of the Whirling Dervishes) intended to disrupt normal consciousness. Christian monks practice inner wakefulness, an attitude of alertness to the presence of God, associated with contemplative prayer and the liturgy of the hours.

Meditative techniques propel the attentive soul into a state of agile receptivity where the active divine influence can reach down to meet and illuminate the human intellect. The awakened heart awaits the presence of the beloved, keeping watch: "Therefore let us not be asleep like the rest, but awake and sober." (1 Th 5:6). The contemplative soul practices the cessation of words and the cultivation of true presence, says the anonymous author of *The Cloud of Unknowing*.

Contemplatives rarely pray in words but if they do, their words are few. The fewer the better as a matter of fact; yes, . . . for now the contemplative must hold himself continually poised and alert at the highest and most sovereign point of the spirit.[2]

Mindfulness is also taught to enhance daily living, as well as to reduce stress, anxiety, symptoms of depression, and other health-related issues. Contemplative practices have been adapted in schools, colleges, hospitals, prisons, corporations, and anywhere there is the intent toward a realized life. It is apparent that without the discipline of mindfulness, the seeker remains disordered. His or her intrinsic, organic order cannot be imposed from outside, but is generated from within.

The variety and scope of mindfulness practices in the world's cultures and religions is vast, which will not be touched on in this chapter. Instead, I provide a general synopsis of three stages or levels of mindfulness: ordering your life, active effort toward divine love, and mindfulness as mystical consciousness. Each stage is not a necessary precondition for the next but can be developed and practiced in a variety of ways.

STAGE 1:
Ordering Your Life

MINDFULNESS IMPLIES seriousness and care in ordering your life according to spiritual principles; and a realization that it is a full-time occupation, not a part-time project that is squeezed in with everything else. Rather, spiritual awareness *is* your work, or vocation: a state of being that inhabits the center of your life. This full-time occupation of spiritual growth stabilizes your soul and allows disparate needs and longings to fall into place more easily, because you are now focused. When you lack inner order, it is easy to be overwhelmed by a multitude of possibilities, all of which compete for attention and time—and none of which achieve the desired peace.

In this first stage of mindfulness, meditative practices are critical for observing feelings, desires, and needs. We learn to become aware of our emotional tone, and to avoid anger and undue passions. We also become sensitive to how heedless and negligent we often are. We are inattentive with our prayer. We are careless in the way we treat people. We rush around. We do not put proper attention on what we are doing.

On a daily basis, the new monk struggles to maintain a contemplative attitude in all he or she does. Yet, disordered states—reluctance, complaint, gossip, disturbance, forgetfulness, jealousy, etc.—of which we often are unaware, derail our intentions. For example, there is nothing more damaging to spiritual growth than the reluctant pilgrim. Mindfulness thrives on attentiveness and concern; it is disturbed by ineptitude, laziness, and apathy. You may experience a kind of internalized inertia or sloppy disregard for what is important to your soul. How often do we say, "I want to meditate today, but I have to go shopping and I have to call this person … ," and then, "Oh gee, now it's midnight and I didn't have time to do that all day." When we are reluctant to find the time to be mindful, in effect we are saying that the spiritual practices and personal relationships that provide meaning are unimportant.

In the *Rule of Life*, St. Benedict discusses the destructiveness of complaining or "murmuring," chiding the monks to dispense with constant gossip. Legitimate complaints, which are a necessary and healthy part of community life, are different than harmful murmuring, which is designed to undermine the community or another person's heart. Complaint often is directed toward a perceived or real authority, which can take many guises, from unexamined family dynamics, religious alienation, personal wounding, social injustice, and so forth. To address these issues honestly is vital to health, and essential to the growth of awareness.

Another way we avoid being mindful is through distractions. A serious spiritual commitment cannot be completely disturbed by every little thing—by gossip, anger, or fear. This does not mean that we remove ourselves in a superior or arrogant manner. Rather, we apply mindfulness to our relations and ask ourselves whether this relation is, in itself, healthy. The same is true with respect to removing ourselves from television, movies, internet browsing, phone calls, text messages, and emails. There is no right or wrong distraction, only what is a distraction for you. You determine what de-centers you or what fragments your inner peace. That is your distraction. That is your disturbance. It is different for each of us. Discover what hinders or interrupts your attention and make a plan to reduce the distraction. Then put the plan into action.

Mindfulness is an important tool that also makes us aware of how we forget. We are not just mindful of what we should be doing, we are also mindful of how we are forgetting what we should be doing. This is important because through study of our forgetfulness, we learn about ourselves. Again, what kind of camouflage or pretense do we use in order to forget? What kind of rationalizations do we proffer? *I was so busy I simply misplaced my mind. The kids got me up early and I didn't have the energy in the evening to pray. I said unkind things at work, but it was stress. I had a raincoat and two umbrellas and didn't realize my colleague was getting wet.* What kind of ego struggle is taking place when we ignore or deny the truth? Striving to recognize the motives behind forgetfulness helps with developing perspective, self-compassion, and acceptance.

We all need healthy egos to survive, but the unhealthy or false ego is an obstacle to wholeness because it is in large part concerned with looking out for itself. In other words, the ego can be a mask that conceals our inner fears and damages, conceals how afraid we are to know ourselves and to love, and conceals the brutal honesty of the mind at rest. Somehow and someway, mindfulness guides us through those aspects of our personality that we did not know and will be surprised (if not shocked) to learn. And yet, it is with an aware heart and an attentive mind that we discover freedom.

STAGE 2:

Active Effort Toward Divine Love

WE ALL WISH SPIRITUAL growth were easy, but it requires work. The person who seeks a self-reflective manner of living recognizes the importance of striving to achieve divine love. This seeker devotes time and energy to exploring the capacity of love to empower the soul and to resolve painful or tense situations. Akin to other forces of nature such as gravity, love is held by many to be the greatest power in the cosmos, a living reality and a universal energy that governs all aspects of existence.

The quest of attentiveness to divine love can be wrenching to the contrived personality. Worldly success cannot match the achievement of spirit. The greatest societal award can feel empty if the person has not found meaning and love. For the most part, the spiritual life is hidden, and often the holiest people are unrecognized. Yet, in their depth they have accomplished something for all beings; they are climbing a mountain toward Mystery. Aware mindfulness reorders priorities, helping us to be serious about our time and more sensitive to the lighter aspects of life as well. Seekers must prepare to be alone because no one may join or know them. Yet, even the difficult moments can be joyful because their quest is the gateway into wisdom.

The capacity to grow in love is assisted by spiritual community, a wise counsel that every monastic lineage has embraced. Buddha placed right association (*sangha,* community of monks) as the precursor of the Eightfold Path (way of enlightenment). That is, living among or being associated with people who also are seeking truth is critical to self-transcendence. When we are not around people with whom we can share our spiritual intention, it is hard to maintain focus. There is a sense of loneliness. Through participation in a common aspiration, alienation can be healed and the heart opened. When we have the great blessing of the companionship of other seekers, we are very enthusiastic because we know how solitary the journey has been. We have gratitude for community, however perfect or imperfect.

Another effort toward awareness of divine love is making provisions for solitude and for silence—to be disengaged from the demands of the world, and to be centered in one's inner hermitage. For monastics, praying many times a day, chanting the liturgy of the hours, or practicing zazen (sitting meditation) is the fuel that ignites the embers in one's heart. It is this intense commitment to do all in our power to grow closer to the divine—longing to know truth, to be holy—that continually inspires us to give up lesser pursuits and center our intention on the divine quest.

Of course, repetitive mindfulness exercises and spiritual rituals can become monotonous. Monastic literature is replete with stories of boredom and tedium—Christian monks call this struggle, *acedia*, the "noonday demon"—and other rebellions of the person chafing against the narrow path. And yet, what I notice in the most peaceful of monks is a kind of reverence for monotony, even when they have heard, for example, a particular passage of Scripture hundreds of times over the years. The beauty of monotony is that it is the result of eliminating distraction, helps to condense all the senses, elevates the vitality of body, mind, and spirit, and releases a fragrance in the soul.

For contemporary people, the quiet repetitiveness of awakened practices can be a particular challenge. Our busy societies are based on diversity and complexity. We are not accustomed to monotony. We like a million possibilities, a million distractions. The norm then is busyness; the default is external affirmation, stimulation, and a frenetic pace of life driven by endless to-do lists. What is important is reversed. Those aspects of life that generate peace and inner joy, and are nourishment for our souls—quiet contemplation, rapt attention, awe—instead are relegated to a secondary place in the daily round of events and activities.

Due to the absence of solitude and quiet in our daily lives, it is not always easy to decipher whether you actually are pursuing divine love or your own self-will. No doubt you are aware of the difference between the happiness that comes from doing what is spiritually right, and the material happiness you get when you buy or accomplish something. These are different levels of happiness. Discernment is a form of mindfulness that helps in distinguishing between interior happiness and material or superficial happiness. We are so habituated to seeking worldly success that we often dismiss spiritual fulfillment. It is offered, and we ignore it. It is available to practice in the simplest and most humble ways, and we reject it. The aware person allows the Divine to show him or her how to relinquish transient forms of happiness that the ego craves and discover the freedom that only Spirit can reveal.

Mindfulness is not a chore, but a joyful endeavor. The active effort that we make toward celebration of the sacred is not a substitute for secular life. It is not an imitation of the spiritual life in the secular life, but rather the inner rest that is the purview of the true seeker of God. We tend to think that mindfulness is something that we have to jam into our regular life. But it is not possible to expand our capacity for goodness—kindness, compassion, humility, etc.—and continue to be as busy, fragmented, and psychically unmoored as we were before. Contemplative awareness is not supposed to be another thing added onto everything else we are doing. Rather, it is an experience of resting in and *within* all things, seeing the cosmos through the expansion of its Mystery.

Just as we realize that the spirit offers a different kind of happiness than that provided by the accumulation of material things, similarly we recognize that the love we have for transcendence may be different than what we think love is or should be. When we discover this pure divine love, we realize the potentiality for love in all our relations, and in all of life's moments. Mindfulness then becomes an intense longing to be faithful to the gift of love, in unceasing adoration of the sacred.

Mindfulness is the ordering of our lives according to what we know to be true. When we are disciplined, we mirror the universal order. True discipline refers to an interior state, not the discipline that is harsh and imposed from outside, but the spiritual discipline that is in line with a consistent effort to know our Creator. Nature is disciplined. Trees, for example, do not pull up their roots and declare, "I don't want to be a tree!" This may seem ridiculous, but it allows us to understand the discipline of nature. The tree practices stability. The tree *is* a practice of stability. It is rooted in a particular place for the duration of its existence as a tree. The tree is actively practicing stability. It is also practicing unconditional receptivity because it is taking in whatever comes to it—sun, rain, insects that bore holes in its bark, birds that build nests in its branches, and dogs that wet its trunk. In nature, we encounter the ordering of the divine mind. We as human beings have the free will to be disordered, but it is the discipline of our minds and hearts that joins us in the great cosmic circle of all beings.

STAGE 3:
Mindfulness as Mystical Consciousness

THE DEEPEST STATE of mindfulness is mystical consciousness, what we might call pure contemplation in which our whole being is possessed and transfigured by the transcendent, in which word and thought take place within the inner life of the Divine. Mindfulness at this level expresses a high degree of solitude, which is simultaneously available even now in the depth of the heart. Here are some signs of transformed consciousness:

* We cling to the Divine without any forgetfulness, in those illuminating moments when we glimpse and understand reality. There is no forgetting. We have had an immediate experience of the Divine Presence.

* The memory that we have of Mystery is without any trace of weariness. We are not weary. We are not burdened. We experience reality in a state of exuberance and joy.

* Mindfulness that is an act of love, or what is called infused contemplation, when our experience arises because the Divine has already called us to love. It is a moment of co-mutuality, without separation.

In this state of transformed consciousness, memory is not just the activity of retrieving information, as in the mind, but conveys the residual imprint of mystical presence. This is why prayer and meditation are so vital to the monastic life: they are the means of directly experiencing the sacred realm. In this state, your soul becomes a mirror of peace and love; your presence is healing. Your being becomes transformative for the consciousness of other beings because you have been touched by the holy light. Why have you experienced this? Because through ceaseless prayer or meditation, you have surrendered your self-will to God. Mindfulness as mystical consciousness is not something done with your will or mind. It is the upwelling of the Divine in your soul. Maybe you will never be able to express in this life what you feel, what you experience, but you are able to transmit through your countenance and behavior.

In this reordered state of consciousness, our disloyalty is healed—our unfaithfulness to ourselves and to others is changed by a divine gift. We tend to think of ourselves as troubled or unstable. *Why am I not ordered? Why can I not control myself? What is wrong with me?* This level of self-awareness and the subsequent blessing of self-order come about through an act of grace. Thus we pray for grace, we meditate on our capacity to be given and the willingness to accept the gift of fidelity, the blessing of not forgetting. Instead of focusing on our flaws and errors, and being angry because we are not ordered, we practice praying—and ask the Spirit for help: *Show me, guide me, empty me.* This becomes a giving over of our will instead of its suppression.

Such mystical surrender finally leads to a theophanic consciousness—one that reveals the presence of God in the world; a path that leads us from the external and superficial to the depth of reality that elevates and informs everything. We step into the world of the Divine, and we look at this world from a holy perspective, which includes greater understanding and compassion. Here, not only is your awareness of the world raised, but your conscience—your moral fiber—is raised. Life becomes simpler and more innocent.

Contemplative awareness is a return to the inner purity that you may fear is lost, and a releasing of the grief that you harbor of never being blameless again. But now, you are able to confront your pain because you realize that the true self is never lost, and you have the courage to heal your wounds.

Mystical awareness will bring about repentance and remorse—a conscience that realizes how we violate holiness. It also provides the means to reconcile our heedlessness, the things we do every day where we simply lose our minds for a moment. We are just not paying attention. It is not done necessarily out of the worst effort or the worst intention, but nonetheless, it creates pain. Maybe the other person did not even expect to bear the brunt of inattentiveness, but you know you could have done better and this becomes the raising of conscience—not just the raising of awareness. Those two things go together in the spiritual life. We have to raise our consciousness, but also our conscience—our moral fiber—every day.

With respect to others, if we do not understand our own moral resolve, we are not able to recognize it in someone else. We cannot guide someone else if we cannot guide ourselves. We cannot help others to be virtuous if we are morally inept, morally inattentive, or hiding shortcomings "under the rug," covering them with something that appears clean but underneath harbors garbage and debris. If we are not honest and truthful with ourselves, then we should stop the spiritual charade.

True mindfulness aims to uncover those inner, secret impulses that we may think are innocent, but are dangers leading us away from our life in God. It is the diagnosis of self-truth.

Have I really put the Divine at the center?
What are my motives for doing what I am doing?
Are my motives sincere or are they self-aggrandizing?
Do I have a hidden agenda, and why does it matter that I know this difference?

If a person seeks liberation and holiness, then he or she has to recognize the difference between false motivations (that lead the seeker away from Spirit) and true motivations that draw one closer to the Divine. Mindfulness is, ultimately, a high state of mystical awareness, a sensitive attunement to the gentle mercy and precious gift of being born. It is inner discipline applied to daily events, which compels each person to discover the abundant, exuberant, noble, sublime freedom of being fully alive.

. ◆ .

May I begin each day mindful of peace
attuned to the divine flame within
May I share love with all whom I meet,
in gratitude and compassion.

May my soul, broken open by the glory
and suffering of the world
Be transformed into a
wish-fulfilling jewel.

May my heart illumined by fire
and anointed by wisdom
Burst with joy,
a bouquet of flowers in full bloom!

Amen.

PART THREE

Energy and Healing

❖

The universe of cosmic forces speaks to our intuitive minds, visits us in visions, and touches our hearts in silence. The various practices handed down through tradition teach about our bio-spiritual capacity for transformation. Sometimes healing comes about after years of living in community, sitting zazen, or chanting the psalms. But at other times it is necessary to know, now, what is tormenting us, bringing injury into the light, and allow it to dissipate. These healing modalities are born into the world with us. It is not so much that we labor to find them, as it is a miracle already within us that heals and transforms.

It is this to which the following chapters point.

❖

TWELVE

Theology of Energy

UMANS ARE MULTISENSORY beings. Alongside awareness of
physical reality, every person has interior senses or faculties
that are attuned to unseen worlds, and to the unspoken emotions, energetic disturbances, and the stories told by the posture, eyes,
and face. This mystical, unitive kinship with the life force that permeates
creation and resides within us is a natural power of the self. When we are
in harmony with these inner capacities of knowing and seeing, we participate in the vibrant energies around us and open our hearts and minds
to wonder. Simultaneously, we unlock the imaginative force within us,
enhancing our soul's integration of the physical-spiritual worlds.

People are usually more connected to multiple ways of knowing during their early years. Such an experience began for me through the intimate connection to nature I found in the woods and waters around my
childhood home. In these youthful experiences, I felt the earth breathe
around and in me, I saw the harmonious energy among all beings, and I
knew that this was where my spirit belonged. One striking example was
my utter fascination with the interdependent relationship among trees.
They spoke, touched, and shared energies in a grace-filled dance. The
aura of an oak bent and intermingled with a nearby hickory, sassafras
communed with black walnut, generating patterns of light that intensified the atmosphere with a mysterious intelligence.

No doubt many of you have had similar feelings of kinship with the natural world and can recall childhood experiences of awe. Yet, a rational mindset and educational training may have blunted, ridiculed, and perhaps even shut down your natural capacity to truly feel, know, and see. These offenses to the mystical, intuitive senses damage our self-understanding and curtail full engagement with the vibrant interplay of multiple realities. Blocked from spiritual access to the complex systems that govern life on Earth, we learn to evaluate our lives and goals from a limited, materialistic perspective. While we grant credibility to rationality, we dismiss and often denigrate artistic, mythical, or mystical knowledge.

I am of the opinion that the conversion of life that identifies and stabilizes monkhood and all seekers of truth is dependent on a restoration of our inherent multisensory, mystical sensitivity. In fact, the person's call to monastic life is wholly based on a deep spiritual aspiration that by definition cannot be fulfilled by the things of the world. This means that a significant element of the new monk's formative path requires a recovery of our natural and intrinsic capacity to read the unseen—that is, to enter into communion with the universe of energies.

Monastic communities foster the turn inward through the discipline of thought, word, and deed. Silence and solitude protect the holiness of members and provide monks and their communities permission to dispense with contrived social pleasantries in favor of the search for God. Ideally, the great gift the monastic atmosphere accords monks is the freedom to seek and know their divine source without having to explain or defend; thus, to be at ease in one's own depth.

The rules that govern monastic life protect against the intrusion into another seeker's emotional, psychological, or spiritual space and dissuade those situations and people that gossip or disturb the balance of peace. The commitment to inner solitude is safeguarded in various ways: a schedule which keeps daily life ordered; established periods for prayer, meditation, and chant; consistent rhythm of religious rituals; yearly calendar of liturgies and scripture readings; regular work assignments; shared meals often taken in silence; and time for personal study and solitude. Further, silence is valued as the milieu or effective spiritual atmosphere that holds everything together. In this way, the monk's body, mind, and spirit is trained hour by hour, day by day to live differently, to preserve the integrity of openness to divine energies. Personal commitment to authenticity is maintained through the consistency of spiritual practice.

Elders know that it is not enough to wear a monastic habit, or to sequester with holy books and sacred practices. The commitment to seek truth requires conscious facility with the ordering of the person's life and protecting the integrity of the divine within. These monastic rules of guarding the heart can be replicated in those living outside a formal monastic setting by developing the skills of energetic discipline and emotional integrity, which require insight into the mystical intuition of visionary worlds that swirl around us in each moment. This is the path to becoming a vibrant, centered person, open to the sacred universe incarnated on Earth.

We Are Energy

THE HUMAN BODY—and every life form on our planet—is composed of interdependent physical and spiritual or energetic bodies. In fact, there is no physical form that is not also an energetic one. Body, mind, emotion, spirit—each—is energy oscillating at different frequencies. Everything that takes place in the human energy field is recorded and imprinted in some aspect of the body-mind-spirit. Physical effects (injury, illness, death) and personal consciousness, including thoughts, emotions, intuitions, dreams, actions, etc., are composed of and generate specific energy signatures or equations. Such that, for example, fear lodges in a person's energy field as one type of vibration and love as another. Each energy signature is disrupted or dissolved by a higher vibrational field. The highest frequency energy is Divine, which transforms all other energies vibrating at slower, more physical levels. It is the supernatural energies— *Dao*, Great Spirit, Sophia, Buddha-mind—that effect transformative and sometimes miraculous change, including physical and spiritual healing, which are often invoked through prayer or meditation.

My experience is that first and foremost we are *spiritual* bodies—animal, human, plant, mineral. As quantum physics has demonstrated, the table where I write is not solid, but consists of the movement of electrons and subatomic particles vibrating at different rates. Similarly, our bodies are both tangible and intangible, representing the dynamic configuration of physical energies swimming in a sea of spiritual energies.

Everything in this world vibrates with spiritual presence. As we read these words, each of us is pulsating in a unique energetic pattern. We are the incarnation of multiple energies, from the slower vibrations of matter to the higher vibrations of soul and pure spirit. When I say we are "spiritual energy," I am not intending that spiritual energy is opposed to bodies and the material world, but something more fundamental: everything exists because it is composed of the energy of spirit.

Energy awareness implies, first of all, that we know our unique energy signature. Most people—particularly beginners on the path—do not feel or experience their own energy. Each body has an energy signature, such that the self-aware person is able to recognize: "This is me. This is my energy." Energy is not confined to a person's family or cultural identity, but the vibrational field and inner sensation of being itself.

To know the self, we have to understand and harness our own energies. Religions accomplish this through meditation and prayer, sacraments and rituals. Spiritual practices are designed to balance the energy of the Earth with that of our bodies and higher mystical states. When we have too much psychic or spiritual energy, we can become ungrounded. In contrast, when we have too much earthly energy, we may become stuck in our habits, or rigid and fixed in our attitudes. When we are not in our energy, when we don't experience the inner "rightness" of being, we do not feel at home. Many of us grew up feeling "not at home" in our bodies, in our energy.

Religions employ sophisticated vocabularies to describe the relationship between spirit and matter, and to map the etheric or esoteric dimension of body-mind-spirit. Especially in the religions of Asia and the Indian subcontinent, human beings are thought to be composed of three elements: the physical body, the subtle or energy body, and the soul or spirit that is one with the divine. The energy or esoteric body is composed of etheric channels and pathways: *auras* and *chakras* of Indo-

Tibetan-Chinese religions; Shamanic techniques of ecstasy; Ayurvedic *doshas*, energies that govern all physical and mental processes; *kundalini*, described in the Tantric tradition as the "serpent power" or vital energy that is awakened at the base of the spine; and Chinese acupuncture, with its emphasis on pressure points located along invisible meridians throughout the body.

These subtle or esoteric bodies are considered to be contiguous with, and also prior to and extensions of, the physical body. In some sense, they are more real than the material body itself, and exert influence over it.

An important element in the formation of the new monk is recognition of one's spiritual body and how it is constantly in dialogue with and extends to include the human physical body. The soul's spiritual faculties—visionary, intuitive, empathic, knowing, etc.—coincide and interact with the physical body's senses—sight, smell, touch, hearing, and taste. The vital, primordial interaction of spiritual and physical is often brought into conscious awareness by experiences of awe or mystical insight. In fact, many people drawn to the contemplative life report prior awareness of the visionary worlds within and beyond the everyday realm.

Mystical Effects on the Body

MYSTICAL EXPERIENCES have profound repercussions on the human body. Divine energies activate the energy of our bodies to vibrate at a higher rate than is normal for cell physiology. As a bio-spiritual form, the energetic configuration of the body is expanded by the influx of the sacred. In fact, the spiritual exercises and practices that are integral to mystical growth are designed to help the body not only to *know* about— but also to sustain and *be*—spiritual presence, raising the vibrational rate of body, mind, and spirit. Because the holy simultaneously exceeds and is embedded in phenomenal forms, it subsumes patterns of consciousness and lifts us to a higher, more elevated, state of being. It is an energy that is "outside" the earthly realm (more comprehensive than it) and "inside" the material world, igniting the divine sparks that liberate and heal.

Religious accounts of physical debilitation and sensate effects—light that blinds, fire that consumes, love that overwhelms, etc.—associated with intense mystical or enlightenment events are numerous. Two areas of special interest are how mystical events influence bodily states, and how physical sensations can trigger spiritual experience.

John of the Cross held that physical manifestations of spiritual events are first felt in the soul: "God usually does not bestow a favor on the body without bestowing it first and principally on the soul."[1] Using St. Francis as an example of this effect, John describes how the fiery six-winged archangel, or Seraph, appeared to Francis on Mount LaVerna and pierced his body with the stigmata—the five blood wounds that Christ received. The imprint of the stigmata on Francis' physical body was an outward manifestation of the wounds imprinted on his spiritual body by the power of the Seraph. John writes:

When Francis' soul was wounded with love by the five wounds [of the crucified Christ], their effect extended to the body and these wounds were impressed on the body which was wounded just as the soul was wounded.[2]

John held that due to the purity of Francis' soul, and the compassion he felt for the crucified Christ, his body was fully conformed to the spirit. Thus, the spiritual wounds inflicted by the fiery Seraph resonated in the compassion of his physiology. Here, the physical manifestation is the result of a prior cause in the soul or spiritual body. Especially in a person of profound sensitivity, the positive or negative effects to the subtle energy bodies will filter down to the slower vibration of the physical form.

Bankei—a seventeenth-century Zen master—describes a similar account of physical infirmity resulting from spiritual anguish. As a schoolboy, Bankei was overcome with doubt about the concept "bright virtue" taught by his Zen teachers. He didn't understand the meaning of "bright virtue," and decided that he couldn't live without solving this puzzle. At a young age—possibly eleven—he built a hermitage behind his parents' house and locked himself in, asking people to bring him food. Thereafter, for many years, he wandered from master to master in search of wisdom and consolation.

Yet, he found no one who could help him. His desire to know truth was so intense that he could not bear to go on any longer without resolving this dilemma. Meditating excessively, to the point of starvation, he became quite ill with tuberculosis, unable to swallow or keep food down, and was spitting up blood.

Here is a disciple's account of his story, told in *The Unborn: The Life and Teachings of Zen Master Bankei*:

The master, frustrated in all his attempts to resolve the feeling of doubt which weighed so heavily on his mind, became deeply disheartened. Signs of serious illness appeared. He began to cough up bloody bits of sputum. He grew steadily worse, until death seemed imminent. He said to himself, "Everyone has to die. I'm not concerned about that. My regret is dying with the great matter I've been struggling with all these years, since I was a small boy, still unresolved." His eyes flushed with hot tears. His breast heaved violently. It seemed his ribs would burst. Then, just at that moment, enlightenment came to him—like the bottom falling out of a bucket. Immediately, his health began to return, but he still seemed unable to express what he had realized. Then, one day, in the early hours of the morning, the scent of plum blossoms carried to him in the morning reached his nostrils. At that instant, all attachments and obstacles were swept from his mind once and for all. The doubts that were plaguing him ceased to exist.[3]

Bankei describes a spiritual anguish ("great doubt") that becomes an intense physical suffering ("death seemed imminent"). Yet, after fourteen years of struggle, once he is awakened, his anguish disappears like a dream. Notice that he doesn't recover gradually. He remains ill for quite a long time, but when the spiritual crisis is resolved through achieving enlightenment, his physical suffering dissipates.

The physical senses also can initiate or influence mystical events. The scent of plum blossoms wipes away all obstacles and doubt, cleansing

Bankei's mind of attachments. Similarly, the first awakening of Japanese Zen Master Hakuin (1686–1768) began after practicing Zen one night. Shocked by the sound of the temple bell, he later wrote, "It was as if a sheet of ice had been smashed or a jade tower had fallen with a crash," precipitating enlightenment. Soon after, he became seriously ill:

> My ears were filled with ringing, as with rushing water of a swift river in a deep canyon. My inward organs felt weak and my whole body trembled with apprehensions and fears. My Spirit was distressed and weary, and whether sleeping or waking, I used to see all sorts of imaginary things. Both sides of my body were continually bathed in sweat, and my eyes were perpetually filled with tears.[4]

The intimal relationship of body and spirit—so entwined and within each other—illustrates the mysterious symbiosis and intelligent wisdom that animates life in a continuum of energies. We tend to associate spirituality with the abstention from physical senses. But in the mystical journey, physical senses are harnessed in order to experience the super-sensual. When the attraction of the lower senses or passions—jealousy, greed, possession, hatred—is stilled, the soul opens to the super-essential, the Divine's passion in and for us. The person's emotional reaction to the inflow of the divine can become so intense that the body registers these spiritual touches as anguish or ecstasy. Divine energy is almost too intense for the physical form to hold.

Like Hakuin, Teresa of Avila complains that she cannot concentrate because of noises and rushing waters in her head.

> While I'm writing this, I'm thinking about what's going on in my head with the great noise that I mentioned at the beginning. It makes it almost impossible for me to write what I was ordered to. It seems as if there are in my head many rushing rivers and these waters are hurtling downwards, and many little birds and whistling sounds, not in the ears but in the upper part of the head where, they say, the higher part of the soul is.[5]

Another physical effect that Teresa recounts is pain or stiffness of the limbs, and the cessation of the beating heart:

> Sometimes my pulse almost stops according to what a number of Sisters say who are at times near me and know more, and my arms are straight and my hands so stiff that occasionally I cannot join them. As a result, even the next day I feel pain in the pulse and in the body, as if my bones were disjoined.[6]

The spiritual senses associated with the subtle body generate effects in the physical body—overflowing in tears, piercing of the heart, stiffness in the limbs, and rushing waters in the head. Yet often, while the body suffers physical turmoil, the spirit experiences silence, and is still able to pray. Teresa writes: "For all this turmoil in my head doesn't hinder prayer or what I am saying, but the soul is completely taken up in its quiet, love, desires, and clear knowledge."[7] Even in the midst of suffering, she is able to pray and find solace.

Many people experience some type of mystical event, but don't have the words to explain what happened. They may also fear such experiences are superficial, should be hidden, or indicate a need for medication, rather than evidence of a transformation of being. Again, it takes self-knowledge and discernment to understand when an experience is authentic and when it is not.

Variety of Religious Experiences

THE MONK'S DAILY LIFE involves various types of religious experiences, both personal and communal. Guidance in the quest for the Absolute is thus directed to the entire range of religious phenomena common to the spiritual life: prayer, meditation, vision, inner voice, techniques of contemplation, feelings of grace and awe, ritual, liturgies, fasting, healing, etc.; as well as the more intellective events, such as insight through reading of sacred texts, study of scriptures, and scholarly learning.

One of the quintessential effects of mystical experience is the overwhelming feeling of unity with and love of the divine, people, nature, and all creation. The emotional stirring is so intense that it pierces the heart and wounds the soul. It is sensitivity toward all beings, and attunement to the unity beyond division that is felt in the person's depth. We experience that all creation is one, indivisible energy flowing into and through us. And this inner moment of the stirring of love can bring a person to tears, and usher in a totally different view of reality. The soul has been touched—wounded—in its inner nature by the energy of divine love, which manifests in physical effects. Mystical union is the fulfillment of intoxication by the divine, so writes the Andalusian Sufi, Abu al-Hasan al-Shushtari (1212–69):

> O desire of the one mad with love,
>   by God, I love no one but you
> In you, I made my heart's abode.
>   Make my eyes see you.[8]

Religious personalities also have documented many other types of mystical touches. Among these are the third-eye visions, trance states, yogic postures, prostrations, and *chakra* and *chi* energies known to the religions of India, Tibet, and Southeast Asia. In the Abrahamic monotheisms, using different vocabularies, religious experience also includes visionary states (seeing with the inner eye), locutions (hearing with the inner ear), experiential prayer forms, sacred dance (such as the Sufi Whirling Dervishes), and mystical illuminations or trance. For example, in *The Book of Her Life*, Teresa of Avila explicitly distinguishes three kinds of visions and three types of locutions.

Three Types of Visions:

1. Intellectual, that can be "felt" and known (Chapter 27.3).
2. Imaginative, perceived with the "eyes of the soul" through imagination or "phantasy" (Chapter 28).
3. Corporeal, seen with the bodily eyes (Chapter 28.4).

Three Types of Locutions:

1. Explicit, heard with the sense of hearing (Chapter 27.2ff).
2. Explicit, not heard with the bodily ears, although they are understood much more clearly than if heard (Chapter 25).
3. Not explicit, just as in heaven one understands without speaking: "God and the soul understand each other only through the desire His Majesty has that it understands Him, without the use of any other means" (Chapter 27.10).[9]

Light

LIGHT IS A UNIVERSALLY experienced effect of mystical touches. In Sufism, the first emanation of divinity is the primordial light of Allah constituted by the fourteen immaculate beings of light who—in the eternal succession of their births—bring forth the worlds. Every world is created out of light; and, therefore, humans are beings of light.

When you meditate or pray, the forces of light raise awareness. For example, if you are attached to a painful self-identity ("I am worthless"), it is composed of certain energy vibrations. But every identity is a construct that is vibrating at a slower rate than the Divine Light. Therefore, the act of awareness is itself a result of divine energy within a person burning through whatever is untrue, liberating that energy equation and transforming it into light.

I often have claimed that nothingness is condensed light, the strongest point. Therefore, a moment of nothingness condenses the light within a form or idea, breaking apart its fixed-ness, and releasing falsehood, that is, what is not of the divine. The fourteenth century Dominican theologian, Meister Eckhart, says that one moment of "naughting" is worth all the "aughting" that you'll ever do in your life. As we willingly unravel our "somethingness," divine energy pours in, which changes whatever obstructs the free emanation of light. The power of light to transform is affirmed in this passage by Thomas Merton:

The reason why this light was blinding and neutralizing was that there was and could be simply nothing in it of sense or imagination. When I call it light that is a metaphor which I am using, long after the fact. But at the moment, another overwhelming thing about this awareness was that it disarmed all images, all metaphors, and cut through the whole skein of species and phantasms with which we naturally do our thinking. It ignored all sense experience in order to strike directly at the heart of truth, as if a sudden and immediate contact had been established between my intellect and the Truth. . . . But this contact was not speculative and abstract: it was concrete, and experimental and belonged to the order of knowledge, yes, but more still to the order of love.[10]

The light mysticism Merton describes is a direct experience of reality that cuts through and is above desire. For this reason, the mystical traditions emphasize that the highest states of wisdom occur when we become empty of all ideas and images, because what we seek is beyond the mind. Merton again:

The strange thing about this light was that although it seemed so "ordinary" in the sense I have mentioned, and so accessible, there was no way of recapturing it. In fact, I did not even know how to start trying to reconstruct the experience or bring it back if I wanted to, except to make acts of faith and love. But it was easy to see that there was nothing I could do to give any act of faith that peculiar quality of sudden obviousness: that was a gift and had to come from somewhere else, beyond and above myself.[11]

In a number of Mahayana Buddhist scriptures, aspirants are taught visualization of the light. The Sutra on Visualizing the Buddha of Infinite Life (*Guan wuliang shoufo jing*) specifically describes visualization of Buddha Amitabha (Infinite Light) and his Pure Land called "Sukhavati" (Ultimate Bliss). In the chapter, "Mahayana Buddhist Visualization," scholar and Jōdo Shinshū priest, Kenneth K. Tanaka includes the full text of the Sutra. Below are two excerpts on visualizing light:

The Buddha said to Ananda and Vaidehi: "When you have accomplished visualization of the ground, next contemplate the jeweled trees.... Visualize each one and then form an image of seven rows of trees...high and adorned with seven-jeweled blossoms and leaves.... From the beryl-colored blossoms and leaves issues forth a golden light. From the crystal-colored issues forth a crimson light. From the agate-colored issues forth a sapphire light. From the sapphire-colored issues forth a green pearl light.

The Buddha Amitayus possesses eighty-four thousand physical characteristics, each having eighty-four thousand secondary marks of excellence [that] emit eighty-four thousand rays of light; each ray of light shines universally upon the lands of the ten directions, embracing and not forsaking those who are mindful of the Buddha.[12]

In Tibetan Buddhism, a white light or the "clear" luminosity of emptiness can occur at the moment of death. Professor of Indo-Tibetan Studies, Robert Thurman, in his translation of *The Tibetan Book of the Dead*, describes clear light (transparency) as "the subtlest light that illuminates the profoundest reality of the universe. It is a light like glass, like diamond, like the predawn twilight, different from the lights of sun, moon ... It is an inconceivable light, beyond the duality of bright and dark, a light of the self-luminosity of all things."[13]

Here again, we have the experience of the macrocosm-microcosm. We are part of Mystery and yet it is beyond us. We are both infinite and finite. We are eternal and temporal. We are everything, and it is All: more than us, more than we can name. St. Augustine, in chapter seven of *The Confessions*, captures the transcendence of light:

I entered into my inmost being...and by my soul's eye, such as it was, I saw above that same eye of my soul, above my mind, an unchangeable light. It was not this common light, plain to all flesh, nor a greater light, as it were, of the same kind, ...not such was that light, but different, far different from all other lights. Nor was it above my mind, as oil is above water, or sky above earth. It was above my mind, because it made me, and I was beneath it, because I was made by it.[14]

Fire

INNER FIRE is another spiritual effect experienced in the body. The divine fire is described as the inflow of the Divine into the soul. The Russian mystic Theophan the Recluse (1815–94) puts into words the "burning of the spirit." Jesuit theologian, William Johnston, says, "Just as physical fire applied to a damp log causes ugly smoke to belch so the fire of God's love at first causes suffering because of the impurity of the person. But when the impurities are burned out, the whole person is set on fire with love. After speaking about the log, [Theophan] writes:"

> So it happens with human beings. They receive the fire and begin to burn—and how much smoke and crackling there is only those who have experienced it can know. When the fire is properly alight the smoke and crackling cease, and within reigns only light.[15]

We let go of our impurities: attachment, loneliness, and jealousy. We discover forgiveness, love, and beauty. The soul begins to dry out. The inner self is enkindled with love of the Divine, with its desire to be a living flame. And this flame that ignites the soul causes it to suffer, as it heals whatever is not in harmony with a person's true nature. Symeon the New Theologian (949–1022), a Byzantine Christian monk, also describes how the divine fire affects the soul:

> Among those in whom this fire is burning the fire arises with a great flame and reaches up to heaven, not allowing the one who is embraced any pause or repose. And this is not in an unconscious manner . . . but possesses full feeling and knowledge and having in the beginning an unsupportable suffering, for the soul is endowed with feeling and reason.[16]

Because we have conscious minds and are capable of suffering, the effects of the soul's flame are felt in the psyche. Thus, we feel our soul's suffering, but also the suffering experienced by others, because our whole being is enflamed with love for God.

These energetic events remind us that an entire spiritual realm co-exists with our ordinary perception of reality. We gain entrance into its territory through receptivity and desire. Often, these mystical experiences—arising from the deepest core of the person—awaken us to aspects of our personalities that we ignore. It is the eruption of the "inner world" (the divine world) into our knowledge and senses, which overturns our categories and necessities, our evidences and norms.

The upsurge of the Divine into our conscious life cannot be perceived by ordinary knowledge, nor proven or disputed by means of ordinary argument. It is hearing with something other than physical ears, seeing with more than our biological eyes, knowing with that which is greater than the rational mind.

Every human is created with spiritual senses through which he or she appreciates, identifies with, and experiences the feelings of others—their suffering, joy, fears, love, etc. Each of us has the capacity to enter into the universe of another being and come back with understanding. When we suspend chronological time (beginning and end, linearity) and the false homogeneity that we impose on the teeming worlds that constitute reality, we enter qualitative time, the soul's time. It is this inner world that charts the history and expanse of the spiritual senses, where we learn how to be a spiritual-physical person in time and space.

Just as humans have external senses—sight, hearing, touch, taste, smell—we also have inner senses. These include inner seeing, hearing, touching, smelling, and tasting, as well as inner fire, inner wound, inner inebriation, etc. While these inner spiritual senses are connected to the outer senses, they are not identical to them. The consideration of non-physical or spiritual senses is a common theme in the world's wisdom traditions.

In the Sufi tradition, the creative imagination is an organ of the spiritual senses that is connected to the spiritual heart. The heart as the organ of the creative imagination is regulated in its own right to the spirituality of our bodies. In the spiritual senses, the material or external world is a veil. Our external thoughts and feelings are covering something more timeless and authentic. Christian Orthodox mystics speak about God's "uncreated energies," where we are touched by the divine fire of love and thrown off-balance by the splendor of a reality too profound to name. We can only be devoted; we can only learn to read the spirit's signs.

Religious experience, however, is not confined to conventional notions of the religious but is more aptly understood as an awareness that is present whenever there is an immediate apprehension of truth, divinity, or awe. Such moments may occur during meditation, communing with nature, in response to animals and other living beings, in times of trauma or emotional stress, and in other situations that take us outside our usual frame of reference.

Further, religious experience also can involve conflict, pain, dividedness, despair, fear, anger, doubt, and impasse. These painful and often "dark" experiences can be areas of intense spiritual growth, for here too we are called to an awareness of something deeper and more profound. It is through the variety and scope of mystical events, and the increasing awareness of these deeper feeling and visionary states, that we come to wisdom, and to an understanding of the intimacy that we share with all creation. These moments—whether of joy or sorrow, conflict or illumination—change our orientation, and often are accompanied by feelings or intuitive visions that cannot be fully captured in language.

John of the Cross describes how dark and painful "rapturous visits" torment the body:

> The torment experienced in these rapturous visits is such that no other so disjoins the bones and endangers human nature. Were God not to provide, she would die. And indeed, it seems so to the soul in which this happens, that she is being loosed from the flesh and abandoning the body.[17]

In certain kinds of raptures or intense mystical events, the thread between spiritual and physical life is thin. The person is not fully in-body. The soul is transported above the body, in communion with the Great

Mystery. The intimacy experienced between the soul and its beloved is so profound that attachment to the body is weakened, which can be experienced as pressure, pain, and even torment. An experience of the soul's separation from the body, when the veil between the physical and spiritual is almost erased, defies conscious recollection and articulation.

Yet, when ecstasy is present it does not necessarily presuppose that the divine action is more intense than when it is lacking. In fact, as the aspirant matures in his or her practice and devotion, ecstasies may either cease altogether or become less frequent and intense. I believe this happens because as the person becomes more spiritually integrated, the body is able to contain more of the divine energies, and extraordinary experiences become a natural outpouring of the heart. This is why ecstatic or visionary experience is not definitive evidence of mystical union; sometimes such experiences can be distractions, and sometimes a very transformative divine event may not include any of these signs. Nonetheless, it is important to study the various energetic manifestations of mystical experience because in your life, or in helping others, you may come upon these and need to be able to read the signs.

Attunement to the energetic systems and their manifestations in the psyche and body is pivotal to spiritual balance and human wholeness. This is especially significant for new monastics, again, because stability of life and spiritual growth in the first instance comes from within. Lacking the foundational wisdom of a religiously affiliated monastery, the modern monk turns to these ancient resources as guides to form a practical and serious contemplative orientation to everyday life.

• • •

Miracle of Sun
Mystery of cell
glorious body
Blessed are you!

Mother of matter
Radiant of flesh
within you, Spirit
Dwells on earth!

Earth is my body
Spirit my soul
Mystery unending
Joy of great light!

Amen.

THIRTEEN

Spiritual Practice:
Obstacles & Solutions

AT SOME POINT in our lives, it is not uncommon to become
dissatisfied with prayer, meditation practice, and spiritual development. We may despair of attending church or synagogue, be
repelled by groups that we use to enjoy, or find ourselves bored with
spiritual advice. We may invent excuses for why we are uninterested,
lazy, or just disgusted with our lack of progress. We may avoid seeing our
therapist or spiritual director or stop confiding in a friend. Prayer can be
a chore, and while previously we brought our troubles to a trusted guide
or to silent contemplation, now we spend more of our time avoiding
these activities.

Wise elders know that while there are good reasons why a person
finds previous commitments distasteful, it is equally true that the aversion may also arise from deep roots in our character. This can be a reaction to a need to conceal or deny hidden layers of wounding. Awareness
of our resistance to spiritual practice, then, can serve to reveal unac-
knowledged or unconscious dimensions of the psyche and spirit. Thus,
at the same time that we seek spiritual maturity, we may be compelled
to begin again, to turn away from accomplishment and toward mystery
instead. Unless we are content to be a humble, curious beginner who
knows little or nothing, it is difficult to face the real challenges of life
and the disturbances in our personality. The fear of confronting the self,

to become aware of doubt and confusion, can create an all-consuming spiritual and psychological crisis.

Various types of resistance—among them inertia, discouragement, confusion, avoidance, addiction, and willfulness—are indicators that our spiritual practices have gotten off-track and are being used to avoid the unpleasant or fractured places within. Whatever arises becomes an important tool of spiritual maturation, and the remedy I suggest is to meditate on and address the cause. If we feel lost, if we feel hopeless, if we feel discouragement, if we do not feel grounded in our divine center, as before, then that is where our prayer goes. Suspend old practices and pray directly for realization. Because, in every case, awareness of these impediments plays an important role in leading us away from the mind and rationalization and instead guiding us into a more healthy and peaceful life.

Inertia

One of the obstacles to spiritual practice is spiritual inertia, the letdown that happens when meditation and prayer become difficult or do not result in obvious benefit. Inertia can generate feelings that you are not doing the practice correctly, you are inherently wrong, or your life is not progressing. In the past, efforts led to results, but now your spiritual practice is spinning in circles.

Spiritual inertia may be the result of contemplating yourself instead of God. In other words, your practice has become so internalized and convoluted that you are actually meditating on yourself instead of contemplating the Divine. Self-referential practice is static; it shields the ego from insecurity and dreads surrender to that which is greater than the self.

One antidote to spiritual inertia is the realization that your inner depth and your external actions are not aligned. The fracturing that is pulling you in opposite directions creates a stalemate that is experienced as inactivity or impasse. We tend to think that the interior life is not available to us or that it is hidden. However, what is ripping us apart is that the deep self is crying out to be heard—but we are not listening. Traumatized by our refusal, the soul's anguish breaks through the psyche, alerting us to the need for change.

Discouragement

Related to inertia, discouragement is a distinct emotional state where you find yourself derailed, stymied. You are disheartened and cannot connect to the source of your being. You no longer experience passion or longing for the divine quest. People will confide: "I used to love attending church, or sitting in silent meditation, but now I am listless, uninterested. What is going on?" We find here, too, loneliness, despair, and anguish. If Spirit or a loved one has been your closest friend for many years and, all of a sudden you do not feel connected, stop and think about what has happened and why. Divorce, death, loss of job or community, and other ruptured relations generate heartbreak—and feelings of abandonment and betrayal—whereby the person feels he or she cannot depend on prior happiness or knowledge.

Confusion

Spiritual obstacles can be related to the deconstruction of the self, when the soul grows deeper into contemplation. We may feel unmoored, as the disjuncture between our old and new reality is not yet resolved. We may become lost in a confused helplessness and, imprisoned by an old self-identity, are unable to escape. The impasse can be overpowering. We cannot go back to what we once were, but we cannot go forward either. Here we need to discern whether disorientation is the result of being bound by or stuck in the false ego, or whether it is part of a more profound transformation (such as the dark night) when the Divine is drawing us deeper into faith, along a path we cannot see or know.

During these times, it is easy to succumb to despondency and boredom, a dejection that seems to arise without cause. The temptation to give up the spiritual life is strong and lures the person away from his or her monastic commitment by inwardly whispering, *Aren't you bored with all this prayer? Isn't meditation leading to a monotonous life? Find something more exciting, more fruitful.*

Avoidance

When practice touches on unpleasant feelings or painful memories we may devise strategies to avoid uncovering hidden motives and injury.

Trapped by the powerful emotion of fear, our perspective is altered so that we cannot see that it is easier to pass through the pain, than to resist. And, yet, we have learned so many forms of resistance that we do not recognize that our resistance is what impedes us. If your prayer or meditation has become repetitive or rote because there is resistance to delve more deeply, then this is the time to suspend your practice. Let the practice go and instead pray about why it is that you are in avoidance. The adage "As you ask, so shall you receive" is quite true; it is always helpful in situations such as these to turn the entire problem around and to pray for guidance: "Help me to understand why I use diversion to hide my despair or wound. Show me my resistance." Ask directly, instead of feeling that you are letting God or yourself down. In this way, with the help of Spirit, obstacles can be transformed.

We forget the power of simple prayer because we tend to believe that the spiritual journey is "out there" and we are going *toward* something. Instead, all our struggles are part of the transformative process, taking place *within* us. The truth in our center is pushing harmful aspects of our personality from the unconscious into the conscious mind, so that we become aware of our impediments and have the capacity to change them.

Addiction

When does a spiritual practice become a type of addiction, an imposition of the will, or an accomplishment of the ego, and not an act of liberation? When a practice is adhered to excessively, is used to bypass inner troubles, or overrides other aspects of life, these are symptoms of addictive impulses. Frequently, compulsive practices are those that require undue attention, bolster the false personality, or provide something to the self. For example, let us say that you are performing life-affirming activities—feeding the poor, fasting, intensely practicing yoga. If you are not acting with a pure heart, but instead being motivated by something the ego wants—to build self-esteem, be noticed, or set yourself apart as superior or worthy—then you may fall short of your stated ideal and your efforts will not advance moral strength. Please remember that I am referring to subtle states, not saying that everyone who is performing a good deed is in an addictive spiritual practice.

Rather, become aware (whether within the solitude of your home or during social activism) of what motivates you. Is the practice being motivated in order to grow closer to truth, the Divine, or is it to enhance yourself? Perhaps you tell yourself something like *"I am a helping person and can ignore the other aspects of my personality that I have not worked on."* If you find this happening, then reflect: *What am I getting from all the activity?*

An addictive personality can use anything, including spiritual practice, as a substitution—albeit a healthier one. But compulsive behaviors still obscure the gentle, humble, motiveless, and nondual consciousness that underlie deeper states of contemplation. Being attached to the outcome of our labor may have its roots in a fear that we are not inherently good or in a desire to dominate others; that we must prove ourselves. In many people, belief in unworthiness is the result of such a deep psychological and spiritual injury that as life progresses, new layers of woundedness are uncovered. Perhaps you have been a spiritual practitioner for many years, and also have sought therapy, believing that as a result your problems have been resolved. But, like an onion, as you probe further, more subtle and subversive levels of insecurity—that you are not going to heal, that you are not doing the right thing—start to peel away. This is how and where addictive practices usually grab hold and take root: in the place where we lack experience of our fundamental dignity, the original birthright of everyone.

These subtle issues are significant because contemplation infuses the soul with Presence, and infinite divine care, which is one of the most difficult things to accept: that the Divine loves us unconditionally and without our effort.

Willfulness

When we bury fundamental truths about the self, spiritual practices can become entangled in furthering the willful desires of the ego. Our willpower is used to suppress the unpleasant, the negative, and what we consider to be the unholy. When we use spiritual practice as an imposition of the will, it does not lead to fullness of the self, but rather to diminishment. We do not realize this because we have become habituated to a certain way of being and also to the stories we tell to create a mask for the world. Eventually, layers of suppressed personality rise to the surface, disturbing the façade that our determination is keeping in place. In other words, our will is using spiritual practice to conceal those hidden fears and false identities that we do not want to unmask.

The will often is described in many religious texts as having two aspects: the lower will, or those desires that are directed by the seeker's relationship to the world; and the higher will, which expresses the passion of the divine intent in us to love. The desert monks of early Christianity called this commitment *"intentio cordis"* (intention of the heart), concentrating one's whole being on truth and following one's longing to love.

When the lower will takes precedence over the divine intention within us, we develop destructive patterns of behavior that harm the self and others. For example, the career you are pursuing violates your ethical code. Or a poor decision leads to morally questionable behavior, ones that society has designated as crimes such as drunk driving or domestic abuse. In these cases, the higher will is subverted or restrained by the choices the lower will makes and upon which it acts.

Suppression of authentic emotions—jealousy, fear, anger, etc.—is a further example of how willfulness blocks the true self. Prayer or meditation naturally elevates the energetic vibration of body-mind-spirit, and rather than being used to clarify one's heart, it can instead reinforce denial—*I should not be jealous or angry*—or self-righteousness. We are most honest when we ask for divine guidance: "Why am I jealous?" Because we do not *experience* the gift of love already imprinted in us, it is painful to confront authentic feelings and seek help.

Usually a situation arises to upend willful behavior. Life events occur that will simply require you to go deeper. The imposition of the will is never for freedom but is an act of aggression that we impose on ourselves to suffocate conflicted emotions, thereby veiling deeper truths. When a person reaches a spiritual block, he or she will feel unclear motivations and uneasiness of heart—a jarring of the inner life—as a reminder that he or she is not on the right path. Contemplation is truth, and therefore it is a contradiction to seek self-knowledge using the will to suppress painful issues one doesn't want to confront.

Henri Nouwen's story is instructive. A Catholic priest, Nouwen left his position at Harvard Divinity School to spend his last decade at L'Arche, a spiritual community for the disabled. At Harvard, he was a well-known speaker and spiritual director, whom many sought for wisdom and healing. When he moved to L'Arche, he completely fell apart and suffered a profound depression. These events helped him to realize that his life had been constructed on top of a fundamental wound: that ultimately he was not loved and there was no safe place for him to let go. It was at L'Arche that he discovered freedom—true freedom that had been repressed by an entire archeology of feelings and attributes related to his status as priest and teacher.

Thus, in all manner of life, the contemplative person seeks truth— inexorably, even against the lower will. You can flow with or resist the movement of wisdom, but once you step on the path, you will be relentlessly drawn to authenticity. The sooner a person accepts this, the easier life becomes, because you then embrace the hidden parts of your nature, honoring your quest for meaning, and relinquishing self-harm. If you are willing to enter the wilderness of your being, the miracle of transformative grace may be yours. In this blessed state, wounds are healed, and hearts and behaviors are changed. If you have tired of your willfulness, ask in prayer or silence: "Please help me to have the strength to be truthful. God, please change my willfulness to willingness." This will be more powerful and more useful than anything else you do.

OUR RESISTANCE to the change that spiritual practices can generate becomes a window into the ways in which we conceal our faults and limit our capacity for grace. If we want a different life, if we wonder why there is so much suffering on our planet, we have to be alert to the subtle ploys of avoidance that exist in us and promote self-forgetting. By becoming aware of how resistance is the manner in which the deep self is communicating its dysfunction, we cultivate inner strength and a greater capacity for compassion.

In this look within, confession can be an antidote for the obstacles and painful actions that derail us, for we admit we have done something not in line with our better selves. The shame that occurs when we are aware of, but cannot disclose, the grip of our various stumbling blocks translates into pride, arrogance, and illusion. Repentance, however, overcomes resistance. Authentic sorrow changes our heart and the hearts of those we have injured. It is a force for lifting up our moral fiber and leading us to liberation. Orthodox Bishop Kallistos Ware describes its positive influence on the soul:

> To repent is to look, not downward at my own shortcomings, but upward to God's love; not backward with self-reproach, but forward with trustfulness. It is to see, not what I have failed to be, but what by the grace of God I can yet become.[1]

The confession of error pierces the soul and often leads to a heightened sensitivity to, and awareness of, our culpability in the infliction of pain. Voluntary disclosure helps repair the heart by awakening the person to the underlying oneness of creation and a new sense of responsibility for the conditions of the world. Always, in these moments of self-reflection, it is helpful to pray for assistance, and to allow feelings of sorrow, regret, guilt, remorse, etc. to surface. Humility is the remedy to help overcome fear; it provides the strength to explore what is beneath the façade of personality. Meister Eckhart's sermon on poverty of spirit—"to want nothing, know nothing, and have nothing"—is a prayer that exhorts us to deny the impulse of the lower will that wants to forget, and to instead harness the life-changing power of self-emptying.

For good or ill, what we do and bury inside ourselves adds to the collective storehouse of consciousness. By having the willingness to face what is hidden, we open a portal to the possibility of change, and offer a welcoming heart for the birth of the holy among us.

The philosophy that I hold and live is this: every one of our painful or self-destructive emotions and behaviors is built on top of a fundamental wound that distorts the intimacy of divine love. If you are willing to look

within, the Divine will guide you through darkness and into your true goodness. The gift of truth continues to surface throughout our lives, despite denials, calling us toward wholeness and healing,
The universal force of love never abandons us.

. ◆ .

May the Divine anoint our souls
with the perfume of devotion

May the fragrant Heart of divinity
hold us in tender embrace

May the wisdom of Mercy fill us with gratitude
in all things may we be worthy
of your gifts.

Amen.

FOURTEEN

Freeing the Spiritual Imaginary

O VER THE YEARS, I have noticed that much of our spiritual work involves understanding and healing painful or distorted views of reality that block access to the Divine within us. Due to the influence of psychology, mind-brain research, cognitive therapy, yoga, etc., seekers are more knowledgeable about and attuned to the impact family and social history exerts on the self. Today, traditional and non-traditional monks recognize that prayer and meditation practices are not, alone, normally sufficient to transform inner distortions and hidden fears. The work of being a whole person is enhanced by integrating the gifts of spirituality with other healing modalities.

In an attempt to provide a visual way to convey this idea, I adapted the notion of the "moral imaginary"—advanced by philosophers and psychoanalysts—to the spiritual life. Grace Jantzen, British feminist phi-losopher of religion, defines the moral imaginary as "the space—literal and figurative—from which moral thinking is done and which frames what we think in relation to moral attitudes and behaviour."[1] "It includes the norms, assumptions and prejudices, and prejudgements which give content to our dispositions to act and think and 'determine what is actu-ally morally thinkable.'"[2]

These deep-seated modes of understanding provide the normally unexamined frameworks within which people imagine their social group

and collective life. Each culture has its own moral and religious imaginary, which appears to be permanent or inviolable, but is—in actual
fact—constantly evolving, overcome or replaced by novel insights and
religious worldviews. The process of identifying previously unexamined
ethical, religious, and social norms can help to remove engrained patterns of behavior that block the inflow of divine energies. In mentoring
people living an in-the-world monasticism, I have developed three concepts to frame this exploration into transforming religious and emotional
symbols or states: the spiritual imaginary, spiritual genetics, and spiritual
miasms. These categories are the result of my engagement with one type
of practice that can assist in the healing of inner wounds and other types
of dysfunction, but they are not exhaustive of the many ways used to
establish wholeness of self.

As in all things, for the monk these processes are not ends in themselves but practices that bring us closer to the hoped-for living with and
for the Holy.

Spiritual Imaginary

THE "SPIRITUAL IMAGINARY" I define—based on Jantzen's writings—
as the space, literally and symbolically, from which religious thinking is
done and which frames what we think in relation to spiritual attitudes
and behaviors, the spiritual journey, stages of growth, moral virtues, and
the divine nature itself. I'm not referring to imagination as illusory or
unreal, but to the collective representations by which we define ourselves
as subjects.

The spiritual imaginary involves the norms, assumptions, prejudices,
prejudgments, as well as the divine figures, metaphysics, religious commandments, symbols, and mythic consciousness that gives context to our
disposition to act spiritually and determines what is actually spiritually
thinkable. This includes the way a person understands the self, and the
religious life that he or she imagines is possible to live. The entirety of a
religious worldview—symbols, texts, theologies, and scriptures—forms,
informs, and controls what we can imagine and think. This symbolic

universe is so deeply intertwined with cultural identities that it cannot be dismantled or transcended simply by virtue of retrieval or reconstruction. The seeker who is already functioning outside a religiously accepted symbolic universe, most likely is aware of how norms that are discordant with one's inner truth lead to conflict, alienation, and pain.

Each of us inherits a certain type of spiritual imaginary from our parents, culture, and religion. It is, in a sense, imprinted in us or born into the world with us, and thus involves an unconscious level. However, I am not referring to reincarnation or karmic patterns, but to something more basic: when a child enters this world he or she is imprinted with particular family, cultural, and religious signifiers. This inheritance has an impact on the construction of self-identity and thought processes, often without conscious awareness. We imbibe and carry with us a self-definition that mirrors both the virtuous and immoral aspects of human nature expressed within our religions, secular cultures, or beliefs.

The implications of the spiritual imaginary are most deeply felt in the person's inner life or soul, where spiritual practices and theological beliefs implicitly or explicitly repeat our personal and collective symbolic inheritance. The capacity to transcend the imposition of the spiritual imaginary in the world's religions is described as enlightenment or salvation: *samadhi, sunyata, nirvana,* or *unio mystica*. Nonetheless, even in these high spiritual states of consciousness, an element of repetition occurs, the person reflecting aspects of his or her primary religious experience. Of course, there are extraordinary instances when a person does break out of a cultural and religious paradigm. Although these events tend to be rare—usually involving some form of transcendent intervention or revelation—we each have the capacity to open and transform the spiritual imaginary and to cross a threshold into an uncharted world.

The story of Gautama Buddha is instructive in this regard. Born to a noble Hindu family, he left riches and comfort to follow an ascetic life. Initially he practiced meditation and physical austerities with Hindu holy men, seeking enlightenment. Yet, after six years and at the brink of death, Gautama realized that he would not find what he desired within his religious training. Leaving his companions, he set off to find his own way, eventually settling down under a Bodhi tree at a place called Bodh

Gaya, determined not to move until he found the answers he sought. On the night of the full moon, he awakened to reality as it *is*—reaching complete enlightenment. Now Buddha ("he who is awake") is a master in his own right and devotes the rest of his life to spreading the *dharma* (truth). Buddha's experience of breaking through or discovering a new enlightenment is a moment of *extraordinary mysticism*. His consciousness is not rooted to the same place or looking at the world from the same vantage point as his predecessors. The *dharma* that unfurls before him is distinct from the path of Hindu mystics, complete and whole unto itself.

The lineage that results from Buddha's enlightenment experience— the disciples who follow him, the trajectory of his teachings, the various Buddhist schools, Theravada, Mahayana, Vajrayana, and the masters who come later—Bodhidharma, Milarepa, Nagarjuna—all drink from the same spring and draw from the same source that Buddha brought into this world. This unfolding of a living tradition, from its founding moment through its development across the span of centuries, occurs within the context of what I call *normal mysticism*. That is, normal mysticism reveals a new aspect of an existing religious tradition or enlightenment experience. In Christianity, the saints—Francis, Ignatius of Loyola, Therese of Lisieux, John of the Cross, and Teresa of Avila, etc.—are recognized as having lived and articulated a unique mystical trajectory within the overarching paradigm of Christian consciousness. They were extraordinary individuals whose spiritual wisdom grew out of Jesus' life, death, and teachings.

Today, many people are experiencing a breakthrough into a new symbolic universe of faith, in which the boundaries of religions are stretched. These herald an extraordinary moment in human consciousness, when the paradigm of existing traditions is broken through to a new spiritual vision of life. Elements of this shift are evident in the vibrant stream of converts around the world, practicing two or more religions, founding new religions, and living humanistic or secular practices. One example is a monastic lineage based on two or more traditions, such as that lived by Bede Griffiths—a Benedictine monk who became a Hindu-Christian *sannyasi*—and found in the depth of his soul a breakthrough into a multi-religious ascetic life in India.

But what is striking about these various approaches is that they emerge from numerous grassroots spiritual movements. In our time, we are pushing beyond inherited spiritual imaginaries, turning back to our lived experience, and to our souls.

Spiritual Genetics

IN MY EXPERIENCE, the spiritual imaginary can be transmitted across generations, which I visualize as a type of instruction that is psychically "inherited" from parent to offspring. Thought forms, emotional reactions and tones, and physical expressions and postures are composed of certain energetic patterns (equations) that can be passed from person to person. I call these "spiritual genetics," to specifically place attention on the soul and mystical dimension of this transference. This transmission occurs intellectually, emotionally, psychically, and spiritually through energy equations; errant or unstable spiritual equations, much like the biological units of heredity, can be re-configured and healed.

For example, if I say: "I am envisioning a tall blue spruce growing by a lake, with fully open branches laden with pine cones," you are able to visualize the scene. Or, if I describe a situation where a mother in the supermarket grabs her son by the arm and angrily yells, you could imagine not only the scene but also perhaps feel the emotional tone. Why is that possible? Because thoughts and feelings are exchanged nonverbally through energetic patterns, pulses, and waves.

As another example, let's say the emotional tone of a parent is primarily one of despair. Or the parent believes in a judgmental and punishing god. These thought forms and emotional states have specific configurations (equations) that are transmitted not only with words and gestures, but also energetically, infecting the relatively unconstructed conscious patterns of the child. Here, I am not referring just to psychology, but to an imprint in deep structures of consciousness, which can be identified with the soul or the true self.

Children's identities and souls are permeable and receptive. A child whose parents express verbal or nonverbal feelings of unhappiness, betrayal, anger, or despair cannot control or ward off their energetic trans-fer, which form actual impediments to the development of the healthy self. These constructions of reality could be defined as giving rise to the false or contrived personality, and operate in multiple states of being from the cellular to soul levels. In addition, because the transmission of spiritual genetics not only is psychological, emotional, and intellectual, but also occurs in the soul, psychotherapy alone may be insufficient to reach the deeper mystical dimension of injury or injustice.

Spiritual genetics is based on a mystical worldview that affirms that the fundamental state of the soul—and of life—is Divine. That is, the human person's external life—with its many manifestations—is founded on and composed of indivisible, inner qualities or virtues, which include love, mercy, compassion, benevolence, joy, and humility. We can discuss the qualities of love, for example, but we cannot break love down into component parts. Love *is*. The same is true for mercy or joy. How do we dissect joy? It is not divisible, because it is a state of divinity. I think of these indivisible qualities as the foundational building blocks of spiritual consciousness or the table of divine elements, which I identify as true virtues, or simple emotions when expressed in a person.

If a simple emotion is an undiluted expression of a divine virtue, complex emotions, on the other hand, are a combination of truth and falsehood. These complex emotional equations are divisible, meaning they can be broken down into their component parts: 1) a virtue or simple emotion that is mixed with 2) a faulty thought or idea. Thus, complex emotions—that is, the combination of an untruth or negative expression mixed with fact and/or virtue—are mis-equations that agitate the person, violate the integrity of his or her deep self, and deny what one's soul knows to be true.

Here is an example. If we are gathered in a room with painted yel-low walls, and I refer to the walls as blue, and continue to speak about the blue walls, you will notice my distortion of reality, which generates a mis-equation—something that disturbs your true self, even if you are not consciously aware. Or, if a pastor tells you that in the eyes of the Lord you are unworthy, this is a lie, because no one is unworthy in the Divine. Deep within—made in the Divine image—you know this is not true, but the mis-equation rattles your being, reverberating in the physical cells, thoughts, emotions, etc.

And precisely because it is untrue, and composed of truth and lie, it has an added weight on your being. It is actually not possible to be unworthy in the eyes of God. In truth, you may have sinned, committed violence, or other wrongs. But in the depth of the self, where you are one with transcendent mystery, you are eternally held in holy embrace. When you take in or accept a lie, it mixes with your emotions and affects consciousness because—at the same time—your soul or deep self knows that this lie is *ultimately* or *divinely* untrue. This tension between the imbibing of falsehood and the often-unconscious realization of its untruth creates inner dissonance, which you struggle to resolve through denial, anger, resistance, grief, among others. These emotional responses, however, are not strong enough to dissolve the full impact of imprinted patterns. Complex emotions are difficult to break down because they are intertwined with an original lie or untruth, which you have forgotten, but now believe to be true.

One way of unraveling complex emotions is through repentance or confession. I believe that the purpose of this time-honored religious practice is precisely for this reason: to uncover the divinity within that is more merciful than the sins we commit and the falsehoods we accept. The healing process can require many instances of repentance, which is nothing more than sorrow over the violation of the Divine in others and in us. Experiencing deep sorrow over the abuse of our own and others' divinity is the catalyst for breaking down complex emotions and opening the process of healing.

Keep this in mind: if you are having trouble understanding an emotion or are acting out a persistent pattern that you can't easily overcome, it is probably the result of a complex emotion that has compromised the truth of who you are. This untruth may have been purposely imprinted or branded in you by another person, or it could be the result of a person's distorted observation or analysis of you, an event, or a situation.

The point is that these complex emotions become intertwined with self-knowledge, and are the ones that we can't unravel yet. We have trouble dismantling them because we don't understand what the original lie is. This is why I say we should never be afraid to confront our pain or fear because it will help us to uncover the violation of our divinity. Unfortunately, many people fear that if they really look within, they are going to find out that they are worthless or nothing, so they resist looking. And that does not help, because avoidance has on its own energy configuration, which solidifies the negative imprint already present.

Once again, awareness of false or painful emotional states is important for stabilizing the vocation of the contemplative or the monk in the world. Having clarity about how the mind works and how disparate and often unwelcome energies or thoughts can disturb inner peace is the work of being pure of heart. This process is not tangential or external to the vocation of monkhood but, from my experience, critically important to it.

Spiritual Miasms

THE SPIRITUAL IMAGINARY and spiritual genetics occur on multiple levels, and it is easy to become overwhelmed in thinking about the extent of their reach: "How am I ever going to unravel all of this? It is happening on too many different levels." But I have found that there are some identifiable characteristics and fundamental similarities that underlie many of these inherited spiritual diseases.

I call these characteristic patterns that underlie and inform spiritual dis-ease, "spiritual miasms." I take the word "miasms" from Samuel Hahnemann, the founder of homeopathic medicine. In 1828, he introduced the concept in regard to the underlying causes of many known chronic diseases that were caused by a derangement of the vital force. According to Hahnemann, miasms are passed down through generations, but the inheritance of a miasm is not biologically genetic but is transmitted down through energetic fields that weaken a person's life-sustaining force.

The word "miasm" means a fog or cloud or pollution in the being. Hahnemann isolated three miasms—psora, syphilis, and sycosis—each of which he contended was the root cause of the variety of diseases in humans. He viewed the treatment of illness from two perspectives: treatment of acute illness, such as the flu or measles, which may or may not be the result of an underlying miasm; and the treatment of chronic or long-term illness, which he claimed definitely was the result of an underlying miasm. Hahnemann maintained that treating diseases by directly opposing their symptoms is ineffective because it doesn't address the latent, chronic, and inherited tendency. Rather, the underlying miasm still remains, and deep-seated ailments can be healed only by removing the deeper disturbance of the vital force. Thus, he proposed the technique of "like heals like." That is, minute doses of diluted strains of a disease—for example, measles—is an antidote to the disease states associated with the parent miasm.

I have found that spiritual miasms, which I define as discrete energetic patterns—beliefs, attitudes, archetypes, energies, vibrations, and so forth—can be used to inform, diagnose, and heal the variations of spiritual or soul diseases. My sample is primarily drawn from the consciousness of peoples from Europe, and the polyglot populations of the United States, Canada, and Mexico. If I lived in Asia, Africa, or the Middle East, I might identify more or different miasms. It is difficult to bring these spiritual realities into a language adequate to their depth, because this requires an excavation of the soul. For this reason, I am not able to articulate the totality of what I have experienced or what is possible, but the following explanation is the best approximation I can offer at this time.

I conceptualize spiritual miasms as wounds or tears created in the vital collective force field of the person that distort or damage divine wholeness, dissipate soul strength, and generate errant strands of energetic data. As they infiltrate the rapidly oscillating bodily energies, they impede or stop their flow, forming specific thought, emotional, psychological, or spiritual patterns in us. These patterns can be difficult to uncover because once established, they proliferate in innumerable and varied ways.

Recognition and naming of one's specific miasm or miasms, and applying the appropriate antidote, can be helpful in correcting the imbalances that impede soul growth, and in healing the vital force of the person. Over the years, I have referred to seven levels in which injuries to consciousness can take place: physical, emotional, mental, psychological, religious-spiritual, soul, and mystical. Because spiritual miasms can be imprinted in any or all of these seven states, the person who seeks to heal and restore his or her inner light must be patient in working through these multiple states of being. But, on a spiritual level, the most important states on which to concentrate—and the ones I employ—are the religious, soul, and mystical, because the remaining four are more frequently addressed in other healing modalities.

Often, in the practice of spiritual guidance, a person—let's call her June—describes years of work on a core issue of parental betrayal, using various techniques—psychotherapy, psychiatry, yoga, journaling, Reiki healing, exercise, prayer, etc. When June seeks mental clarification, there are unresolved emotional issues. Then she delves into psychotherapeutic models, searching for answers, recognizing in a rudimentary way that a wound still exists. Thus, June laments: "I keep spiraling into the issue again. I don't understand why these years of work have not resolved the issue."

What is the reason? Frequently, it is because the deeper soul and mystical states have not been touched.

Like June, perhaps you have investigated a psychological injury, but haven't addressed its impact on the soul, or a soul injury that you have not connected to its effect on your physical health. Since the self wants to be healed and made whole, you will continue to spiral through various impediments until you are strong enough to allow in the inflow of divine light. At the mystical level, healing comes from the divine within; if a wound or disease has penetrated your soul consciousness, then until you open to the Divine, full healing cannot occur. Here, the remedy is to offer your wounds to prayer, to surrender, to release and let go, accept vulnerability, and trust.

In many cases, if the person seeks to know the original lie imbedded in the soul—for example, unworthiness—awareness, in the form of self-confession, alongside intense meditation or prayer can help to uncover its causes. Here, self-confession simply refers to a willingness to become conscious of how feelings of inadequacy or being undeserving are present in a person's daily life, and then directing the heart's intentions—or what can be called the "will"—to be free. It is as if small, diluted doses of self-awareness of and reflection on unworthiness eventually strengthen the ability of the person's will to resist and heal the untruth. This is "like healing like." Occasionally, a person has a major breakthrough whereby a wound becomes instantly healed. But, usually, this is not the case.

When the person is able to address the soul and mystical dimension of injury, especially when the other levels of consciousness have been attended to, miasms can be healed, dissipated, or dismantled. Then a miasm disappears to the point where you can't even remember what it was you were feeling or why you had those experiences because it is erased. It is a profound and incredible event, and it does happen.

I like to think of the dismantling of a miasm as an enlightenment moment, an extraordinary salvation event. There also are smaller or micro enlightenment moments that are just as important, because every release of pain leads to transformation and the opening of the heart. And, since chronic soul disease can be passed from members of one generation to the next, whatever we heal in ourselves reverberates in the collective consciousness and releases miasmic patterns.

The Spiritual Miasm of Loneliness

EVERY MIASM is the result of a prior wound to the divine image within a person and, thus, afflicts his or her integrity of being. I approach my consideration of spiritual miasms in this way: as approximations, and as guideposts to lead us deeper into self-reflection, not as absolutes or ends in themselves. While I have observed other miasmic patterns, in what follows I describe the miasm of loneliness.

The manifestations of loneliness can include abandonment of others, wanting to belong, over-giving, deception, resistance to inner truth, obsessive-addictive behavior, possessiveness, grasping, uncontrollable urges or needs, greed, and/or lust.

I'm describing the elements of loneliness in this way to help illustrate the condition. For example, Josh shares a problem during spiritual guidance, where I learn that his excessive, almost addictive over-giving is destroying his life. He gives money to strangers or friends who never pay him back, invites out-of-work or unsavory acquaintances to use his apartment, in several cases to people with drug addictions that lead to police intervention. He denies or subverts his own best interests and intelligent feelings in order to be likeable and loved.

Eventually, Josh recognizes that his over-giving is not the cause, but the manifestation of, and defense against, loneliness, and that much of his addictive behavior stems from his desire to stop the anguish. In addition, the actual feeling state—even the energetic vibration—of the loneliness he experiences is reminiscent of his father's, and Josh feels it was transmitted to him with "his milk." Because loneliness permeated the family environment, his mother viewed Josh as her savior, the one innocent person to cling to, which masked her unhappiness and led to a cycle of unclear intimacy between mother and son. This, in turn, became another confusion for the child, Josh.

Perhaps like many of you, Josh always felt different from other people. One day at work, he suddenly had an imaginative experience of being abandoned by his young playmates in the woods behind their homes. He was scared that he was on the planet all by himself! Where were the rest of the people who cared for him? Soon after, feelings of profound loneliness surfaced. When I asked about these feelings, he said it felt like loneliness was consuming him, a giant energy that absorbed him and everything around him.

His spiritual homework was to pray to know, what is loneliness? In a subsequent visit, he told me that over a period of weeks he kept "saying and praying: 'I'm not afraid of you, loneliness; I'm going to see who you are.'" The more he prayed and stayed with his feelings, the more he experienced the unraveling of loneliness. "By just being present to this state of feeling," Josh recounted, "I realized that loneliness literally was an illusion of my mind—the illusion that I am separated from love, from God, which I think causes many of my patterns."

It was also important for Josh to realize that the process is essentially contemplative, not cognitive. That is, it is a spiritual process, an interior, often imaginative, engagement with the deep self. It is non-active, in the sense that the mind cannot solve or resolve the issue. It is experiential and affects interior feelings. It is soul awareness, recognition from the silence within, from God within, of that which is more enduring and more holy than the pain.

If you apply this contemplative process to your life, you also may find that you wind up at the miasm of loneliness. As a representative human pattern, it has its own specific energy. Loneliness is not resolved in its manifestations or offshoots, because it is a state of consciousness that has an all-consuming impact on the soul. The way to heal one's self of this trauma is to face it directly: "Show me the nature of loneliness. I want to feel the pain of what loneliness is." Repair of a false identity often takes a continual offering of prayer, a sustained effort to seek one's true nature, and a commitment to resist the desire to forget and deny. (Note: This confrontation is best achieved with a companion or spiritual guide who can help you to remain strong when healing is not immediate, or the desire to give up sets in.)

Remember that the miasm of loneliness is always healed by this fact: God is always present in the center of our souls, loving us and communicating to us from within. Thus, every soul injury is based on a primary disassociation or blockage from the Divine Presence.

Ultimately, loneliness is not an absolute state of being; it has relative truth given the condition of our lives. However, in the Divine, loneliness is an untruth. Thus, the more we resist understanding the miasm of loneliness, the stronger and more imbedded it becomes and the more stubborn is its pattern of thinking and feeling.

What we learn through the practice of contemplative self-awareness is that many of the feelings, actions, and behaviors that we consider painful or untrue represent some soul wound that we experience as separation from the Divine. Every emotion, negative thought, feeling of shame or anger or despair is a clue that forges a way back to God. That's why we have to be brave in order to look at ourselves, but more important, to be our selves. People are afraid to look within. Yet, it is the very thing that we fear about ourselves that is actually the key—clue—to an original wound, or inaccurate understanding of self or of reality.

Healing is intrinsic to our nature. Within us, ever-present, is the force of Divine love sustaining our souls and uplifting our hearts. Understanding the role that the spiritual imaginary, spiritual genetics, and spiritual miasms play in the formation of personality and self-awareness can lead to a practice of liberation and to a path of healing. It is within our capacity to transcend painful or negative beliefs and energetic states, and to restore access to our blessed and sacred inner lives. It is imprinted in our souls from the beginning that we are one with the Divine, shining and ever new.

∴

Let us gather our energy for a few moments
and breathe in the beautiful clear air.

Let us welcome the spirits who come to our aid
in the hermitage of the heart.

May we rest in the Eternal, truly at home
in the secret teachings of Love.

Amen.

FIFTEEN

The Wound of the Soul

MBEDDED IN THE PATH of every religion is not only the inevita-
bility of our suffering, but also our liberation. Changes in spiritual
outlook, wounding of the heart, or illness, pain, and death impact
every person's life. During these times, we become aware as never before
of how profoundly we suffer, and how healing involves physical and spiritual elements. The body may be repaired but the soul may be pained or
in need of sustenance. This realization that we all have an inner life, a life
that responds to and is sustained by non-material factors, is at the core
of self-transformation.

The subject of this chapter—the soul and its wounding—calls
attention to an experience that comes to all of us on our earthly journey.
Adapting a concept of the soul found in Christian mystical texts, the following pages describe the difference between lower and higher states of
soul consciousness, the various actions that wound the soul, and Teresa
of Avila's insight into the healing power of the Divine Wound of Love.

Although the soul is not a universally common term, especially in
nontheistic religions, it is my hope that the topic of inner pain or soul
wounding finds resonance in your lived experience.

Lower and Higher Consciousness or Soul

IN SPIRITUALITIES that affirm a personal deity (Judaism, Christianity, Islam, Hinduism, etc.), the soul is variously described as a jewel in the heart of God, the Spirit and Light of the Holy, the palace of Divine Love, or *atman*, the indwelling presence of Brahman. In general, the soul is understood to refer to the transcendent, spiritual depth in us, the microcosm of the ultimate, and as a bridge between the Divine and the person. It is conceptualized as being composed of a revealed and unmanifested dimension, in so far as the soul relates to physical life and to the mysterious transcendent.

Although the entire soul is one and divine, Christian mystical texts frequently describe the soul as a composite of lower and higher dimensions or states of consciousness. The lower soul turns toward the world and is affected by actions or inactions occurring on the physical level. The higher soul is composed of progressively more refined, supernatural states, culminating in mystical union or intimacy with God. While the lower soul can sustain injury from the world, the higher soul always remains untouched and pure, with God in its center. The various levels of the soul interpenetrate and influence each other and comprise an organic whole.

Because the lower soul is related to the world but is also connected to the Divine, the pain, error, and injustice inflicted on the person reverberates in that person's inner life. Bodily sufferings are felt on one level of consciousness, but another, greater suffering also exists that "isn't felt where earthly sufferings are felt," writes Teresa of Avila, "but in the very deep and intimate part of the soul."[1] Since the core of the person is always in touch with divinity, even while he or she may be unaware, soul consciousness operates at a heightened level of feeling, knowing, and understanding, suffering more than the body because of its greater sensitivity. At the same time, the higher soul cannot be harmed or destroyed because it is supernatural, always replenished by the Divine in its center. The entire soul—higher and lower—is a luminous reality of incredible refinement. Therefore, we always approach another person with love, kindness, hospitality, gentleness, and awe.

Soul Wound

I USE THE TERM "soul wound" to refer to actual injuries the lower soul suffers from the trials and injustices of life. The soul experiences afflictions to its most receptive nature, sustained from bearing the sin and violence of the world. These wounds create a fracture or blockage that separates the lower soul from the higher soul, and prevents the person from connecting with or experiencing the great love in its center.

A soul wound is different from, and more anguishing, often, than bodily pain. Teresa of Avila writes:

> Another type of prayer quite frequent is a kind of *wound* in which it seems as though an arrow is thrust into the heart, or into the soul itself. Thus the wound causes a severe pain which makes the soul moan; yet, the pain is not in the senses, nor is the sore a physical one; but the pain lies in the interior depths of the soul without resemblance to bodily pain. I mention the interior depths this pain reaches, because spiritual sufferings are extremely different from physical ones ... [and] much greater than ... bodily sufferings here on earth.[2]

Soul wounds provide a glimpse into the generous gift of grace—that every wound exists against the backdrop of infinite love. We experience fractures because they are reflected in the mirror of what is whole and untarnished. We feel the pain of failings because they are embraced and upheld by mercy. Whatever the person does to move away from their divine source, the way to healing and restoration is through the original disavowal, through recognizing the injustice that has been suffered and moving back to the center, not avoiding it.

Wounding, even the pain of sin, is held within a matrix of meaning that is wholly and utterly on the side of love. Love is at the center of being; our essential core is pure, verdant, growing love. The Divine reaches down into every suffering and lifts us up. The fourteenth century English mystic, Julian of Norwich, emphasizes that God wraps all of creation in love, caring for even our humblest bodily needs, so that "we, soul and body, [are] clad and enclosed in his goodness."[3]

She experiences the great compassion God has for our sins, and the immeasurable joy that comes through realizing that divine love transforms and heals injustice and injury. Here Julian describes what I call the *mystical method of suffering and love* and how pain and comfort are juxtaposed as we progress deeper into the inner life:

> And after this our Lord revealed to me a supreme spiritual delight in my soul. In this delight I was filled full of everlasting surety, and I was powerfully secured without any fear. . . .
>
> This lasted only for a time, and then I was changed, and left to myself, oppressed and weary of myself, ruing my life so that I scarcely had the patience to go on living. I felt that there was no ease or comfort for me except hope, faith and love, and truly I felt very little of this. And then presently God gave me again comfort and rest for my soul. . . . And then again I felt the pain, . . . now the one and now the other, again and again, I suppose about twenty times. And in the time of joy I could have said with Paul: Nothing shall separate me from the love of Christ; and in the pain, I could have said with Peter: Lord, save me, I am perishing.[4]

The fact that we suffer, or experience pain, failure, or despair, is not necessarily an indication that we are doing anything wrong; it could even be an indication that we are moving into deeper soul dimensions, which will yield great joy. Nothing is lost. "God showed that sin will be no shame but honour to man," Julian proclaims, "for just as there is a corresponding pain for every sin, just so love gives to the soul a bliss for every sin. Just as various sins are punished with various pains, the more grievous are the sins, so will they be rewarded with various joys in heaven to reward our victories over them, to the degree in which sin may have been painful and sorrowful to the soul on earth."[5]

Types of Soul Wounds

As WE HAVE SEEN, Teresa of Avila describes soul suffering as more intense, visceral, and immediate than earthly, bodily, or psychological suffering. Although related to and intertwined with each of these injurious experiences, it is important to become aware of soul wounds in our quest for healing. I describe below three types of wounds felt in the lower soul: personal injury, social injury, social injustice.

Wound of Personal Injury

The type of wound most often described in religious texts comes under the rubric of purification or purgation of sin. Included in this category are sins and other *hungry ghosts*, to use a Buddhist term: greed, lust, addiction, pride, selfishness, ignorance, and illusion, which can fracture the unity between the lower and higher soul. Much of the literature on spiritual transformation focuses on purification of moral failings through ascetic practices like penance, prayer, poverty, celibacy, and even the meting out of physical injury as a means of taming the errant desires of the *samsaric* or deluded, ignorant self.

The wound of personal injury causes a feeling of alienation between the inner and outer life and a restless heart; a heart that's divided in itself, and a wounding that is at the center of the personality. It leads to self-alienation and an inability to be centered in one's being. Often, we blame ourselves for inner conflict and are unable to find language to describe the experience. We can become spiritually mute and have difficulty connecting to our emotions. We may be at an impasse—unable to go back to who and what we once were but unable to move forward either. We may despair and the body may become ill.

This traditional focus on the person and individual sins or errors, however, is only a truncated or partial view. In particular, it does not allow for an understanding of how injury is often administered by others, how we take in and are subjected to injustice, and the influence of societal and cultural sins on the health of the soul and our inner lives.

Wound of Social Injury

Life on Earth involves a series of injuries of various type and intensity from birth to death. Actions that uplift or harm us continually take place. Soul wounds often are impressed early on and most people who are subjected to these indignities blame themselves. Social injury is perpetuated when one person or group intentionally or unintentionally betrays, humiliates, strikes, harms, destroys, or belittles what is sacred in another. Examples in families are rife: the parent who is jealous and thwarts a child's healthy growth and accomplishment; an older sibling, relative, or friend who sexually abuses or rapes a child; a father who brutally whips his son; a mother who shames her daughter.

Wounding directed at the core of a person occurs in institutional and cultural settings as well. You might have colleagues who betray your trust or plagiarize your work; be a member of a faith tradition that excludes you from religious authority; belong to a culture that denies you full equality and dignity, especially if you are disenfranchised because of gender, ethnicity, race, or sexual orientation; be caught in a materialistic economy where the value of ecological sensitivity or spiritual meaning is shamed or ridiculed. All of these things are injuries, other-inflicted, directed at the well-being and sanctity of personhood.

Sadly, social wounds are reenacted and passed on through families, generations, societies, cultures, and nations. When parents do not take responsibility for their own pain, children often assume family disease, creating lifelong soul wounds. The soul can become possessed by these energies and cannot find its own ground. We learn to inflict soul damage, the way it was inflicted on us. The spiritually mature person makes a conscious choice to refuse and resist passing on the pain.

Wound of Social Injustice

Soul wounding can become socially or culturally legitimized; here power is derived from aiming the weapon of exclusion or demonization to entire groups of people. Patriarchal societies in which females are inferior to males, prevented from learning, denied food, sexually mutilated, or treated as slaves (trafficking) are examples of the wound of social injustice inflicted on our souls. Included here are rape and sexual assault

of persons, rape as a consequence and spoil of war, and violence directed
at marginalized communities.

Other culturally endorsed forms of profound soul oppression include
segregation, poverty, homelessness, racism, sexism, homophobia, anti-
Semitism, colonialism, and ecological degradation. In each of these cases,
the perpetrator(s) (intentionally or unintentionally) destroys or attacks
the sacred, divine image inherent in the person, group, or creation.

Dr. Martin Luther King Jr. was attuned to the infliction of soul suffering. He insisted that civil rights alone, without addressing the scarred
souls of African Americans, would not revolutionize individuals and
provide the strength to effect change. His attention, especially during
the Montgomery Bus Boycott (1955), was "on remaking black souls on
the route to the whole society's deliverance."[6] He said:

> The system of slavery and segregation caused many Negroes to feel
> that perhaps they were inferior. This is the ultimate tragedy of segre-
> gation. It not only harms one physically, it injures one spiritually. It
> scars the soul and distorts the personality and inflicts the segregated
> with a sense of false superiority, while inflicting the segregated with
> a false sense of inferiority. But through the forces of history, some-
> thing happened to the black person. He or she came to feel that
> the important thing about a man is not the color of his skin, or the
> texture of his hair, but the texture and quality of the soul.[7]

The most extreme wound of social injustice has been called "radical
suffering"—suffering that has no redeeming purpose, such as torture,
genocide, and holocausts. Radical suffering is designed to rob a person
or a group of soul, to make them inhuman by suffering, and to create an
incurable wound of despair that annihilates the future, severs relationship, and holds no possibility of meaning. Radical suffering destroys the
notion that there is some "reason" for suffering, that there is a correlation
between suffering and punishment, or that this unutterable display of
violence is the consequence of wrongdoing, sin, or karma.

These egregious sufferings have led to national and international
cooperation, and the creation of organizations directed to finding solu-

tions to cruelty and the destruction of life. For humanity's capacity to change situations of harm is dependent on the power of compassion, which resists suffering; it does not justify it. Suffering is resisted by two means: through identifying the causes of suffering and defying its hold. We do this every time we "see" our wounds and resist them through direct awareness. We also accomplish this through acts of social protest, civil rights, and nonviolent disobedience. We discover through suffering a connection with the source of goodness, when we help each other to imagine and build a better world, what Dr. King called "The Beloved Community."

In situations where one cannot transcend suffering—a fatal disease, a death, etc.—resistance takes the form of dignifying the person, of upholding their right and the need to live. If suffering cannot be wholly resisted, changed, or ameliorated, then it is important to honor, affirm, and protect the holy presence and divine light in each being.

Wound of Divine Love

THERE IS A LONG HISTORY in Christian spirituality of another type of wound—of healing and liberation—initiated by God. This is the Wound of Divine Love that draws the person into the inner life of divinity. Harking back to the Song of Songs 2:5, "Strengthen me with perfumes, surround me with apples, for I am wounded with love," Christian writers like Origen and Gregory of Nyssa imbue the wound of love with a christological meaning—"Christ the Word is both arrow and sword, wounding the soul from within."[8] The emotional effect of this wounding is compared to love's "bittersweet piercing" and is explained through a variety of metaphors, sensations, "unfulfilled longings."[9]

The Divine Wound refers to the action of love that both heals the soul of suffering, and causes it to urgently long to be closer to its Beloved. Wounding is an appropriate metaphor because it signifies the intensifying of pain that results from the fiery touches of love, which transforms every anguish into honors.

In the context of Christian spirituality, the wound of love often is a precursor for mystical union, in which we experience deep states of intimacy and inner divisions are mended. The wound of love has two effects: it heals and transforms the soul's worldly afflictions, and it anoints the soul with divine love, which dilates and magnifies its capacity to receive grace. The wound causes any barrier between the soul and the Divine to dissolve and quiets the soul's faculties of knowing. Here, the person experiences life not through the rational mind or the five senses, not even through the spiritual senses, but directly through God's own language. This divine language can include different secondary effects such as visions, tears, intuitions, and the inner voice.

The wound of love is God's great favor to the soul and not, despite its painful aspects, a trial. The soul knows the wound is something precious. Even though the pain is intense, it does not want to be cured of its suffering. The wound leaves the soul in quiet certitude, fortifying it with a great determination to move forward. Only in this way can the person achieve the freedom of mutual life in the Divine.

The soul goes through a period of unknowing, as if it's been hollowed out and made empty. The things that we hold onto—religion, faith, God's names, our lives, our pain—are shed, and it is here that we begin to feel the effects of a profound, yet elusive apprehension of transcendence. Ultimately, the purpose of the wound of love is to invite us to the banquet of solitude, offering to the world the fruit of our experience.

This dissolution of the soul into the ocean of divinity begins the process of integrating the inner and outer life. All that we long for, all that requires healing, all that yearns for wholeness, Teresa claims is resolved in the Divine Wound of Love. Not by austerity, not by repression, not by coercion, not by sacraments, not by liturgy, or erudition, but only by becoming vulnerable to God. As the Divine shares all of our troubles, cares, pains, and triumphs, we share in divine gifts and bear God's suffering for the world. There is mutuality and reciprocity, and it is that desire to be a disciple of holy intimacy, that literally changes our life.

Progression of Love's Wounding

TERESA OF AVILA'S many experiences with the wound of love are immortalized in *The Book of Her Life*, in which she recounts an angel plunging a fiery "golden dart" into the deepest part of her heart.[10] The intensity of pain and excessiveness of bliss she undergoes are symbolic of her ontological transfiguration and the spiritual significance of the wound. She establishes that this wound of love is not self-activated— "there is clear awareness that the soul did not cause this love"—but is ignited by "a spark from the very great love the Lord has . . . making it burn all over."[11] Since the wound is divinely caused, it cannot be relieved by bodily or mental penances, but by God alone, whose desire it is that the soul dies to the old self.

Teresa takes up the wound of love again in *The Interior Castle*, contending that it is the necessary precursor to freedom of being. The suffering is caused by the anguish of her whole being to be drawn not just closer to God, but to be with God. It is marked by an intensity of longing and an increasing awareness of the interior and exterior pains she must endure. She labors to reconcile Jesus' loving graces with her confessors' suspicions that her experiences were from the devil, a fact that caused Teresa to be "deeply tormented and disturbed."[12] These external, social wounds teach her that only God can mend the doubt that grips her soul, and only God can transform her weary heart.

The suffering Teresa feels is not, however, the effect of divine punishment or chastisement. Rather, the soul is wounded by divine love in order to bring it to true happiness: to receive in and accept goodness. It is thus that she progresses from self-wounding and the world's wounding into the deeper divine wound in which she shares in and perceives the world from God's perspective. Certainly, one of the most compelling aspects of Teresa's wisdom is her insistence on the soul's capacity to empathize with, assume, and transform suffering. Like God bears the world's pain, the fully realized soul participates in the intra-divine suffering when God weeps with our weeping. Through the inner eye of love, the soul is given the gifts of divine vulnerability (to bear the wound of love) and divine strength to resist violence and affliction.

The following is how Teresa describes four effects of the wound of love.

Expands the Soul

The first effect of the wound is to dilate and expand the soul in order to make it capable of receiving in God's immensity.[13] This wounding is "far different from all that we can acquire of ourselves here below and even from the spiritual delights that were mentioned."[14] The soul knows the wound is spiritual and even though the pain is intense, it does not want to be cured of its suffering. Experiencing the divine wounds both as an intense suffering and an intense joy in its most intimate depth, the soul feels an overwhelming love as God draws these very depths into its own nature.

> The desire for the Lord increases much more; also, love increases in the measure the soul discovers how much this great God and Lord deserves to be loved. And this desire continues, gradually growing in these years so that it reaches a point of suffering as great as that I shall now speak of. . . . And, in my opinion, it isn't felt where earthly sufferings are felt, but in the very deep and intimate part of the soul, where this sudden flash of lightning reduces to dust everything it finds in this earthly nature of ours.[15]

Always concerned that her path is above reproach, Teresa seeks to distinguish God's awakening of her soul from any worldly activity. She notices that only God has the power to join pain with the spiritual delight of the soul. Similarly, God's action leaves the soul in quiet and certitude, fortifying it with great determination to suffer for God. These capacities, she notes, are not within the person's power to effect. Divine benefits, however, are both more interior and hidden and express special forms of communion between God and the soul. Among these, Teresa mentions an infusion of the senses with a "delightful enkindling" that generates "intense acts of love and praise of our Lord."[16]

Deeper Communion

The wound of love generates a deeper communion, which Teresa describes, respectively, as the prayers of quiet and union. Beyond these prayer forms, God draws the soul to betrothal, speaking to its beloved through a variety of locutions (silent words from God), raptures, and intellectual and imaginative visions. Each of these means of communication instills in her a greater understanding of the divine mysteries and a more integral embodiment of her co-creation with God.

Cocoon of Unknowing

In more advanced stages, the wound of love blinds the eyes of the soul and wraps it in a cocoon of unknowing in order to leave "the soul annihilated within itself and with deeper knowledge of God's mercy and grandeur."[17] Through the wound of love, Teresa's soul is hollowed out and made empty to receive in the realization of her participation in building a sacred community on Earth. Through moments of illumination, the soul is taught that there are no closed passages between the lower soul and the luminosity of mystical marriage in the higher soul. Like rain falling into a stream or a river that enters the sea, the soul is inseparably at home, one with its divine source. "Through some secret aspirations," Teresa writes, "the soul understands clearly that it is God who gives life to our soul. These aspirations come very, very often in such a living way that they can in no way be doubted. . . . when the soul reaches this state in which God grants it this favor, it is sure of its salvation and safe from falling again."[18]

Live Like Christ

Teresa explains that the purpose of the wound of love and the delightful favors is to live like Christ, offering to the world the fruit of good works. The dissolution of the soul into the ocean of divinity effects Teresa's action in the world as her outer works emerge from this inner root. For Teresa, the mutuality and intimacy experienced through the wound of love is more primordial, more fundamental than mystical union, which speaks of joining and uniting. She is quite clear that this reality is not the joining together of two separate entities, but the fount and source discovered by way of love.

God cannot create or lead the soul to the true reality that has been there all along but must suffer and wait for human cooperation—until we love our selves with such an intensity of love that we break through inferiority and self-doubt. Then, the divine being is manifested in our being, co-liberating God into the world. God is curtailed by our oppression, just as God is freed by our dignity and empowerment. Teresa's description of the soul's journey vacillates in *The Interior Castle* between the sensible idea of a predetermined reality to which the soul is led, and a dynamic, interactive reality constantly being co-created by God and the soul.

Teresa discovers that all that is longed for, all that requires healing, all that yearns for wholeness is resolved in the Wound of Divine Love. The wound signifies both God's absence and presence; God's transcendence and intimate friendship; God's excessive benevolence and assumption of human suffering.

THE REALIZATION of and attention to the wounding of the soul, and the healing balm of Divine Love, are significant for our spiritual progress. Too often, we are unaware of how we participate in suffering, how we hold onto and bear the world's injury and injustice. The "friends of God suffer," so says the anonymous Christian monk. We must harness our pain for the transformation of our societies, for "the human race is a solidarity," writes Grace Jantzen:

> There is not only a psychosomatic unity within each individual, but a unity of human beings, and, even more widely, a unity with all of creation. The fracture at the heart of humankind is a fracture that is contributed to by everyone and that has consequences for everyone. The suffering of a particular individual is therefore no indication of that individual's sinfulness or otherwise; it is, however, an indication of the sinfulness and suffering of the whole of humankind of which that individual is a member. . . . In other words, our sin is both by own choice and because of the damage done to us by others.[19]

It is because of an inner fire that we throw ourselves into life and, of necessity, experience the wounding that leads to greater compassion and love. It gives us the courage to find our original dignity. Wounding puts us in touch with compassion for others and for their suffering. It helps us to understand more intimately and more completely the mystery and the grace of being born. Because the mystic heart is close to God's unconditional love, suffering is understood differently. It is the gateway to healing of the whole person.

When one recognizes the subtle gentleness and sweetness of existence, then we become aware of how far we diverge from it. Even if we have a wonderful life, when we come face to face with Mystery, we recognize the many things we have done that harm the holy in our midst. As our contemplation deepens, there will come a point where a Great Light will shine on the smallest deeds we have committed—which to others may seem inconsequential—but in comparison to what we now *experience* form a wound in one's being.

There is the pain of realizing that we are divided between our deepest desires and the actions that we perform. Each of us knows what it means to suffer something that we do not understand—the punishing God who does not speak to our tenderness; the loss of faith—*Why do we suffer? Is God real, or am I living an illusion?* Yet the hope of transcendence, of higher meaning, of transfiguration, is present even in those moments when we fear we are lost and lack understanding.

We advance through suffering because God wants to strengthen our souls. In the beginning of the spiritual life, St. John of the Cross says Sophia, Wisdom, like a mother nurtures us at her breast. She holds us, rocks us, and helps us take our faltering steps. But as we mature, like a good mother, Sophia weans us and sets us on our own path. The soul is purified by the fire of her loving Wisdom. Love itself infuses us with transformation.

Only someone who has been there and experienced this can really understand how literally true this is. It is not a convenient platitude to make us feel better: "Well, it really is love. It looks like pain, but it is really love." In fact, it is because we are able to bear the source of pain, that we cultivate the compassion and wisdom that only love can bring.

．◆．

May my heart expand to hold the sorrow
of the world
May my presence be a healing balm
of gentle hope.

Touched by the Wound of Love
a chorus of prayers liberates my sins
I am anointed with sweet oils.

O Holy One
May I be worthy of your gifts.

Amen.

SIXTEEN

The Mysticism of Healing

When the gods spread the sacrifice with the man as the offering, spring was the clarified butter, summer the fuel, autumn the oblation.

They anointed the Man, the sacrifice born at the beginning, upon the sacred grass. With him the gods, Sadhyas and sages sacrificed.

From that sacrifice in which everything was offered, the melted fat was collected, and he made it into those beasts who live in the air, in the forest and in villages.

From that sacrifice in which everything was offered, the verses and chants were born, the meters were born from it, and from it the formulas were born. . . .

With the sacrifice, the gods sacrificed to the sacrifice. These were the first ritual laws. These very powers reached the dome of the sky where dwell the Sadhyas, the ancient gods.[1]

A S THE GREAT-GRANDMOTHER of spiritual thought, the above creation story from the sacred Hindu text *Rigveda* tells of the sacrificial generosity of the gods. Its visionary cosmology is centered on the emptiness of both being and knowing, from which five sacrifices arise: the sacrifice of the cosmic Man born at the beginning; the sacrifice of the animal creatures; the sacrifice of language, word, and writing; the sacrifice of the gods; and the sacrifice itself. The *Rigveda* sings that the entire creative realm is the result of primordial offerings, which every human contains in his or her depth.

Beyond the forms in which the sacrifice is contemplated, is the sacrifice itself. At the center of reality, at the cosmic point of convergence, rests an unconditional gift in which everything gestates and is born. It is to the sacrificial generosity of this offering that we are called to return, and in which the healing of the self takes place.

From time immeasurable, the spirit world speaks of humanity's inborn capacity to grow in love, repair injury, and be enlightened. Within us is the secret of all secrets: that as we give all of ourselves, so the universe gives in kind. This is because the most precious things in life cannot be bartered but only gifted. This is healing. In giving ourselves away, we discover a new path of heart.

Healing as Spiritual Autobiography

EVERY RELIGION TRACES the human quest for wholeness. The spiritual journey outlines an autobiographical account of how each person travels from birth to the dying process, ever closer to the source of meaning, ever closer to the source of truth. From a mystical perspective, the highest form of healing is the person's direct experience of Divine Presence— *unio mystica* (the soul's union with God)—or enlightenment (*satori, nirvana,* or *samadhi*) described in Buddhist and Hindu texts.

While healing can involve cultural and social factors, it is, even in those instances, highly personal because it is always experiential, affecting the heart, mind, and totality of the person. Within us is the capacity to change the story of our lives, reminding us that the spirit is not limited or restricted by the pull of physical embodiment.

At times in every life there is oppression of the spirit, violence inflicted on the heart, and wounding of the soul. Sometimes, because we do not have access to the language of the spirit, we lack words for what we are suffering and are unable to communicate our pain. Because our culture tends to neglect the suffering that often accompanies physical and spiritual healing, it is not part of conventional thought to discuss, for example, the agonizing dark night of the soul that St. John of the Cross writes about, or *fana*—the "passing away" or "annihilation" of the self— that our Muslim sisters and brothers experience.

We do not talk about the embarrassment or the shame we may feel attempting to share these deep inner states. We do not talk about our passion to find meaning and love. Often, we do not have the words to name the wounding that intense levels of healing provoke. Our inner nature may be shrouded in silence and mystery, and in our need for forgiveness and reconciliation. It is our willingness to open ourselves to these sufferings and fears, and then to share them with others, that is vital to the whole process of healing.

Many gifted people have functioned as mystical healers, assisting others through the suffering of their souls. Jewish texts refer to the *tzaddik,* or righteous one, who repairs the soul's wound by cleaving to and guiding a person's journey through nights of despair. The Indigenous shaman, or soul healer, undergoes a mystical process of loss and reintegration that is necessary to heal mental, physical, and emotional imbalances. And, the Zen roshi or Tibetan *lama* teaches about the transformation of the mind, alleviating the root cause of suffering. The sacrificial offering of self also is the work of the saint, who assumes the pains of world, and heals those hearts of stone capable of inflicting wounds.

The Transformative Archetype in Healing

SPIRITUAL HEALING involves an archetypal process of transformation that is inherent in being. From our original beginnings in the generosity of self-offering (sacrifice), we are constantly able to give; we are constantly able to change.

The shamanic journey offers a classic example of the healing archetype, which involves a spiritual and symbolic dismemberment and reintegration that generates powerful physical effects. The Yakut shaman Tiuspiut describes the metamorphosis of being required to shamanize:

When I was twenty years old, I became very ill and began "to see with my eyes, to hear with my ears" that which others did not hear or see; nine years I struggled with myself, and I did not tell anyone what was happening to me, as I was afraid that people would not believe me and would make fun of me. At last I became so seriously ill that I was on the verge of death; but when I started to shamanize I grew better; and even now when I do not shamanize for a long time I am liable to be ill.[2]

Another archetypal image, in this case of the alchemical transformation of copper into gold, is described in the Sufi tradition. The seeker's conditioned view of reality and egocentricity is the base metal that is transmuted into the gold of liberation, or freedom from the self. Jalal al-Din Rumi, Sufi mystic and poet, describes the healing journey in this way:

Once having entered the way [of healing] the disciple begins to undergo the process of inward transformation. The alchemy of the way will transmute the base copper of one substance into pure and noble gold. The science of transformations undergone is the science of the spirit's journey to its true source in the Divine.[3]

The archetype is expanded beyond the person to include a cosmological healing of the Earth in the twelfth-century spirituality of St. Francis of Assisi. Francis' lifelong meditation on Christ crucified reaches fruition when he receives the stigmata on Mount La Verna. In 1225 (six to ten months later) Francis, almost blind and tormented by mice, receives a vision of the Earth transformed into gold. The circumstances are described in the *Scripta Leonis, Rufini et Angeli*:

He could no longer see in the daytime, . . . and had great pain in his eyes. . . . The mice plagued him both day and night and did not let him go to sleep . . . One night deeply distressed and sorry for himself, he said inwardly: "Lord come to my help and look on my infirmities so that I may be able to bear them patiently."[4]

Francis' prayer was answered by a voice assuring him that his sufferings would be rewarded, and to rejoice, for he is promised eternal happiness in the kingdom of heaven:

> Tell me, brother, if anyone were to give you for your infirmities and tribulations such a great and precious treasure that, if the whole world were pure gold, all stones were precious stones, and all water were balsam, yet you would consider all this as nothing . . . in comparison with the great and precious treasure given to you, surely you would rejoice greatly?[5]

The next morning, Francis told his companions that he wanted to make a song of praise to the Lord for his creatures. Soon after he composed his famous prayer, *The Canticle of the Creatures*, in which he associates his inner healing with the healing of the whole Earth, and with the radiant presence of the Divine in and through the sun, the moon, and the stars, earth, air, fire, and water.[6]

Transformation of base metals into pure gold symbolizes the process of mystical separation of the spirit from the physical body through purification of one's inner life. The separation and purification are an intermediate state followed by integration in which one discovers the Divine image at the center of the self. This capacity of transformation, from one centered on the ego to a state beyond the self, is infinite and always moving forward.

Gregory of Nyssa, fourth-century Christian mystic, uses the Greek word *epectasis* to describe the process whereby the soul is called toward "the continual striving forward to what lies ahead."[7] For Gregory, the soul's journey toward healing is constantly moving ever deeper into the divine nature, an infinite process without end. Even though in the beginning the soul despairs of never arriving at the final truth, "she learns that the true satisfaction of her desire consists in constantly going on with her quest and never ceasing in her ascent."[8] The mystery that can never be contained, and discovery of the incomprehensible and unhoped-for beauty, *is* liberation.

Further, the transformative qualities of healing are intimately connected to our physical bodies. While we may never completely grasp this relationship, nevertheless, we know that transformation is simultaneously bio-physical, embedded in our daily lives. Healing, therefore, does not point to an ideal state to be discovered, but deeper toward the wonder of finitude and infinity, temporality and eternity that we experience every day. Healing is mysteriously imbedded in the cells of our bodies, in our minds, and in our hearts. The path of healing embraces the paradox of existence, in all of its splendor and glory, in all of its questioning and travail.

We are able to heal because in our depth we are one with the universal transcendent. We live simultaneously in two worlds: the world of pure being and the world of conditioned reality with its struggling inconsistencies. We are born capable of moving from one dimension of consciousness to another; we are born for healing. And because of this, we also have within us the techniques of transformation necessary to guide us on the right path.

All of these attributes of mystical healing lead us to a different state of being. The *quality* of life that a person lives who is oriented to healing of the whole self is a different quality than one lives without it. Healing, of course, does not promise freedom from all physical, mental, or even spiritual ailments. But a healing perspective reminds us of the well-being, *the pureness*, at the center of our natures. As we live in the spirit of healing, we find the courage to risk giving up old patterns of thought and behavior. This qualitatively different state of being touches, however momentarily, on the true potential of the human spirit.

Buddha, for example, frequently used analogies of disease and healing to explain various facets of the Dharma. According to Buddhist thought, a person who is not liberated, who is still subject to the sufferings brought on by insatiable craving, is considered ill.

In the Pali Canon, the Supreme Physician is the Buddha; the healing treatment—the medicine and therapeutic regimen—is the Dharma; and the attendants are the members of the Order [Sangha].[9] This is the Triple Gem: Buddha, Dharma, Sangha. In *The Healing Buddha*, professor of Buddhist Studies, Raoul Birnbaum, writes:

Again and again, the Buddha reminds his disciples that they are ill, that they should diligently seek to be healed, and that they can turn to the King of Medicines (the Dharma) and the Supreme Physician for aid and relief.[10]

The sage Vimalakirti—a central figure in the *Vimalakirti Sutra* and a contemporary of Gautama Buddha—discusses healing as perfect enlightenment, not to be confused with the transient illness of the physical body. "The *Tathagata*-body arises from countless types of purities. O Virtuous Ones, if you desire to attain the Buddha-body, and be rid of all illnesses which beset living beings, you should aspire to attain perfect enlightenment."[11]

The Mahayana vow to forfeit enlightenment until all beings are free from suffering is described in the sage's moving comments that his own illness is a result of his self-offering:

> I am ill because all sentient beings are ill. If the illness of all sentient beings were to come to an end, then my illness would be ended. Why is this so? Because when the Bodhisattva enters into the realm of birth and death for the sake of all beings, he becomes subject to the laws of this realm. . . . When all beings are cured, then the Bodhisattva will be cured.[12]

In order to initiate this process of transformation, we have to be willing to mystically die and to physically let go. Healing involves a shift in perspective in order to live in the world pure of heart. It is a process that leads us away from the superficial personality to the true Self, from selfishness to relinquishing of the ego, and from separation and estrangement to interdependence and belonging. As a radical shift in the orientation of how we live, inner healing takes us back to the *Rigvedic* prayer: the sacrifice and offering that was born in the beginning.

Sometimes mystical dying to the old self is indistinguishable from physical ills. A stunning example is Julian of Norwich, who prayed for the recollection of Christ's Passion and to suffer the savior's bodily pains. She tells of her desire to have "by God's gift a bodily sickness to be so severe that it might seem mortal, for I wanted no comfort from any human, earthly life. I intended this because I wanted to be purged by God's mercy." Soon after she writes, "God sent me a bodily sickness" that pierced her body and soul with an intense sorrow, and "in which I lay for three days and three nights . . . . Truly I believed that I was at the point of death." Suddenly, all pain was taken from her, and her health was restored, "that was by God's secret doing and not natural."[13] She had been received by Christ the physician, the great physician (*magnus medicus*), who healed her wounds with compassion.

In chapter twenty-three of the Lotus Sutra, we find a similar physical response in the practice of *danaparamita*, the "perfection of giving" described as the first of the Bodhisattva perfections. "The 'offering of the Genuine Law to the Tathagatas' is the offering of the body or physical vehicle, the sacrifice of the self to the Buddhas."[14] The theme of self-surrender is repeated in an anonymous fourteenth-century Christian text, *The Cloud of Unknowing*. Here the author speaks about the sorrow that we feel in knowing that we *are*, which constantly weighs on our hearts and minds.

> Every man has plenty of cause for sorrow, but he alone understands the deep universal reason for sorrow who experiences *that he is*. Every other motive pales beside this one. He alone feels authentic sorrow who realizes not only *what he is*, but *that he is*.[15]

While dying, particularly in Western cultures, can be difficult to grasp as a mystical form of healing, spiritually dying refers to our capacity for transformation and realization of our divinity. If we did not have the capacity to die, if we did not have the capacity to let go, we would never be able to understand what it means to "float in the vast ocean of being." We would never understand what it means to have a moment free from the egocentric notion of reality. It is our willingness to spiritually die that signals our ability to love, to seek truth, and to yearn for the Divine.

And because this is so, offering of the self is always involved in healing (in one form or another). Whether we sacrifice our view of reality or the way we approach disease and illness, healing requires a letting go of the attachments of the mind, and of the mental impressions the mind causes. More than deconstructive, healing evokes an offering of our hearts to be more loving, forgiving, and peaceful.

Spiritual Stages of Healing

HUMANITY'S SEARCH for healing traces a mystical path that shares similar states of consciousness and psycho-spiritual levels of growth across cultures and religions. As we know, the healing process does not always progress smoothly. It is the path that teaches about abandonment, conversion to spiritual likeness, and ultimately oneness or union with *reality*. When we awaken from this period of darkness, we undergo not only a change of mind and thought, but also a change of heart. We *become* a new person.

Such radical, life-changing transformation has its own spiritual methodology. For example, Pseudo-Dionysius, an anonymous Christian monk writing in the fifth or early sixth century, clearly identifies a method of spiritual growth that progresses through three stages, which he called purgation (or purification), illumination, and union.[16] Other mystical writers concur that within every person a path of spiritual transformation is imprinted. Examples include Teresa of Avila's seven degrees of contemplation, the refinement of the mystical journey expressed in John of Cross' active and passive nights of the soul, and the seven mystical valleys found in *The Conference of the Birds*, authored by the Sufi writer, Farid ud-Din Attar.[17]

These diverse approaches to the soul's journey trace how the conditioned self will be alternately purified and illuminated by its intense search for meaning. Designed to uncover "our face before we were born," the mystical quest brings the heights of ecstasy and the depths of pain and despair. It is a spiritual method by which the self gives up the illusion of "I-hood" in order to experience reality as it truly is.

Although there are innumerable ways of describing the stages of spiritual growth, I will concentrate on four of the five stages outlined by the English writer and pacifist, Evelyn Underhill: purgation, illumination, dark night, and union.[18] For the sake of clarity, I will present these stages in a linear fashion. Naturally, healing is dynamic and organic and is seldom sequential or linear. We may experience one state of the healing process, and then repeat another state. As healing grows in us, we may undergo purification, experience an illumination, and return to another purification.

The initial stage of the path usually involves a period of awakening to our egocentric impulses, and the strength of the ego's will. During this purification, we experience the discrepancy between what the mind wants and what the spirit needs. We are purged of our attachment to reality as our social environment and false self believes it to be. We have to let go of attitudes that impede healing and instead open our hearts and minds to new ways of seeing. We may experience distaste for the lies we live and the hopes that we have abandoned. We *know and feel* that there is another way, a more holy and healthier way, to live. We desire to rid ourselves of all that impedes authenticity. We gather the courage to confront our weaknesses, illusions, and fear of letting go.

Healing ushers in another stage, illumination, that includes an immediate experience of truth, or the blazing light of the Divine. The illuminative consciousness opens the windows of the soul to *see* what previously was unseen: the ever-present realm of holiness behind the veil of ordinary existence. It instills a desire to be more divine-like because we have glimpsed a reality that is not bound by time and space or by the separation that blinds us from knowing the sacredness of every moment. It causes regret, and a desire to be healed of illusion, for the heart has been touched by something extraordinary and profound.

Highly intense, illuminative experiences frequently lead back to further purification. We have glimpsed something *other*, we have seen the nature of truth, and now we cannot bear the way we are living any longer. The juxtaposition of purification-illumination-purification involves our senses, intellect, will, and understanding. But there is an even more intense level of transformation that takes place in the deep self, in the soul.

St. John of the Cross calls this mystical transformation *una noche oscura*—a "dark night"—of the soul. It is at this juncture that the purifying process moves from letting go of external attachments, the errant will, and "I-hood," to the action of the divine in the soul. This is the stage where our efforts are unable to free the soul from its thirst for separate existence. It is the Divine alone that heals. The will, which seeks its own direction and demand, is subjected to radical experiences of not knowing, loss of faith, and fear of love's abandonment; these may continue for some time.

Healing at this level entails suffering and pain because the self is attached to its identity. "From day to day," St. Augustine writes, "I deferred to live in you, but on no day did I defer to die in myself."[19] We are attached to knowing and to being able to name reality; but we are not very clear about unknowing, about what is beyond the mind's ability to grasp. We are attached to *our* will and not to that Endless Ocean of Being that calls us toward wholeness. Attracted to being in control, we are uncomfortable with mystery, with uncertainty. While we think that the journey toward enlightenment resolve all paradoxes, in the dark night we surrender to and *bear* paradox.

The healing of the soul teaches how to withstand ambiguity until we hold in our hearts all those things that do not "add up." This is the uniting of our inner divisions, which ultimately leads to uniting divisions in the world. The dark night of the soul brings us to an experience of peace. It shows that we are able to withstand wounding and pain, because something greater—compassion and love—is always at work in the deep self.

More difficult is the sense of divine absence or withdrawal that many people experience in the passages of night. The awareness of Spirit we had in the illuminative state or the ease of our prayer can suddenly be taken away. We feel an aridness of heart; we feel a great desolation in which the soul seems abandoned by its god. Often described as a spiritual death, the self is pressed to surrender its own will. To find your life, Jesus said, you have to lose your life.

The wrenching uncertainty that lays our hearts bare is designed to prepare us for the experience of mystical union, enlightenment, or intimacy. We discover a state of oneness with all life and compassion for all beings, especially for those who suffer and are lost. In this state, we not only perceive and know—we become *one*—with the Real. This is the healing toward which all the prior transformations have tended. We have found what we have only dimly hoped for and sought. Whether we are physically well or ill, whether disease transforms our living or prepares us for physical dying, our journey toward union allows us to *be* the miracle that is life, which is the true goal of healing.

WE HAVE COME FULL CIRCLE. The release of our small selves is a mystical reenactment of the sacrificial offering mentioned in the *Rigveda*. We are reminded of our capacity for healing, and of our participation in the great cosmic journey of sacrifice, offering, and rebirth. May we all be drawn into the healing circle of life's ultimate longing for itself.

PART FOUR

A Vowed Life

✦

These chapters explore the practical steps that assist the person's desire to live differently, in a contemplative mode of being. It includes examples of a daily schedule, personal vows, a rule of life, and a ceremony of profession that stabilize and affirm a new monastic way of life. It also outlines how a disparate group of people from diverse religions, cultural backgrounds, sexual orientations, and family and professional responsibilities came together, stayed together, and eventually formed a new, nonresidential monastic community.

✦

SEVENTEEN

Creating a Monastic Schedule

I T CERTAINLY NEVER occurred to me that one day I would take monastic vows, be the founder of a new monastic community, or become involved in the global dialogue of the world's religious traditions and spiritual wisdoms. But twenty years ago, under the guidance of Sr. Theresa Schumacher and seven additional Benedictine women monastics, I professed vows as a universal monk of peace. As written elsewhere (*The Monk Within*), the ceremony of profession was life-changing and profound. Due to the intense impact this process had on my inner life, even after many years of teaching and practice, it felt important to share with others the benefit of becoming nontraditional monks.

Thus, a two-year course of contemplative study and monastic formation was created, which focused on deepening the life of the spirit and the monastic archetype in each of us. The process included a structured and an organic dimension. By that I mean that there was a foundation of study, reflection, written work, and critical analysis on classical and contemporary monastic wisdom that was connected to the seekers' freedom to approach their Divine Source directly, creatively, and with an open heart. To find their spiritual rhythm, to speak the language of the mystics, to meditate from their hearts, to write prayers, and to ask for guidance in forming a personal rule of life, and finally a personal set of vows.

The community of participants functioned like a band of far-flung hermits bound together by a mutual love of the Holy. Since most everyone lived in a different location around the country, each person had to take responsibility to develop a strong spiritual center and practice, keeping alive the desire that brought them to pursue monkhood. We gathered in person once and usually twice a year. During our residential retreats, days were a combination of silence, shared liturgy, contemplative talks, dialogue, questions, spiritual exercises, and meals. The unifying factor in these retreats was to preserve the solitude and silence of each member.

For example, during teachings the goal was to listen to the entire presentation without asking questions until the end. This method was critical because it allowed participants to absorb what they were hearing—to truly listen—deeply, in their own way. It prevented intrusion of another's thoughts and questions into the group energy. The goal was to take in the words, allow them to sink into one's heart. It created an atmosphere of receptivity and quiet. It fostered soul thinking and soul integration. It was about adjusting to integration (not revealing personal or psychological issues).

This method, which is the essence of every true "time away," generates a rhythm in our bodies and reorients the mind and emotions to a centered, quiet way of being. It is through solitude and silence that we find the resources within us to reach out to the Divine, listen for the inner voice, and become courageous in embracing a monastic way of life that is both practical and spiritual. Thus, an important part of retreat time is to foster and practice being in solitude while being with others. This requires attention on how we conduct ourselves in relation to our surroundings, and how we honor the bond of solitude each person has with his or her God.

In the interim periods when we did not meet in person, we remained connected through an online portal where I posted contemplative selections for study and reading suggestions, and members communicated with each other and submitted their reflection papers.

During the final year, participants were given a reading list of the vows and rules of life of traditional and new monastic communities drawn from a variety of religious traditions. And, in dialogue with their assigned mentor and/or spiritual companion, they spent many months praying about the meaning of taking vows and writing their own. We concluded with a ceremony of profession; afterward, the new band of eight monks chose a director and a community name.

Developing a Personal Monastic Plan

DURING THE MONTHS of spiritual formation, the community of participants dialogue about ways to adapt and integrate the centuries' old wisdom of monastic cultures, with the creation of a contemporary horarium (Latin for "of/related to the hours"). For the person who has joined with others to pursue monastic vows, it is paramount to maintain spiritual focus and intention in his or her daily activity. The questions I hear from participants, especially after a ten-day contemplative retreat, are: How do we preserve this deep centering, how can we continue to honor our true nature? How can we prevent our obligations back home from intruding on inner peace or even canceling everything that we know and have experienced here?

We usually begin with a discussion on what we hope and need spiritually to include in our lives. What will keep us focused on the contemplative mind and heart? What type of practices are helpful? Where are the challenges that prevent or subvert our intention? We brainstorm methods that encourage reflection on developing a monastic plan. In addition to prayer and meditation, these can include journal writing, sketching a free-form map, drawing or painting, creating a chart, making a collage, walking in nature, or writing a list. The idea is to give yourself time to devise a blueprint that works with your actual life commitments and then modify areas where needed. The monastic plan facilitates the creation of a spiritual rhythm for your day, and then can become a guiding principle that is expanded into finding God-time during the weeks and months ahead.

The process of mapping out a schedule of study and practice is usually undertaken in conversation with others in a community setting but also can be accomplished alone, with self-reflection and prayer. The creation of a spiritual plan of action involves giving yourself time and space to think about how to re-order your life in a very practical way. In a traditional, residential monastery, a schedule of rituals, prayers, and obligations organizes the day and directs attention to the soul's spiritual need. The in-home, nontraditional seeker can replicate living in sacred time by making a conscious effort in this direction.

The tool I've used with participants is the "Nine Dimensions of Practice," which I first drew free-hand and later had revised into a graphic design. It is one example of a regular horarium that can help with the change of life and the transformation of soul that monasticism evokes. The nine dimensions are listed here, followed by the graphic design and a sample monastic plan that is a compilation of ideas from participants. Spend time in contemplation and prayer. Journal or write a first draft of a plan, creating or adding your own practices.

Create Holy Space and Holy Time

Claim Passion, Longing for the Divine

Practice Daily (Prayer and Meditation)

Simplify Life Schedule

Engage in Spiritual Reading

Honor and Celebrate Body and Earth

Explore Creativity (Writing, Art)

Receive Spiritual Direction

All Centered on Silence and Solitude (The Monastic Heart)

Nine Dimensions of Practice

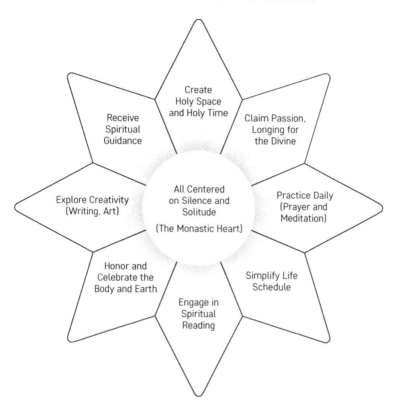

Sample Monastic Plan

Create Holy Space and Holy Time

- Reclaim a guest bedroom and turn it into a meditation and study sanctuary.
- Consecrate an outdoor space where you place stones and build a fire for prayer.
- Create a mini altar in one or each room of the house.
- Build a chapel or meditation room on your property.
- Set aside a period to rest in God's Time, without the pressure of things to do and places to go.

- Reserve a day or several days to be in silence.
- Attend a prayer group or services at a church, synagogue, mosque, interfaith center, etc.

Claim Passion, Longing for the Divine

- Find your voice in creative writing; knowing and stating your truth. Perhaps you are better in writing than in speaking or in speaking and art than in writing.
- Reflect: How do I live in the world and can be who I truly am?
- Find a way of practicing social justice from your deep, spiritual center.
- What is true nonviolence? How do you embody it?
- Pray for guidance in opening your heart further to the Divine Call.
- Discover resources that ignite your longing to live with and in the Holy.

Practice Daily (Prayer and Meditation)

- Our community uses a common book of prayers to recite five times a day. Choose or create your own book of prayers from scripture, the liturgy of the hours, a sacred text, poems, etc.
- Rise early to recite the morning vigil. Take a long walk. Listen to nature. Feel your heart open—feel that you are part of the vastness of the sky.
- Light a candle and/or burn incense, then recite the morning prayer for the day. If you have time, read a spiritual passage and journal about it.
- Before work, spend ten to twenty minutes in meditation.
- At work, incorporate "prayer breaks"; create a way to fit them into your day. Recite noon prayer.
- Consecrate the simple things—time in nature, eating, working in the garden.
- Recite evening prayer before dinner.
- Before sleep, spend twenty minutes or more in meditation.

- Each evening, before sleep, reflect: Where or when was I most aware of the Holy One today? Where or when did I feel separate from the Holy One? Take a moment to rest in gratitude for the ways God was present *through* you and *for* you via experiences of people, animals, nature you encountered.
- Recite the night vigil, in prayerful waiting for the coming of the Divine. Some find solace in waking in the early and dark hours before dawn—say, 3 a.m.—to pray vigils.

Simplify Life Schedule

- Help to reorient your day by arising in the morning early and going to bed early.
- Find support from friends or family if you have important obligations to fulfill—such as taking care of an elderly parent or a child who is ill.
- Limit interactions with organizations, government, or other bureaucracies when possible.
- Limit evening and weekend engagements.
- Practice saying "no" to requests and demands on time and attention that take you outside of your purpose and are done out of obligation.
- When feeling overwhelmed, honor your daily commitments, but pray for space and reprieve. Be amazed at how God answers.

Engage in Spiritual Reading

You will find an extensive Bibliography in the appendix. Here are several authors who explore aspects of a new monastic life in the world (full citation in Bibliography):

- Bruno Barnhart, ed., *Purity of Heart and Contemplation: A Monastic Dialogue Between Christian and Asian Traditions*
- Joan Chittister, *Wisdom Distilled from the Daily: Living the Rule of St. Benedict Today*
- M.K. Gandhi, *Vows and Observances*

- Rory McEntee and Adam Bucko, *The New Monasticism: An Inter-spiritual Manifesto for Contemplative Living*
- Patrick Hart, ed. *A Monastic Vision for the 21st Century*
- Beverly Lanzetta, *The Monk Within: Embracing a Sacred Way of Life*
- Diarmuid O'Murchu, *Religious Life in the 21st Century: The Prospect of Refounding*
- Raimon Panikkar, *Blessed Simplicity: The Monk as Universal Archetype*
- Wayne Teasdale, *A Monk in the World: Cultivating a Spiritual Life*

Honor and Celebrate Body and Earth

- Become more aware of what your body needs and honor what you discover. Perhaps it is more rest or exercise, better food, walking in nature, etc.
- Eat a healthy diet, keeping it simple to fix and shop.
- Reserve your energies for things you love and minimize other obligations.
- Take time for a bath, or a massage, or simply sitting in quiet.
- Dance! Practice yoga or tai chi. Or otherwise move in joyful ways.

Explore Creativity: Writing, Art

- Discover your creative spirit—poetry, music, art, dance.
- Play with paints or try sculpture, pottery, knitting, weaving, woodworking.
- Write from your heart—prayers, poems, music, liturgies.
- Let your inner creativity guide you into new areas instead of forcing or planning.
- Pray with icons. Paint your own icon. Set it on your altar.
- Affirm and listen to the inner voice of the creative spirit that guides decision, intuition, health, and the monastic way of life.

Receive Spiritual Guidance

- Seek spiritual guidance once a month. It can help very much to enrich your inner life.
- Read books about spiritual companionship. Learn more about religious experience and how the spirit's subtle voice communicates with you. (See Bibliography in Appendix)
- Notice areas where you close down or are afraid to share your true spiritual desire.
- Practice *lectio divina*—divine reading—savor the words and ruminate over them during your day.
- In tandem with spiritual guidance, therapy can be very helpful. Some people say that therapy helps them to name and lay bare their wounding. Spiritual direction can then help to discern how to move through the wounds (an ongoing process) in an integral, embodied, sacred way.

Center on Silence and Solitude: The Monastic Heart

- Take a regular day of silence. If you cannot do this every week, then take partial days without speaking, at home alone.
- Periodically spend one to three days in solitude on retreat at an established retreat center, zendo, or house of prayer.
- When time allows, spend entire days camping or hiking in the most natural environment possible.
- Fasting—literal and/or digital. Take specific times each week away from digital devices, social media, television, and screens. Designate a day to fast from food.
- Sit in a church, synagogue, or other sacred place when no one else is present and the building is silent.
- Practice sitting in emptiness.

EIGHTEEN

Lectio Divina:
Mysticism of the Text

O NE PRACTICE I ENCOURAGE monastic seekers to pursue is the ancient art of slow, prayerful recitation of sacred texts. This type of spiritual reading has been part of the daily schedule of monastic traditions for centuries in many of the world's religions. The monks usually spend a few hours in private reading of their tradition's holy books, very slowly savoring the words, sometimes in silence, sometimes aloud. Their goal is not to finish a passage but to be attentive to the deep meaning, ruminating on it, allowing it to sink in. If something in the passages strikes them—a word or a phrase—they are to pursue it, moving into meditation, prayer, and then, contemplation.

Reading at a slow pace, with a contemplative state of mind, nourishes the inner path and opens us to become aware of the movement of spirit. We do not rush through the text to gain details or knowledge but seek instead through words the Divine presence and action in our lives. A gentle, prayerful attitude opens the door and unlocks the text, so that we may pass over to our journey into the sacred.

In the monastic traditions of Christianity, the fourth-century desert monks are thought to have practiced *lectio divina* (Latin, divine reading), which can be traced to the veneration of the *Torah* and meditation on the sacred scriptures by Jewish ascetics in Egypt and Palestine. Central to the practice of the desert monastics was the reading of Scripture, which was the tangible bond that united life and prayer. This is because Scripture was seen as the foundation and moral order of the monk's life, and the path to being Christ's disciple. Each day in receiving God's word, the monk becomes the mind of Christ, to see the world as God sees, to love the world as God loves. Scripture was the sacred connection between prayer and life as it should be lived.

This tradition of divine reading later becomes ritualized in St. Benedict's rule for religious, in which hours were set aside each day for studying the Psalms. Texts were committed to memory so that every monk would be well equipped with a stock of favorite scriptural passages from which prayers and guidance were to be gleaned as occasion warranted. The monk was to silently preserve those passages that had special meaning, in order to act as a reminder and to share when a need arose. Well equipped with wisdom, no matter what happened—suffering, war, poverty—the monk's heart was where Scripture was kept, and so could never be taken away.

As a contemplative way of reading Scripture, spiritual reading is a meeting place for a personal encounter with God and is widely practiced today. One begins by approaching Scripture with reverence, realizing the divine Word in and through words of the text. Christians call upon the Holy Spirit to help them hear what God is saying in the practice of reverential reading. Seekers find ways to ritualize time for *lectio divina*, perhaps right before going to sleep, or in the morning before breakfast. With one word or phrase, they listen for the Divine speaking through the text for a period of time. At the end of the period, readers choose a word or phrase that is meaningful to them and carry it in their heart through the day. The process of sacred reading is completed with a closing prayer of thanksgiving, reverence, or awe.

Unlike reading for content, *lectio divina* approaches the text as a form of prayer, guiding us closer to union with the Holy One. At its simplest, *lectio* is not reading intellectually to gather information or instruction, but with the intention that the reader be formed in the divine likeness. In and through text, one comes face-to-face with Spirit. Through slowly reading, we allow words to penetrate our hearts and fill us with wisdom and love. Sometimes we are pulled clean out of our ordinary state of mind. We may awaken to new truths or insights, suffer compunction or shame, or be forgiven and bathed in light. By whatever means, when we read with meditative attention, communion occurs through surrender and rest. We do not hurry reading, trying to find the thesis, underlying cause, or doing critical analysis. We stop. We remain still in the presence of mystery.

Symbolic Interpretation

It was always understood that God speaks through Scripture in many ways, using various means of communication in order to reach each soul at its own level of understanding. Central to the practice of spiritual reading is that Scripture, its letters, words, and context, has transformative power as a living energy or reality. Reading holy words generates spiritual effects in the soul, drawing the person to take part in divine energies. For instance, you might be reading the story about Jesus' healing of the blind man. As you enter the scene, you can imagine revealing your wound to Jesus and awaiting his healing touch. In this practice, you enter a symbolic world in which language, spirit, and imagination combine to generate inner change in the seeker.

Three additional stages are practiced. Meditation, *meditatio,* is reflective engagement with a text. For example, let's say you read the passage from the Sermon on the Mount, "Do not resist an evil person. If someone strikes you on the right cheek, turn to him the other also." During the day, you carry the passage with you, ruminate on it as you are walking, at work, or running errands. It becomes your *meditatio,* as you listen for the Divine speaking through Scripture and learn how the passage relates to your life.

Prayer or *oratio* gives over to God the wisdom gained in meditation. Thus, one prays to be led to truth and virtue, to practice the principles discerned from the day's reading, and to express praise and thanksgiving. Ultimately, *oratio* moves into *contemplatio,* or contemplation. Here you are not "doing" anything but opening yourself to receive and rest in God. You can move into a passive or receptive form of knowing, where you may experience the text coming directly from the divine mind and heart into your being.

Of course, from the slow reading of a text there is no need to curtail how the spirit moves you from one stage to the next. You can remain in any of these stages for the duration of the practice, and you can move spontaneously, and not linearly, from reading to meditation, prayer, or contemplation.

In the thirteenth-century devotion to the humanity of Christ, another type of *lectio divina* flourished. This practice focused not on the reading of a written text but on contemplating the mystery of the historical event of Jesus' birth. St. Francis of Assisi is credited with staging the first nativity scene on Christmas Eve in 1223. The historical account we have of Francis' nativity comes from *The Life of St. Francis of Assisi,* by St. Bonaventure, a Franciscan monk and theologian. According to Bonaventure's biography, Francis received papal permission to set up a manger with hay and with two live animals (an ox and a donkey) in a cave in the Italian village of Grecio and invited villagers to contemplate in wonder upon the scene, which spilled over in affective prayer.

Franciscan spirituality of the thirteenth century advocated meditation on the life of Christ as a method of discerning a moral lesson. In *The Life*, Bonaventure uses the Tree of Life as a symbol to represent Christ's journey on Earth, "on whose branches blossom twelve fruits, which include such virtues as humility, piety, patience, and constancy presented to us for imitation."[1] In meditation on the birth of Christ, theologian Ewert Cousins writes that "Bonaventure paints a graphic scene and even draws us as participants into the drama of the event," evoking love for the infant Jesus, wonder at the host of angels, and a prayer of praise for God Most High:

> Now, then, my soul,
> embrace that divine manger;
> press your lips upon and kiss the boy's feet.
> Then in your mind
> keep the shepherds' watch,
> marvel at the assembling host of angels,

join in the heavenly melody,
singing with your voice and heart:
Glory to God in the highest
and on earth peace
to men of good will.[2]

Early Christians also read Scripture as a rich layer of symbolic meaning: literal, allegorical, moral, and mystical. By the Middle Ages, this was known as the fourfold interpretation of Scripture: literal (what the text intends to say directly), allegorical (how an event or person is a metaphor for or foreshadows something else), moral (relates to the life of virtue and perfection), and anagogic (mystical fulfillment in the afterlife). In *The Life of Moses*, Gregory of Nyssa used the moral interpretation in order to illustrate how Scripture should be read symbolically by choosing a passage that refers to the Jews' exodus from Egypt and their escape over the Red Sea. Gregory employs the moral interpretation in this passage about the army of soldiers:

> For who does not know that the Egyptian army—those soldiers, chariots, and their drivers, archers, slingers, heavily armed soldiers, and the rest of the crowd in the enemies' lines of battle—are the various passions of the soul by which man is enslaved? For the undisciplined intellectual drives and the sensual impulses to pleasure, sorrow, and covetousness are indistinguishable from the aforementioned army.[3]

While spiritual reading usually is undertaken in relation to Biblical scripture, any sacred text can be read with the same spirit of prayerful attention. In the religious traditions of Southeast Asia, millions of Hindus daily recite the *Bhagavad Gita*, Daoists and many others around the world consult the *Dao dejing* for wisdom and guidance, and Buddhist monks chant the *Dhammapada*. Similarly, Jews invoke the blessed *Torah* as God's message to the people, and Muslims practice *ta'wil*—bringing the soul into the hidden spiritual meaning of its divine origins, or praying *dhikr*, the rhythmic repetition of the name of Allah and his attributes. In the recitation of sacred stories, scriptures, and chants, language is not just textual but fully experiential—it is listening "with the ear of the heart," and reciting over and over until the sound of the words becomes the heartbeat of the soul.

In a broader context, sacred attention is a methodless method of reading the Divine in the faces of human companions, in the wonder of nature, in praying with icons, and in the everyday encounters of life. It is a quality of heart that, in piercing through appearances, is able to listen with rapt attention for a depth of meaning to be revealed. Often our experience of each other is limited, even false. We approach friends, colleagues, and family with personal histories, formed opinions, and blind assumptions. *Lectio divina* reminds us to slow down and experience awe, to listen for the spirit struggling to speak through the book of our lives. We become attuned to listening for the divine in every encounter—in a mother's joy of birth, a child's cry of hunger, or a soldier's prayer of peace. This form of daily reading in the Book of Life is one of the most holy of spiritual practices and one of the most difficult to achieve. It is far easier to meditate in a quiet spot undistracted by noise, or to read Scripture in the comfort of one's living room.

A spiritual book is a mirror of the soul because it reflects not only the itinerary of the spiritual journey imprinted in its depths, but also the image of God. From this point of view, *lectio divina* is a method of reading the life of the Divine itself in the depth of our souls. Spiritual reading involves the many books of creation—the book of the cosmos, the book of nature, the book of the spirit, the book of scripture, the book of sacred texts, and the book of the soul. When we contemplate these books, we move from the world without to the world within. We expand our consciousness as we contemplate the Book of Life, the exemplar of divinity in creation, expressed in various symbols in the world's religions, and in which all the other books are "recapitulated and transformed."[4]

How to Practice *Lectio Divina*

THERE ARE MANY viable methods of entering into spiritual reading and no doubt you will find what works best. To get you started, I offer the following suggestion of how to practice.

Find a quiet place and choose a text to read

Locate a place of silence and sit in a comfortable position. Use whatever meditation or prayer method is best for you and allow yourself to sink into silence. After a period of silent meditation, open Scripture or another spiritual book and choose a reading.

Read
Turn to the text and read it slowly and gently, silently and aloud

As you read, listen for a word or phrase that calls to you. Listen for the still, small voice. Allow it to arise from the passage as if the Divine is speaking to you today. Do not exert yourself or worry. Likewise, do not force this. When you finish reading, pause and recall if some word or phrase stood out or something touched your heart. If so, pause and savor the insight, feeling, or understanding. Then read the passage again because it will have a fuller meaning. Pause again and note what is happening within. We are being taught to listen, to seek Spirit in silence, to be gently invited into a deeper relationship.

Meditate
Ponder the word or phrase in yourself

Memorize and slowly repeat the word or phrase to yourself both silently and aloud and ask how this word or phrase speaks to your life and why it is connected to you. Do not be afraid of distractions; those might be part of your responses. Allow yourself to ruminate on and digest what you have been given, and during the day carry the passage with you, inviting dialogue with God.

Pray
Speak to God as one who knows, loves, and accepts you

Dialogue with your Beloved and offer what you have discovered in meditation. Give to the Divine what you heart has found. Pray to be re-formed into this new way. What do you need to do or consider or give up as a result of the word revealed to you today? Pray for peace and grace to be instilled in your heart; take the prayer into your day.

Contemplate
Wait to be invited into contemplation of the word or phrase

Rest in the Divine presence and rejoice in the knowledge that you are held in words and in silence. *Lectio* has no other goal than being in the presence of the Holy One. Allow your whole being to be filled with the wisdom given today.

Lectio Divina also can be used in a group setting. It is especially effective when a community enters a process of decision-making, and together are able to rest in silence, as well as listen for and receive Divine guidance. One member reads a passage, and those gathered take some time for extended silence, allowing each person to absorb what he or she has heard, particularly noting whether any word or phrase became a special focus of attention. Groups, especially if there is a small gathering, may also invite members to share out loud the word or phrase that struck them. This is done without discussion. Then a different person from the group would read the passage again with a pause for silence. The leader might suggest different emphases after each reading: What gift does this passage lead me to ask of the Divine? What does this passage call me to do? The gathering is usually ended with a closing prayer. Group *lectio* is used in many monastic settings, often during silent meals, when a monk will read aloud a scriptural passage for the uplifting of members. This is another way in which a gathering of people may enter together in communion with the Holy.

THE COMPLETION or fullness of the whole practice of sacred reading is contemplation and action, intimacy with the Divine in this world. It is coming to rest in God's presence, passing beyond words to the gateless path of truth. *Lectio divina* functions as a mysticism of the text and of the body, centering the practitioner in the silence that animates words and speech. As the reader's heart opens, it is as if a living flame rises from each letter, igniting the emptiness from which words flow. It is communion, between the silence of sacred words emblazoned in consciousness and the silence of the one who reads.

NINETEEN

Sr. Theresa on Vows

S R. THERESA SCHUMACHER, OSB, my dear and gentle friend, was
integrally involved with and committed to the spiritual formation
of our nontraditional monastic community. She helped members to
cherish the monk's commitment, to develop a communal structure, and to
prepare for vows. We were honored that she so willingly shared sixty years
of her wisdom as a Benedictine monk with us, which was a great blessing.
I always experienced her presence as the embodiment of the essence of
monasticism, for she was a person of light open to whomever and however God called us to love and serve. Supportive of and enthusiastic about
the vocation of the new monk, which she felt was an expression of the
enduring vitality of the monastic impulse, she embraced everyone in her
compassionate heart. In this transcription from July 24, 2015, Sr. Theresa
addresses the community on the meaning of vows, in particular for the
eight who were preparing for profession the next day.

Sr. Theresa:

I'M SENDING AROUND a piece of paper that has some tunes on it. At
Morning Prayer at our house, we read Psalm 61 and as I was praying that
with the community, I thought maybe this is how you are feeling today.

We could send it up as a little prayer to begin. I did take one section out because it talked about the kings and whatever. But I thought of this prayer if you want to just look at it quickly. You know you are at the place now where you have committed in your heart, there's no doubt about that, but it's a big step so you are perhaps feeling just a little bit like you want to call on the Divine favor over and over again. I'll start with Psalm 61 and we'll do the chant, *Ecce quam bonum* [Behold How Good], later if we have time.

> Here me God I cry out
> Listen to my prayer
> I call from far away
> For my courage fails
> Lead me to a mountain height
> Where I can be safe
>
> You are my refuge
> A tower of strength
> Against my bones
> Welcome me into your home
> Under your wings forever
> God you surely hear my vows
> Give me the blessings of those who honor your name
> I sing your name always
> Each day fulfilling my vows

I wanted to talk to you a little bit today, and you talk to me too, about vows and some of the symbolic meanings of the gestures and words that we use and say. Before I get into your questions, I'll just say a little about vows. You know a vow is both a verb and a noun. It's active and also something you can define as a kind of promise. It's really a binding act and it's a service to the world. Vows have been made throughout the history of all people, really. We interpret a vow as a promise made to God or the Divine One or the One to whom we pray above all and in awe, so it needs to be voluntary. It's very sacred. In it we dedicate ourselves to God, or if we do it with other people, we dedicate to God but also within the community. It is important to remember that there is a kind of obligation to the people with whom we are vowed. Is that how you view your vows? That it has relationship to the people in this community. Yes, God and the community.

You know that vows are common in Buddhism and Hindus, but not always for life. We don't have to make vows for life either. But I think those of you preparing to take vows are looking at this as kind of perpetual, something you want to live by for the rest of your life. And, of course, in Judaism it is very common to consecrate something to God and we are consecrating ourselves to God. Then, of course, we know that in Roman Catholicism and many kinds of Protestantism, vows are common also. Baptism is a kind of vow that continues in many of the sacraments that are taken in Catholic and Protestant circles.

So monastic vows are a giving of oneself to God, an act that defines us, at least in our hearts. We don't have to carry our commitment around with a placard, but what is most important is that God knows what is in the heart of the one who makes a vow. This vowing can be more of a prayer; it can be a vow of austerity. Some people do that. But Benedictines are not asked necessarily to make a vow to do some specific thing, other than to live your life in the monastic way, which means prayer, dedicating your life, your art to a contemplative way of being. Is that how you see it? It is really a mystery that we have been chosen to be in the Divine Presence in a special kind of relationship. Certainly, God has made the initiative and has come calling you and you are responding with your life.

In our Benedictine monastic tradition, it is very clear that the promise of vows is made before God and the saints. We call this the "Litany of the Saints" because we are in a great cloud of witnesses it says in Hebrews [12: 1–2]. I think that many traditions believe in and experience the presence of those who have gone before us. Those who are the angels watching over us and so on, are all part of this category. Another thing is that these promises or vows that you make need to be written out. I know that is very important in Benedictine life and I know you are doing it too. You write it with your own hand. That is such a wonderful thing that even in this age when you can so easily make a copy and put it in a computer; this is more of yourself and more of who you are. So, we write the document and in our contemporary culture, that has even more meaning, I think. And then you put your own name and signature on it, very important. It makes it so strong to write your own name on that document.

After that we say the *suscipe,* a Latin word which means "receive" or "accept." We raise our arms and say to the community and to God: "Receive me, O God, as you have promised, and I shall live! Do not disappoint me in my hope." After you say it, then the community says it three times. Each repetition is an intensification of our promise, our vow, and our willingness to give ourselves totally. And of course, when you do that and with each other, there is a bond that is formed between you and the community and of course between you and your source of all life and desire, God. This act of total surrender is very important.

Then there is a part in the profession when you are going to say with your body what you are doing. This is prostration. First you write your pledge by your own hand and sign your vows, which is very bodily. You chant the *suscipe.* But there is also the prostration. As we put our body flat on the floor in a vulnerable position, you are not able to defend yourself in that position, which is very symbolic that you are giving your entire self. And I think prostration also says something about being one with the earth. We don't do it on the earth itself, but the floor is as close to earth as we can be. In a way, we are professing that we know we are made of earth, we are God's handiwork, and we are vulnerable. While the professing monks prostrate, the community chants, *Da pacem,* which is followed by chanting the Litany of the Saints.

"Humus" is a word that comes from ground, soil, and the word "humility" comes out of "humus": I am made of earth. When some people interpret humility as walking around with your head bowed and your eyes on the ground, that's really not what it's about. Humility is being our true self and if we recognize that we are of earth, God's creation and live whatever that means, that's what humility is.

This is one of the most important things to keep in mind, that in the act of prostrating on the earth, I feel like our hearts are being certainly accepted, but given in a way that is also a shelter. Our hearts are flat on the ground when we prostrate, so even though you are vulnerable, your heart is very strongly kept by the earth beneath you. It is a significant amount of time that you are prostrated. And, again, every ritual or every gesture really means more if you take time for it and so we wanted to make sure that nothing is rushed and that each part of this is done with the best intention.

And then rings: so those who wish may want to wear a ring. Of course, we all know what a ring signifies, unending-ness and a circle of community and a circle of being united with God, who doesn't have a beginning or end. As the prioress or leader places the ring on your finger, we say, "May this ring be a pledge of steadfast love and a sign of your commitment to the monastic way of life." There is another period of silence. Then the newly professed sisters and brothers say the *Magnificat* and we have a closing prayer.

I wonder if you have any questions or if the people who have already done this may want to talk about any part of this.

Q: You were very young when you entered the monastery. Do you ever feel you wanted to take vows at different stages of life?

TS: In the community, we renew our vows once a year. If I miss that particular ritual it doesn't mean my vows are gone. It is not like taking them over again. But at different stages of your life, your vows mean something very different. Ohhh yesss!

Q: Could you talk about that?

TS: Well, when I was a young sister, there was a certain amount of, I suppose, what a young married couple might feel—it all looks good! And the future is all before you. It was something that I certainly did freely, but as life works itself out and there are new relationships [change happens]. I entered a community of one thousand sisters or more. I never knew them all, but our life was pretty much what was called vertical obedience. We were, for instance, assigned to a place to do work whether we wanted to do it or not. Obedience was almost blind. Somehow being with the other women, we went all over the diocese with a small group of women that we were not brought up with, our mothers did not cook the same food. All this mixture of people, so friction happens. I think probably relationships were the hardest for a long time because we got moved to different places and you never really got to know anybody well until maybe the 1970s. We started to live in chosen smaller groups even if we worked somewhere else. That helped because we had time to work out some of the wrinkles that happened.

But I think another thing that was very hard for me in the '70s was the excessive attention or driven-ness in our community about work. We are a German community. Once when I was taking a course in opera, our teacher said, "To understand opera, you have to know this." He brought a chair out in the front and he said, "All right, now here's a chair," and it was a wooden chair. He said, "This chair with the carved legs that looks really nice, that's French. Then he said, "Does anybody have a cushion? And now you've got a good Italian chair. You get rid of all that and you have the wooden chair. That is German." So it is kind of a tough look at life. It's rooted in our community. We're getting better but it is a kind of thing where work could eat us up.

And in the '70s I became very aware of that and I wanted more prayer time and it was a real effort to carve that time out of my life without other people frowning on my efforts. I couldn't imagine if anyone didn't even know that I was doing it. But I would take my calendar and mark off an hour maybe here and an hour there and maybe get spiritual direction and do things that were for my soul and that was really difficult, because I felt more and more that time for contemplation was what my vows were really about. And, certainly, I was in service to the community, but it took me a long time to work that out and to keep on saying that obedience goes this way as well—obedience to my heart as well. Obedience has been a very different call for me when I first made that vow.

Q: When you renew your vows, is it the same as your vows of profession?

TS: Because the vows are to the community, you don't necessarily do personal vows. When we renew our vows, it's kind of a formula and we don't say the same words we say in our profession. It's more that we want to spend our lives in service to God through the community and the world, that's the essence of it. Our vows contain stability, conversion of life, and obedience. That is a good way of looking at it because it is in God's hands and it is for us to be receivers and givers, but the initiative is always God's.

TS: Let's close by singing from Psalm 133. It says, "Behold, how good and how happy it is wherever people [indicates that she changed it to "people" from "men"] live as one." That's an aspect of vows that I've often thought about. One of the monks here is an anthropologist and doing some work. I don't know if I can tell you clearly, but he is seeing less and less gender issues, especially in monastics and he is doing a lot of work on that. The monastic call doesn't wipe it out, but it just brings, I suppose in Jungian sense you'd say individuation. We become more complete, also in the integration of masculine and feminine energies.

(Begins singing and teaching the song to everyone.)

The way I was taught chant, everything had a meaning. *"Ecce quam bonum et quam jucundum"*—"Behold how good and pleasant it is for brethren to dwell together in unity"—would be the kind of narrative where it's just one note on every syllable. The most important is that we live as one. Two notes make it more important than the syllable with the one note. So, we are celebrating that and then *unum* comes together as one. *Unum* is the home note. We could sing this little psalm with the same melody as what is on top if you would like to. We could just sing the first two lines and the last two lines because the middle part is so culturally rooted that it might not mean much to us. So, let's go to "… how good it is, how wonderful, wherever people live as one. There God gives blessing, life forevermore." Amen.

· TWENTY ·

Preparing for Vows

NYONE CAN PURSUE a monastic life without vows or institutional authorization, and many have done so throughout history.
Today people from all religions and professions live as invisible
monks, practicing the hidden vocation that is the same as that of the
professed: to dwell in the Divine Presence through a life of prayer, self-
honesty, and inner solitude.[1]

In fact, the traditional monk living in a monastery often is the most
aware of and vocal about passing over to a phase of life that is beyond
identity and religious norms. Perhaps due to the years of struggle to
plant hope in the dry soil of one's faith, or to quell doubts that surface
over one's ascetic vocation, elder monks who have given their will over
to Mystery realize that ritual, deprivation, obedience, vows, etc., are no
longer needed and may, indeed, be an impediment to their final passage
of holy freedom.

Because too few of my contemporaries have had the benefit of
spending time in prayer, spiritual discussion, study of sacred texts, and
communal life, the desire to strive with others toward a nontraditional
monastic commitment has increased across the globe, and has demonstrated that such communities can provide the foundational stability for
a new and meaningful way of life. In many cases, seekers also want to
take vows in a ceremony of profession. This rite becomes a significant

262

declaration to self and also to others that the central focus of the new monk's life is devotion to God.

The act of commitment yields positive effects on the person's inner life, opening a deeper connection with the Divine centered in one's heart. In the process, it can unmask layers of culturally imposed feelings of unworthiness, fear, betrayal, or rejection as well. This is because the admission of one's longing for God touches on the conflict between the purely secular and the sacred that exists in many of us. The disjuncture can be especially stark or real in people from technologically advanced societies, where rationality and material purchase are held in high regard at the expense of the soul.

The years of study and practice one gives to the important event of monastic profession frequently reveal painful feelings of being an outsider in the dominant culture. The status of "one who does not belong" sensitizes initiates to mend interior division and to reclaim one's original union with the entire web of creation in a holy bond. This healing is profound and deep. It touches the core of self-identity. It restores whatever denies, harms, or steals a person's *imago dei* (divine image), and points the new monk toward re-claiming and integrating what has been lost. Thomas Merton on the inner struggle:

> The idea of a monastic vocation is something distinct from that of a "career." In a sense, you don't pick the monastic life, it picks you. In religious terms, this is expressed by saying that one believes oneself "called" by God to live a monastic life. Translated into ordinary language, this refers to a deep implosion which may even go against the grain of one's conscious inclinations. It entails a fight. There is a considerable amount of doubt and resistance, a great deal of questioning, and at times the whole thing seems absurd. Yet you have to push on with it. There is a sense of one's destiny and identity involved in the struggle.[2]

This assent is not purely about adopting a countercultural lifestyle. It is, as well, a critically important dimension of the monk's vow—the path of striving for a holier manner of being, to be like unto the Great

Spirit, the Messiah, and all the other Sacred Ones. Thomas Merton offers advice, with the "hope these few notes may be of some use":

> I would say that there is one basic idea that should be kept in mind in all the changes we make in life whether of career or anything else. We should decide not in view of better pay, higher rank, "getting ahead," but in view of becoming *more real,* entering more authentically into direct contact with life, living more as a free and mature human person, able to give myself more to others, able to understand myself and the world better.[3]

The monastic journey truly begins with the desire to be "more real." It takes root when we allow the divine fire to burn in us. This solitary work digs at the causes of inner division, unhealthy attachment, and sin. It gives rise to self-knowledge and to the shadow of self-doubt that threatens the quest. This arduous work uncovers the wounded heart—and its projection of a false personal narrative. The willingness to lovingly embrace the distortion of our lives is the radical work of the monk, who seeks total inner transformation. But it is not easy, and some people succumb to simply being in the company of community, but not truly present or devoted to the arduous task of opening themselves more fully to the presence of the Divine, as it is expressed directly, as well as through others.

While people enter monasteries for a spectrum of reasons, the true center of the quest forever assents (writes Thomas Merton scholar, Ness Cannon) to an interior exploration in which monks:

> encounter not only their own heart, but the heart of mankind in which both grace and sin abound. Although they may be aware of the presence of God and the light of grace, they are also in contact with the darkness of sin and its destructive power in themselves, the world, and others. In some small measure, it is their mission to bring this darkness to the light of Christ [or one's Divine Source]. As a consequence of being a conscious meeting point of the light and darkness, monks seek reconciliation for themselves. In doing so, they become instruments of reconciliation for others. Theirs is a never-ending

task. The solitary journey into the center of their own heart becomes a journey into the center of mankind's darkened heart as they seek to discover the center of their true self where they find God. In their journey, every arrival becomes another departure.[4]

For these reasons, during their final year community members are asked to intensify study of monastic life, submit reflection papers, pray our communal liturgy, sit in meditation, schedule days of solitude, and dialogue with their spiritual mentor in discerning the call to monastic profession. This is the period of contemplative communion, to address concerns and fears, and to listen and respond to the Divine voice. *Is this where you are calling me, Holy One?* In particular, an important aspect of preparing for monastic profession is to reflect on the rules and vows of traditional monastic communities, paying attention to those that reso-nate with and are or are not supportive of your inner life.

Participants in our formation process bring a variety of religious and non-religious backgrounds—Jewish, Protestant, Catholic, Buddhist, Hindu, Indigenous, spiritual but not religious, etc.—to communal study, providing a rich foundation for interspiritual dialogue. I've learned from this shared wisdom that the Holy One has a vow and a rule of life unique to every person. In our community, seekers are called to listen for and pray about their vows. While we do have a common community vow, no one takes the same set of personal vows, because each must find what he or she can—with a full heart—profess.

As a movement of the Spirit, a vow is an expression of the heart's deep longing. In a similar way that people vow to be faithful to spouse or partner, the monk vows fidelity to the Divine. In essence, fidelity to God expresses the integrity of one's fidelity to self, and to one's commitment. Many questions surface when we seriously consider what it means to be faithful to monastic vows. Never in this life is a vow absolute. We are always beings "on the way." We will never achieve absolute obedience or absolute charity. The work of the monk is to strive to fulfill the gifts of the Spirit, with ardent and peaceful desire. All we can do is offer our whole being to the quest. Taking vows is a response of gratitude for all that we have been given.

Glimpse of a Ceremony

THERE ARE VARIOUS ways of professing vows, and every tradition has its unique ritual. In our ceremony of profession, the new monk can choose to read his or her vows, followed by acceptance from the community leader. Likewise, that person may prefer to have the vows read, responding, "I am."

What follows is a portion of a ceremony of profession that focuses on the formal taking of vows. This selection is a compilation of personal vows written by members of our monastic community in the form of responding, "I am." The order and content of the ritual draws on many elements of Benedictine monasticism, due to our association with and learning from Sr. Theresa. Naturally, sacred ceremonies from the world's religions will speak to you and inspire the creation of a ritual of profession that is most suited to your spiritual orientation, and your community. It is my hope that what is shared below will assist you to consider and write personal vows, and a ceremony of profession.

All Stand: Officiant leads the Call

Leader: _____ , what do you ask of God and of this community of brothers and sisters?

Monk: I ask to make lifelong profession to the heart of the universal monastic vocation.

Leader: The essence of monastic life is to seek God with an openness that expands our hearts and frees us to be transformed day by day in God's love. By sharing deeply our sorrows and joys, our hopes and fear, and our longing for Divine life, we are called to a continual striving to become lost in Her. Are you willing to commit yourself to this promise of conversion of life?

Monk: I am.

Leader: With unspeakable love we are called daily to listen and respond to the revelation of the Divine in silence and in word. We know that it is to the Divine that we must give our heart. Are you willing to listen to the Spirit speaking through others? Are you willing to commit yourself to the abandonment of your will to live by God's will?

Monk: I am.

Leader: Understanding that the monastic life requires us to continually discern the true from the false, the necessary from the unnecessary, the sacred call from the daily distractions, are you willing to vow yourself to a singular purpose—to live a life of simplicity and purity of heart?

Monk: I am.

Leader: Aware that in the unending process of conversion, the spirit continually remakes us in the Holy imprint of the Divine Heart, are you willing to live devoted to your sacred practice and to answer your sacred call?

Monk: I am.

Leader: Are you willing to vow to put God at the center of your life, to cultivate the virtue of emptiness of spirit, to wade into the waters of transformation, and release yourself into the flow and current of Divine Love?

Monk: I am.

Leader: United by love and in awe of Divine Mercy, we recognize that faithfulness to the monastic way of life continues the dialogue of liberation. By staying with the journey, our life becomes focused on a state of heart that sustains all our relations. Are you willing to commit to this promise of stability?

Monk: I am.

Leader: Increasingly aware of the manner and measure of the oneness of creation we pay homage to the Earth, all of God's creatures, and our human relations. We are called to respond with sensitivity and reverence. We know that our Creator excludes no one from the banquet of love or imposes a priority of person, religion, revelation, or creed. Are you willing to commit to this promise of compassion for all beings?

Monk: I am.

Leader: Knowing what a gift it is to have a living teacher and a community of devoted companions, are you willing to vow your loving support to your sisters and brothers on this path of a new monastic way, to be of service to your beloved community, and to live your life as an extension of benevolence and peace?

Monk: I am.

Leader: Sisters and Brothers, will you join me in acceptance and support of _____'s desire to share the monastic way of life?

Community: Yes, with joy we accept and support _____ in her/his journey to Divine life.

After the call-and-response portion of the ceremony of vows, the new monk signs his or her handwritten promises of vows, witnessed and signed by all attending monks.

New Monk and Leader chant as follows. All repeat.

"Sustain me, O God, as you have promised, and I shall live! Do not disappoint me in my hope."

The next part of the ritual involves the prostration of the monks, invocation of the Spirit, and the chanting of the Litany of Saints. The closing ritual follows.

Leader: Let us Pray
Community responds with, Amen.

Gracious God, look mercifully upon _____ . Grant her the gift of your Spirit as she seeks to live this monastic way of life. Amen

May she commune with the Earth and all creatures in a humble awareness of our relationship with God and all things. Amen

May she serve God with the good things she has been given. Amen

May she seek peace and nonviolence in thought, word, and deed. Amen

May she be patient and steadfast in time of trial. Amen

May she be faithful in prayer and attentive to the presence of God in all of creation and all of life. Amen

May she support her sisters and brothers in mutual love and esteem. Amen

May she walk in the tradition of monastic women and men who have gone before her. Amen

May her family and friends and all who support her be blessed. Amen

May those with whom she shares her life, and all those who have shared life with her, be blessed. Amen

Ever-loving God, Divine Mother and Father of us all, accept our prayers and all our lives. Amen

Now the community blesses the rings and, being placed on each hand, all recite:

May this ring be a pledge of steadfast love and a sign of your commitment to the monastic way of life.

Reading:
Magnificat of Acceptance   Luke 1:38

> My soul trembles in the presence of the loving Creator
>   and my spirit prepares itself to walk hand in hand
>   with God who saves us
>   because I have been accepted by God
>   as a simple helpmate.
> Yes, forever in my life
>   I will sing of this loving encounter;
>   through remembering this moment, we
>   will know all things are possible in God.
> Holy is the place within me where God lives.
> God's tender fingers reach out from age to age
>   to touch the softened spaces of those
>   who open their souls in hope.
> I have experienced the creative power of Her embracing arms
>   and I know the cleansing fire of unconditional love.
> I am freed from earthly authority
>   and I know my bonding to the Author of all earthly things.

Sign of Peace

Closing Prayer:
Loving Creator of the world and of all people, we honor you with praise and thanksgiving. Today, it is right that your house should echo with a new song of thanksgiving for this sister of ours who has listened to your voice and responded in faith and love.

We pray that in the freedom of her heart she may bring comfort to your people. May she look upon the world and see it ruled by your loving wisdom. May the gift she makes of herself hasten the coming of peace on Earth and make her one with you and your saints forever. Amen.

Final Blessing and Song.

TWENTY-ONE

Diksha and the Sannyasin

O N THE EVE OF THE CEREMONY of profession, I addressed the gathered community as we shared our commitment and hopes for the future. What follows is a transcription of my talk from July 24, 2015.

EVERY RELIGION honors sacred time, when the world stops to rest, and our hearts are given over to being in God's time. This is living in the spirit, listening to the intonation of our Creator, of our universe. Following our natural rhythm, we are joined with the rhythm of the cosmos. This is medicine for the soul.

Sacred time is that intensified period that erupts into our daily lives and is dedicated to the holy. The traditional monk is supported by the community's rule to leave behind ordinary time and to live according to the spirit. This is why, for example, in Christian monasteries the monks chant the liturgy of the hours, following a horarium—a sacred liturgy that sanctifies the day.

How much of your day, week, or life have you given over to God's time?

These days in preparation for taking monastic vows form a fulcrum, or an intensified center of energy. There is a concentration and heightening of the Divine Presence. Today, of all days, is a time to let yourself be holy, to be thankful for the gift of devoting your life to the Divine, and to honoring the Spirit on Earth.

I thought, in the context of your monastic profession and what this commitment means, it would be helpful to learn about the monastic tradition in India, especially the initiation ceremony ("diksha" in Sanskrit) of the sannyasis (renunciates). In particular, I will concentrate on how Hindus understand the role of the guru, the symbolism of the sannyasa initiation, and the giving of sacred gifts, including shawls, prayer beads, and the like.

The Sanskrit word, "diksha," comes from the word "disk," which means to dedicate oneself, and is actually the combination of two roots—to consecrate and dedicate, and to grow and expand. Therefore, diksha means to expand one's consciousness through a process of deification and dedicating oneself to Brahman. Diksha is the gateway into the transformation of self, which is activated in the initiation ceremony by the intensification of divine presence that occurs. These elements in monastic formation—transformation of self and conversion of life—are common across religious traditions.

The English equivalent of the word, diksha, is initiation, which includes not only the formal ceremony of initiation, but also the more subtle energies of transmission. In Latin, the word for diksha is *sacramentum*—"that which binds." It is a binding of the deep self to God, and therefore has the same meaning as sacrament. Thus, in Roman Catholic monasticism, a vow is a sacrament.

Swami Satyananda Saraswati (1923-2009)—Indian sannyasin, yoga teacher, and guru—compares initiation or diksha to an extra burst of energy that is required to propel the seeker into the infinite space between the personality and the true self. In Hinduism, this transmission is called *shaktipat*, which can occur through teaching, ceremony, and study. The transmission of energy from guru to disciple is not merely in words, but is the living spirit emanating from the elder, entering into the soul of the seeker, transforming his or her being by an act of love, faith, and divine intervention. In the Hindu tradition, as you well know, the relationship between the disciple and the guru is considered sacred, because transmission from an authentic elder carries the energy of the divine and has transformative power. The deepening of the contemplative life occurs through self-emptying, and giving away of extraneous personal baggage, which increases the guru's capacity to transmit divine energy.

Diksha also means to see, and thereby to see the golden path of the inner life. It makes the spiritual path visible and directs our life journey toward that interior goal. For example, what does it mean to see the inner light in another person? It is not just reacting to the personality but seeking the longing of another soul's quest for authenticity. The role of the monastic elder—or guru—is to see into the heart of others and to empower and inspire them to be their true selves—to leave behind their false personality.

The word "guru" in Sanskrit means the "one who removes darkness," and also one who breathes light into the devotee. According to yogic terminology, darkness means ignorance and ignorance exists only in the mind. It is the mind that separates the disciple from the guru, and the foundation of the mind is the ego. It is the guru's duty to find ways and means to whittle away the disciple's ego, and it is the disciple's duty to allow this to happen without complaining too much.

In Hinduism, Brahman is the first guru. The power of diksha descends from Brahman (God) to the guru, and through each lineage. Even though each lineage is distinct, ultimately all the lineages return to Brahman. In the ceremony of diksha, energy comes from heaven, down the line of the gurus, into the new initiate. It is this link between God (the first guru), through the embodiment of the historical guru, that activates the energetic and ontological transformation of the devotee.

It is also the guru's duty to discern the disciple's karma, and to find a way that karma can be exhausted and one's inner light can shine through. One of the ways the guru works on the disciple's ego and karma is through the community life of the ashram. Living among other monks, dealing with diverse personalities and habits, challenges each aspirant to become more compassionate, considerate, and loving. There is a kind of "method to the madness" of community life and, typically, at least in Christian monasticism, even those members who are more reclusive are usually required to live in community for a certain amount of time before being allowed to live as hermits. Swami Satyananda has said:

I don't like ashrams, but they are absolutely necessary for a stage in our spiritual life because they provide the discipline required for training the mind. In the early stages, beginners often find ashram life like a jungle, a type of survival of the fittest. One gets into constant conflict with responsibility, the areas of communication, and the lines of authority. . . . It is only in adverse circumstances that we come to terms with our emotions, and so begin making the right choices to control our lives.[1]

Community life requires an expanded awareness of personal foibles. As we express our anger, jealousy, or resentment in community, we find others expressing emotion also. Next, we realize that negativity is not helping us or anyone else, and we try to stop these disruptions. We may take a break, go for a walk, chant our mantra, or analyze the situation. During this stage, we see that despite having this unfortunate aspect in our nature, our guru accepts us. This is simply because the guru's relationship with disciples is not based on emotions or personality. The guru is not looking at foibles, but instead seeks God within each person.

In the next stage of the Hindu path, disciples realize how unworthy they are. They wonder how the guru can bother to spend so much time extricating them from detrimental conditions. The penultimate state is when initiates have inner recognition and not just intellectual understanding of the greatness of the guru and the greatness of God. They understand the concept of grace and develop inner gratitude that is beyond words. When the aspirant has reached inner gratitude, he or she works willingly with the movement of the spirit and not against it as before. Even if there is friction, the aspirant accepts his or herself more and realizes that the guru always has been accepting of him or her.

According to the sannyasin tradition, the process of transforming one's karma is dependent upon the development of four essential qualities: discrimination, detachment, endurance, and balance.

Discrimination provides "right understanding" in any situation. It is the slowing down of action and speech, as you differentiate between the right and wrong way of looking at a situation. The slowing-down process that discrimination requires prevents reacting to life's conditions. When the heart is wounded, we react and it is difficult to control emotions. When the heart is healed, we can be responsible and discriminating. Thus, discrimination is one of the four pillars of the sannyasin (renunciate).

Detachment provides emotional distance between you and whatever is happening around you. Thus, one is not so easily influenced or affected by persons and situations. We might imagine detachment as seeking refuge in one's inner monastery. That is, deepen your contemplative life, stabilizing in the cave of the heart, the divine within. The more you rest in the cave of the heart, the more able you are to maintain balance and equanimity in difficult situations. You become calm and peaceful. The physical and emotional senses quiet. You are not as interested in worldly activities as before. At the same time, the disciple does not criticize worldly and sensual activities because just a short while ago he or she was attracted to them as well.

Endurance is developed through detachment and discrimination. Faith deepens. You are more balanced. Whether we are praised or not praised, we have to learn to maintain equanimity. Whether people understand us or don't understand us, we must develop the resilience and strength to push through. Endurance is a quality of the heart, which is able to withstand the rigors of growing in spirit and the challenge of living in the world.

Balance assesses every life situation from a higher, spiritual perspective. We must evaluate praise or criticism without the intellect intervening, causing us to be puffed up or fight back. According to the sannyasin tradition, there are nine different kinds of pride, starting from physical pride and ending with spiritual pride. These are very difficult to shake off. When we are praised we like it, when we are not praised we dislike it. It is our liking and disliking that creates natural imbalance.

To these four qualities of consciousness, I add "**prophetic pathos.**" While the Asian traditions, in particular, have developed significant practices of equanimity and spiritual detachment, there is wisdom in the prophetic voice emphasized in the Abrahamic religions.

The prophet is one who is overcome with divine pathos, who feels and speaks God's suffering. In order to be a prophetic voice, we need the attributes of discrimination, detachment, balance, and endurance. An angry or violent voice is not a prophetic voice. The prophetic voice loves and suffers with the world. Thus, a monk in the world needs to achieve inner balance, because he or she feels with compassion, and bears the injury to life.

The monk gives his or her life to the divine pursuit. The sensitive person cannot help but feel the world's pain. Thus, prayer, meditation, discrimination, and detachment provide the necessary grounding and discipline to face the injustices and cruelties of life on Earth. Without spiritual techniques, it is easy to become angry, imbalanced, bereft, and disenfranchised.

These five attributes—discrimination, detachment, endurance, balance, and prophetic pathos—lead to purification of self, and greater desire for liberation. It is only when the sannyasin has managed to control the senses and develop discrimination that he or she is ready to serve humanity. If the Hindu monastic seeks to serve humanity before developing these qualities, it is understood to be a subtle form of ego at work. A person without awareness thinks, *How nice it is that the monk wants to serve humanity.* The spiritually wise person knows differently. If we try to serve humanity without developing these qualities, we are putting ourselves in the position of superiority. But when the desire to serve humanity comes from harnessing of one's consciousness, it is with humility. The great lesson is that the ego always seeks its satisfaction; it fabricates its web of lies and arguments to prevent the opening of the heart. It is only when one's ego is properly whittled away that the disciple can serve humanity genuinely and eventually become a guru to others. Swami Sivananda Saraswati clarifies the state of humility of the true elder:

I had no ambition to become world famous by any extensive tour or thrilling lectures from the platform. I never attempted to be a guru to anyone. Even before donkeys and other animals, I do mental prostrations. To my disciples and devotees, I first do namaskara. I behold the essence behind all names and forms. That is real Vedanta in daily life.[2]

The Hindu sage Swami Gyanbhikshu Saraswati also reflects on the necessity of surrender in the guru-disciple relationship:

He alone can know you, to whom you make yourself known; and the moment he knows you, he becomes one with you. It is only by your [the guru's] grace that your devotees come to know you.[3]

This is the principle of the guru-disciple relationship. One may be surrendered or empty, but she or he alone can know you to whom you make yourself known. If you don't open yourself to the guru, you will never know the guru and the guru can't know you. Surrender, thus, indicates the opening of the heart, a heart devoid of protection. The moment you are known, you become one with the one whom you know. This is the essence of mystical union or intimacy. In high states of contemplation, the divine opens one's being, and the seeker is known by the all-knowing and the all-knowing knows the seeker.

Every aspect of spiritual growth is related to this important realization. If you pray to open the heart, your life will change. You ask: "What am I protecting? Why don't I want to be known? What do I think is so bad about me that I can't let anyone see?' If you let yourself be known, this is enlightenment. This is sainthood: not hiding, not claiming greatness, simply to be.

We know through grace. Grace cannot be claimed; it is not even deserved. It dawns upon us; it is showered upon the soul. How? Nobody knows, says the guru. It is the secret of the sannyasin. It is the secret of all secrets. And even though grace is a mystery, the guru's purpose is to help the disciple in his or her quest to be known.

We should pray for the courage to be known by the all-knowing, and to welcome each other in our true essence. Amen.

Sacred Gifts

The Mala

DURING DIKSHA, the initiate is presented with sacred gifts from the guru. One gift is the mala, which is specially charged by the guru's spiritual energy. The mala is used for repetition of the mantra given by the guru and is never worn by anyone other than the initiate. It is kept carefully and reverentially in a specially made bag and placed in the *sadhana*, the area designated for spiritual practice—prayer room, altar, or another holy place.

The English equivalent of the word, "mala," is rosary or prayer beads, which many spiritual traditions use for meditation and the repetition of prayers. In the yogic tradition, the *sadhus*, or spiritual seekers, hold that each type of material that is used in a mala has a particular vibration, which can bring about a peaceful and positive state of mind. Therefore, malas are made of various materials, each with its own energy: wood, crystals, flowers, plants, or metal.

A prayer is said on each bead of the mala, which prevents the practitioner from introverting too quickly, allowing him or her to slowly progress through the transformation of energies. Yogic gurus hold that it can be difficult to handle the transformative experiences—visions, illuminations, loss of ego, and breakdown of resistance—that occur in a spiritual life if they happen too quickly. Prayer beads, thus, are a sacred vehicle that facilitates the steady movement into the divine.

The mala also is used to break the monotony of concentration, so you do not lose your awareness while repeating the prayer. Rather, the attitude of witnessing is to be maintained. At the end of the mala is a tassel. When you come to the tassel, the awareness is alerted, and you have to turn around and start the mala once more. Ideally, while praying with the mala, one should be neither fully introverted nor extroverted, but between the two, in that slightly detached place of centering.

With constant practice, the mala will become powerfully charged and, as soon as you take it in your hand, it will prepare your mind positively for commencing spiritual practice or sadhana.

The following represents a ceremony of the sacred gifts, performed on the aforementioned eve of vow taking.

I have brought each of you a gift of a mala that I have prayed over. Instead of my giving it to you, I would like you to take one.

Silence while malas are distributed

We are going to pray with them in a minute. These malas are from India, and inside the package is a description of the plant used to make this mala, which I will read:

The tulsi plant is also known as the holy basil. It is worshipped in Indian and Greek cultures. It has a tremendous medicinal value. Its leaves, wood, and even the air around it, are beneficial. It has been proved scientifically that the tulsi possesses qualities of killing harmful microorganisms. Likewise, malas made of tulsi wood are considered very suitable for meditation, because they eliminate the baser instincts, pacify minds of libidinous passions, enhance spiritual growth, fill the mind with Godliness, clear the aura, balance vatta and kapha doshas, and protect and aide in the pursuit of Bhakti Yoga, the yoga of devotion.

Let's take our mala out of its wrapping. In the sannyasin tradition, the guru gives the disciple or the person taking initiation a mantra—a sacred word. I will not be giving each person a mantra. Of course, if you already have a mantra or a sacred word, it can be used with your mala.

What I thought we could do together is to pray excerpts from *"Prayer to Holy Sophia,"* in the booklet, reciting one line on each bead. So, *O Mother of Compassion, Blessed is your heart of pure love, source of all life,* is three beads. You start at the first bead after the bead on the tassel. Let's say it together.

All pray

Prayer to Holy Sophia

O Mother of Compassion
    Blessed is your heart of pure love,
        source of all life.

O Mother of Wisdom
    Radiant is your sacred teaching,
        known by the pure of heart.

O Mother of Sorrows
    You share in every wound,
        healing every suffering and sin.

O Mother of Light
    Who illuminates all realms
        with inexhaustible sweetness.

Formless, Dark Mercy
    Hidden is your power
    of wordless bliss
    You are the fountain of joy
        and the breath of benevolence.

Holy Sophia, Godhead of intimacy
    Within creation you dwell,
        longing for you alone.

Amen.

Another way to pray Holy Sophia with the mala is to say the first stanza, "*O Mother of Compassion, Blessed is your heart of pure love, source of all life,*" over and again for the entire length of the mala; or "*Blessed is your heart of pure love, your heart of pure love, your heart of pure love, Blessed is your heart of pure love …*" It is letting the words speak in and through you.

I pray this stanza during daily chores or walking down the street: *"Blessed is your heart of pure love, source of all life, Blessed is your heart of pure love, source of all life."* An easy way to stay focused is to wrap the mala around your wrist and take it with you wherever you go.

Praying the mala this way can release a mantra or sacred word. In the above example, one's mantra might be "Blessed is your pure heart," or "pure heart," or "heart," or "blessed."

I will give you a few minutes to pray silently.

Silence. Gong sounds

Don't forget that the mala is your gift, your sacred gift. It doesn't have to be shared. It can be kept in your prayer room or carried with you on your wrist or in the little pouch that comes with it.

After you receive monastic initiation tomorrow and return home, a special place can be prepared for spiritual practice. Ideally, the spiritual place should be a separate room where no one but the initiate enters. However, if this is not possible, a corner of a room can be kept for this purpose. The spiritual practitioner should keep the room or area clean, without intrusion or interference from other people. Through daily repetition of your mantra or prayer, the energy will build up and your room will become pervaded by the psychic vibration and spiritual sanctity of your practice.

Lighting incense or lighting a candle will help create the right atmosphere for meditation and will relax the mind. The chanting of prayers, hymns, and devotional psalms also has a very powerful effect. A chanting recording can be played. The mala or other spiritually charged objects like a shawl, a picture of a saint or guru, a statue, a cross, a special object from nature, and so forth, can also be kept there. This will help focus the mind and awaken the right attitude of the sadhana (spiritual practice).

In addition to the mala and mantra, another spiritual gift offered by the guru to the disciple is a spiritual name. I do not give a spiritual name, but—like the sannyasa tradition—I hold that the true name of every disciple is God. In Hinduism, this is Brahman, *sat-chit-ananda*—being, consciousness, and bliss. In other words, every name is God's name. Even though the disciple is given a particular name by the guru, that name is only the lower vibration of the disciple's ultimate name, which is *Atman*. If an elder has given you a name, or one comes to you through spirit or dream, that is wonderful. But, remember: your true name is *Tat tvam asi* (That art thou).

The Dhoti

In the diksha ceremony, along with the mala and the giving of a sacred name and mantra, the aspirant is presented with a dhoti, which is an unstitched cloth. Like the mala, it is considered to be a sacred gift from the divine hand of the guru and kept clean and carefully in the place of one's spiritual practice. Ideally it should be worn only at the time of spiritual practice to maintain its heightened vibration. The dhoti, like the mala, will become charged with your spiritual energy, and as soon as you put it on it will have a peaceful and soothing effect on your mind. It will also remind you of your spiritual identity and true purpose.

The Vedic and yogic traditions of Hinduism also assign differing meanings to the various colors of the dhotis, but one of the most common is white. White represents purity. The novice or the householder, student, or one involved in society and worldly life, wears white, which represents sincerity and earnestness of desire to know the spiritual truths. When you take diksha, you are embarking on a new beginning, like a white sheet of paper on which nothing has yet been written. So you are presented with white cloth. The guru has given you your first initiation. What you write upon it is up to you.

Traditionally, the dhoti is given to the disciple this way: it is folded lengthwise, with the opening toward the person to indicate the open heart of the giver, and the open heart of the recipient.

I also have a white cloth or dhoti for you. If you wish, you can wear yours for the ceremony of monastic profession. As each dhoti is gifted, let us bow to each other, as they do in tradition.

Silence as dhotis are given to each person

Let us recite this Buddhist prayer three times: "May our bodies be transformed into wish-fulfilling jewels."

May our bodies be transformed into wish-fulfilling jewels.
May our bodies be transformed into wish-fulfilling jewels.
May our bodies be transformed into wish-fulfilling jewels.

Let us together chant a Hindu mantra of peace.

Asatoma sadgamaya
Tamasoma jyotirgamaya
Mrityorma amritam gamaya
Om shanti, shanti, shanti

From ignorance, lead me to truth
From darkness, lead me to light
From death, lead me to immorality
Om peace, peace, peace.

TWENTY-TWO

Rule of Life

I NTRINSIC TO MONASTIC community is a rule of life, or code of
conduct by which the adherents live out their vows, grow in spiritual
depth, and preserve the community. Generally, codes or precepts
governing a monastic lifeform develop organically, from the illuminated
spiritual intent of those seeking the narrow path. Over time, like other
human endeavors, they are susceptible to becoming bogged down in
legalistic interpretation and strict adherence. Then a community or
practice can lose its spiritual life force, become rigid and suffer from a
lack of creativity.

A monastic rule is designed to transform lifelong habits that take us
away from true happiness, and to provide a guideline or anchor to what
is more real, more essential. For the monk, temporal goods of whatever
kind are not permanent representations of happiness. I'm sure that most
people have expressed these concerns: "I purchased this thing, it's nice
but now I want something new." Or, "Now I have a certain spiritual
understanding but it's not taking me anywhere. I still feel unsettled, I
still feel fragmented. I need to try something else."

Spiritually, these mental menaces indicate two things: 1) happiness
is not fulfilled by temporal pleasures or material objects, and 2) something deeper is needed, even beyond spiritual knowledge. Liberation or
enlightenment, or even simple contentment is not sustained by accom-

plishing everything you ever hoped for. Something within is drawing you toward a deeper kind of happiness, one that comes only from the sacred.

Thus, monasteries promote creative monotony that structures a monk's life around activities of prayer, charity, meditation, solitude, ritual, asceticism, silence, and obedience. This daily repetition is intended to reconnect monks with simplicity of heart and teach them how to live in the spirit's rhythm.

The monk's vocation, if you will, is to challenge the prediction that you will never know your true self, and that you always will be separate from your Source. Monasticism—taking of vows, living a rule of life—is radical. It reminds us over and over again that this world is both a veil obscuring and a window into the realm of the holy. For this reason, monastic life requires audacity and courage, and the full surrender of one's heart. It is a way of being that seeks the triumph of freedom.

If vows are the means by which we live out our love of the divine, the monastic rule assists us on the journey. It is the map we follow to become more grateful, receptive, and humble. Monastic rules also are described as codes of conduct, ideals, or standards of behavior to ensure the stability of the community. The variety and scope of monastic wisdom eludes facile summary.[1]

A Rule of Living Conduct

OVER THE YEARS, I have composed and followed a personal rule of life. I include below excerpts from the original and longer rule, which you may find helpful in writing and living your own code of conduct.

1. Be faithful to the Divine in all that you do. Put the Divine will before your own. Ask, "What would God do?" and wait for the answer. Do not allow personal attraction or gain to cloud decision-making, or your soul's intentions to be compromised.

2. Be simple of purpose. The basis of simplicity is centering on God. The heart of the monastic life is to live in God's presence.

3. Love all of creation with Divine compassion. Total commitment brings change. Give to life your unparalleled commitment, and complete love, one that is without self-interest.

4. Offer yourself as a place of prayer. May your presence be one that heals divisions and expands hearts.

5. Be attuned to the splendor of creation, and the gentle web of existence. Celebrate embodiment. Actively work—both within yourself and in the world—to make the holy manifest.

6. Refrain from possession. Remember the transient nature of earthly life. Possession can occur on all levels: physical, emotional, psychic, spiritual. Love expands the spirit, possession contracts it.

7. Pray daily to grow in humility, and to be empty of the false self. Offer over to the Divine your regrets, sorrows, doubts, motives, and unresolved desires.

8. In all you do, practice nonharm. Make a small footprint, tread lightly, become aware of the impact your actions have on others. The refusal to reflect on your motives leads to suffering (for others and also one's self).

9. Treat all religions and spiritual paths with honor and respect. Enter silence. Keep faith alive.

10. Create community wherever you are. Make of your heart a home for the homeless, a refuge for the poor. Pray for the well-being of your monastic sisters and brothers.

TWENTY-THREE

Make My Life a Vow
(A Meditation)

Let us connect to the earth beneath us,
    to the moist, fragrant soil,
    the beauty of trees and birds and flowers
    that adorn our world.
May our living monks of nature embrace us in silence.
May we hear creation whispering solitude in our hearts.
May we feel the blessing of the waters, of the mountains.
May we hear the song of praise that each living being offers
    to its creator.
May all the joyous serenity that surrounds us anoint our souls.
    Breathing in and Breathing out,
Receiving the Earth's invigorating energy into our bodies.
    Breathing in and Breathing out.
Lifting our hearts to the light, to sky, to angels, and
    to the circle of divine beings watching over us,
    Breathing in and Breathing out,
May we give away all that troubles, distracts,
    and prevents surrendering ourselves to God.
    Breathing in and Breathing out.

Imagine a little altar illuminating your inner vision.
Gently place your mystical heart on the altar.
Feel the Holy Ones wash away sorrow, fear, and pain.
Listen to the words your mystical heart speaks.
What does it say?
    Breathing in and Breathing out,
    Breathing in and Breathing out.
Now lift your mystical heart so gently and enclose it in your body,
as it fills your entire being with Light.
    Breathing in and Breathing out,
    Breathing in and Breathing out.
Silently, let us pray: *Make My Life a Vow*
Together, quietly aloud, let us pray: *Make My Life a Vow*
    Make My Life a Vow.

O Divine Mother, for all who are gathered here today,
    show us the way of peace and mercy,
    the way of unconditional love,
    the way of silence
    that our hearts may be one with your beloved heart
    and our monastic vows may bring joy to you
    and to all sentient beings.   Amen

PART FIVE

Spiritual Exercises

❖

The person called to live as a new monk in the world benefits from the assistance of spiritual practices, among them meditation exercises, journal reflections, daily prayer, and a monastic schedule. The chapters that follow offer a series of practices that I have found effective for anyone wishing to deepen his or her contemplative vocation and for those who are preparing for monastic vows.

❖

TWENTY-FOUR

Meditation Exercises

T HE HUMAN BODY, along with every form of life on our planet, is composed of interdependent physical and spiritual or energetic bodies. Recognition of one's spiritual body and how it is constantly in dialogue and coextensive with the human physical body is an important aspect of contemplative development. The spiritual body (often referred to as the universal energy field) functions at a higher frequency than the human body. The soul's spiritual faculties—visionary, intuitive, empathic, knowing, etc.—are related to and interact with the physical body's senses—sight, smell, touch, hearing, taste. The vital, primordial interaction of spiritual and physical is often brought into conscious awareness by experiences of awe or mystical insight. It is not uncommon for seekers to have previously had awareness of the visionary worlds beyond the range of normal consciousness.

The maintenance of energy integrity ideally should be part of everyone's education and is especially significant for people devoted to spiritual growth. Meditation and other energy practices help to center the body-mind-spirit in its inner field of knowing and preserve the person's bio-spiritual integrity.

Included in this chapter are meditative exercises and energy practices I have shared over the years. They are by no means original or exhaustive, and I am sure you could add many to this list from your experience and spiritual background. The practices outlined below assume an understanding of basic meditation, which entails awareness of the breath, centering the self, quieting mind chatter, and openness to receive. They can easily be followed on own's own. Or, even more effective, is to practice in a group setting where a member reads and guides the session.

Foundation Exercises

Centering Your Attention

Sit in a meditative pose. For some of you this may entail finding a comfortable straight-backed chair and placing your feet flat on the floor with hands loosely in your lap. For others, you may feel more comfortable sitting on the floor, in a cross-legged posture, or seated on a Zen meditation cushion. The important point is to find a posture that is conducive to attention and that is sufficiently comfortable.

Begin by breathing in and out with awareness of your breath. Follow the breath as it fills your lungs and as it is released through your nose. When I do this exercise, I concentrate on the energies that are coming up through my feet from the Earth, as well as the energies coming down from the Spirit through my head. I think of myself as a spiritual pump that takes in, mixes, and integrates the two energies.

Allow your whole being to center on your breath. As you breathe in and out, form one word or phrase that feels true to your spiritual life: Silence, Peace, Lord Shiva, Jesus, Allah, Love, God. Keep the word simple. As your mind wanders, gently bring your attention to the word and to your breath. Breathe in and out your sacred word. As the word is repeated with each breath, allow it to fill your whole being. When there is no longer a separation between your breath and the word, you become the divine flow.[1]

Earth Meditation

Sit in a meditative pose. Feel your connection to the Earth and how you and all creatures are sustained in physical reality. Feel your energy connected to the ground, to the trees, flowers, cacti, rabbits, deer, coyote.

At the same time, you are open to the inflow of every living creature. As you breathe in and out, breathe in the Earth's loving energies. Breathe out your love for creation. As you breathe in and out, sit very straight and be centered in your heart.

Evoke one place in nature where you find solace and are at home. Let gratitude fill you. As you feel the healing energies enter your body, of water, sky, mountains, meadows, etc., ask yourself how you would live if you were truly thankful for the natural world's bountiful gifts. Breathe in and let the energy of gratefulness permeate your whole being. Breathe out.

Now turn your attention to your heart. Find the divine flame that is your monastic heart. Where does it dwell? Let the flame in your monastic heart fill your whole body and embrace you in warmth. Let the light expand out to fill the entire room, then expand into the natural world around you. Slowly and gently bring the light back into your heart, back into your body, and remember the glow of divinity within.

When you are ready, open your eyes and gently take several breaths, maintaining the sense of peace.

Meditation of Longing

Sit in a meditative pose. Take as long as you need to meditate in solitude. Feel the silence entering your body, cells, mind, and heart. Breathe in silence. Now focus on the spiritual heart. Gather all the energies up from the heart and let your whole being long for communion with the Divine Mystery. Be in the presence of this longing. Let the longing fill you. Feel that the Divine is also longing for you. Allow the silence at the source of your being to anoint you with peace. Rest your whole being in that place.

Practices of Energy Integrity

THE REMAINDER of this chapter describes meditative practices that I have found to be effective in opening our minds and hearts to the multisensory world and its relationship to self-understanding and the contemplative quest. The important element here is that practices that train us to be aware of our energy also serve to reinforce and preserve the intent of a monastic enclosure. That is, to protect the holy within us, guarding the integrity of our communion with God from unwanted intrusion.

While the practices initially may appear rudimentary or naïve, I encourage you to try them. Energy exercises are not an end in themselves; in fact, over time they simply become part of business as usual, the way that the person *is*, daily. They are tools to remind us of the importance of spiritual training in opening our hearts and minds to the Real beyond everyday reality. Of course, there are many, many practices that are equally effective that you may already use and find more suitable.

The language of Asian religions used to describe the human energy field has become general knowledge in the West, especially in acupuncture, ayurvedic medicine, and tai chi. These include, among others, the following terms: chakras, auras, meridians, doshas, and chi. The most well-known, and the ones I concentrate on in the descriptions below, are auras and chakras.

Aura: Human Energy Field

The human energy field is a manifestation of universal energy in the human body. It is a luminous body that surrounds and interpenetrates the physical body, emits its own characteristic radiation, and is usually called the "aura." The auric field is often depicted as layers of energy composed of increasingly finer vibrations than the physical body. We each have the capacity of *seeing* these layers of light radiating from sentient beings, and the invisible world around us. Sometimes the radiations are of different colors; sometimes transparent light. They convey a living universe that provides knowledge concerning the emotional, physical, and spiritual health of the physical body—whether human, animal, plant, etc. The higher vibrational oscillation of these concentric energy bodies is constantly communicating divinity into the world. That is, they are forces of light that animate the physical form and transmit information about its balance or imbalance. Generally, when radiations are clear, transparent light, the auric field is healthy and unimpeded, but if there are opaque or even dense, impenetrable areas of light, it is blocked or possibly dis-eased.

Chakra: Energy Vortex

The word *chakra* is derived from the Sanskrit, meaning "wheel" or "turning." According to traditional Indian medicine, chakras are force centers or vortexes that concentrate, transform, and distribute the energy of the human astral body (bodies) to the physical form. They represent focal points where spirit and body connect and interpenetrate each other. These subtle energies are connected to the organs and metabolic systems of the physical body via seven or nine principle *chakras* along the spine. Other energetic pathways intersect with the chakra system into various meridians, acupuncture points, and locations of chi. Physical and spiritual practices move energies through the chakra system. One common description divides the chakras into seven vortexes:

First: Base of the spine
Second: Below the navel
Third: Solar Plexus (abdomen above belly button)
Fourth: Heart
Fifth: Throat
Sixth: Third Eye (center of forehead)
Seventh: Crown of the Head

PRACTICE 1: Energy Balancing Meditation

This practice aims to both balance and raise energy. It involves a rhythmic pulsation of Earth and Sky energies through the chakras and the spinal column.

Sit in a straight-backed chair. Place your feet (preferably bare) on the floor. Hands in the lap, palms up. Breathing is from solar plexus. Visualize as you breathe in through the nose and out through the mouth:

Deep breath in,
drawing energy up from the Earth through the soles of the feet, up
the legs, and to the base of the spine (first chakra).

Deep breath out,
simultaneously drawing energy down from the Sky through the top
of the head (crown chakra), down the spinal column, meeting the
Earth energy at the first chakra.

Deep breath in,
simultaneously mixing Sky and Earth energies,

Deep breath out,
simultaneously pumping both energies up the spinal column and
releasing out the top of the head.

Repeat.

Initially, it can be difficult to synchronize the movement of the in and
out breaths, and to feel the pulsating effects. A good way to begin is to
exaggerate the meditative instructions in a sequential manner, without
trying to simultaneously enact: Big breath in, visualize energy up, big
breath out, visualize energy down, etc. This step-by-step process will feel
awkward and contrived. But, as you practice, your breath will become
natural, synchronizing with the movement generated by the pulsation of
energies, and a natural rhythm will develop.

The purpose of the practice is to balance spiritual and earth energies
and to elevate the vibration of the human energy field. That is, the deep
breaths and the pumping action are designed to raise the body's vibration to an unobstructed clarity, free of personal motive or outcome. This
is learning how to *be* at the still point—nothingness or emptiness—letting go of perceived thoughts, feelings, and actions. It is also detachment,
equidistant from all positions.

A Note on the Spiritual Senses

WHEN WE WORK with the human energy field to restore our naturally endowed multisensory awareness, often we use the terms "visualize," "see," or "know." I've found that these instructions can be confusing and frustrating for people who report that they don't *see* anything. So, let's do an experiment with this exercise. If I say, "Visualize a red apple with a green stem," are you actually *visually seeing* in your mind's eye this apple? When I use the term "mind's eye," I mean your creative imagination. Seeing is associated with clairvoyance and the sixth chakra or Third Eye.

Or are you imaginatively *knowing* the red apple? Here, when asked to visualize the red apple, you would intuitively know or understand its apple-ness, but not see a *vision* of the apple via your Third Eye. The faculty of spiritual knowing may be more dominant in you than imaginative seeing. Spiritual knowing is a powerful intuitive sense and is not inferior to seeing in any way. Spiritual knowing is usually associated with the crown chakra, and intuitive, mystical insight.

Another spiritual sense is feeling or an empathic experience of the world around us. Empathic knowing is a subtle spiritual faculty that requires a finely tuned sense of self and development of personal boundaries. This is important because spiritual feeling can be confused with emotions and cause disruption, especially in a body that is more attached to the physical and emotional realm. Sometimes the empathic faculty is called clairsentience, and is associated with the third chakra, located in the area of the solar plexus.

Frequently, one spiritual faculty is more dominant than another, for example, you may immediately *know* and then *see.* Or perhaps your primary mode is empathic feeling, which later you are able to integrate and cognitively understand. Not infrequently, our spiritual senses are used interchangeably or simultaneously, such as seeing and knowing, or knowing and feeling. Understanding how your spiritual senses operate is an important tool to become aware of how you intuit the energetic worlds, and your response to input from people and situations.

Practice this exercise. Place an idea in the creative imagination—maple tree in autumn, sunflower in full bloom, sailing on the bay. Can you identify your first response: is it seeing, knowing, or feeling? A combination?

Remember: The spiritual senses all operate on higher frequencies than the physical senses. This means that information about a situation, person, or the world around us is bombarding our spiritual faculties faster than our physical senses can process and bring those to conscious-ness. It is the vibrational training resulting from meditative constancy that attunes us to these subtle states of seeing, knowing, and feeling.

We All See—Visionary Knowing

To a greater or lesser degree, we all "see" each other. Even though we may hide, deceive, or deny, there is no ultimate escape from the ener-getic signatures of anger, fear, love, regret, etc. It is written on our faces, expressed through our voice, palpable in our auras. In some manner, we are attuned to the vibration of those around us. This is a type of clairvoy-ant knowledge housed in the sixth chakra and referred to as the Third Eye in many Asian texts.

Accepting that we do see into the world around us—however par-tially or imperfectly—is a first step in identifying how our being operates in the intersection of spiritual and physical space. It also can clarify the ways we pick up on the thoughts and feelings of the world around us. Through meditative exercises we learn to differentiate our universe of energy—including thoughts, emotions, beliefs—from those of family, friends, partners, colleagues, etc. Also important is that, through the practice of detachment and humility, we develop an inner certitude, based on humbleness and openness to gifts of the spirit. It is this willing-ness to see into the deep feelings and motivations of others that is the basis of compassion.

Try one or more of these exercises to develop your "seeing" faculty.

PRACTICE 1: Energy Flow Meditation

Once you feel that the Energy Balancing Meditation is stable, turn your attention to any impediments in the energetic flow. For example, you might notice difficulty visualizing and feeling the energy moving from your feet up the left (or right) leg. Similarly, this energetic block may extend up the spinal column or to an entire side of the body. Or, you may find no difficulty with energy until it reaches your solar plexus or heart chakra. It may require days or months of meditative sitting to loosen the stagnated energy, unblock that part of your body, and experience all fields flowing.

While practicing the Energy Balancing Meditation, conduct an energetic inventory. Is it unnerving or maddening to sit and practice "running" energy? Is there any part of your body or energetic field that is stagnant, blocked, or twitchy? What does the particular block reveal? Does it represent a physical injury? Emotional? Is the blocked energy of your own doing or the imposition of someone else's energy in your auric field? How will you tell the difference? Some people visualize that their energy is, say, violet, and energy that is not their own is, say, yellow.

PRACTICE 2: Aura Health Meditation

Related to Practice 1 (Energy Flow) is a meditation to check on the health and vibrancy of the aura. The spiritual body extends outside the physical body as a series or layers of lights of increasing vibration into multidimensional space. The colors and clarity of the aura—as well as its dynamism or stagnation—indicate varying degrees of spiritual health or imbalance. A person capable of reading auras may be attuned to subtle layers of meaning unseen by the physical eye. One practice is to become aware of one's auric balance and rhythm.

Sitting in meditation, visualize that your consciousness is looking at your body and aura from the corner of the ceiling (if you're outside, locate a tree or something similar). Do you "see" or "know" any dark areas? Any areas that have no movement? Any areas that appear hot or cold? Is your aura opaque? If so, where? What does this mean (or represent)?

Using your creative imagination, direct light into the opaque areas or generate movement in the stagnated places, transforming the vibration of the auric field.

PRACTICE 3: Energy Field Cleansing

A helpful spiritual exercise is to clear your energy field, preferably every time you meditate, but hopefully at least once a day. After you have spent a little time in sitting meditation, visualize bringing an intense, blazing blue fiery light (I think of this as the blue sapphire of the mind light) up from your feet, through your entire body and aura. As the light moves, it gathers up and burns away any energy that is blocking the transparency of the Divine light in us. Continue this process until your being is infused with the steadiness of the light, a more unified, golden-hued aura in and around you.

We All Know—Intuitive Knowing

BECAUSE SPIRITUAL KNOWING is more immediate and elusive than spiritual seeing, it is easy to dismiss insights that arrive in such a lightning-fast way. Are we imagining? We don't trust what we know. We have been taught to deny intuition. For example, a child who grows up in a household where painful truths are withheld learns to mistrust his or her inner knowing. The child may be punished or ridiculed for daring to notice the parents' pain, emotional hunger, or sorrow. Confusion settles into the child's systems of perception, until so much is dismissed that his or her natural and immediate faculty of knowing is suppressed or lost. The suppression of intuitive knowledge advances into adult lives, limiting the range of our capacity to create, feel, and be whole. These prohibitions are reinforced in patriarchal societies, where women are expected not to know what they know, and men are expected not to feel what they feel.

PRACTICE 1: Knowing Energy

Visualize a scene from a recent encounter with a colleague, family member, or friend where you were left with an uncomfortable, painful, or agitated feeling. Maybe your throat or jaw was tight, your head or stomach hurt, you were angry or regretful or resentful afterward. Review the exchange. Can you see or know or feel the energy being exchanged? Where did it make contact with your body? What did it do to your aura? Do the same exercise with a positive experience of love, friendship, or trust. How does your body react? When you remember this positive exchange, what does this feeling do to your spirits? As a result of this, what do you know?

PRACTICE 2: Knowing Pain

Visualize a scene where you were rejected or humiliated by another person or group. Hold the interaction in your mind. What do you experience about this situation? When during the interaction does the discomfort arise in you? Can you pin it to something that was said? A look? A gesture? Observe how your sense of spiritual knowing operates. Now using your creative imagination, find how this injury has affected your aura. What does it look like? What color is it? Is there painful energy stuck in your aura? If so, where? Pour love into it. Fill your aura with compassion and soothing. Erase the rejection. Repeat. Do the same exercise with an experience of embarrassment or shame. Each time you visualize the scene, experience the effect on your aura, and then erase it. The process of imagining and wiping away an experience, allows you to become detached from its energetic charge and assists in purifying your aura.

PRACTICE 3: Being Known

At some level we each long to be known as the Divine knows us. Yet, too often our true selves are neither known nor seen; our deep interiority and mystical life is dismissed or ignored. In this meditation, imagine a scene where your inner divinity is completely and truly seen and known. Stay with the feeling; allow it to fill your entire being. Be immersed in the joy of true communion. Feel how you are able to let go of hiding or protecting. Celebrate your Light.

We All Feel—Empathic Knowing

IN EVERY SPIRITUAL JOURNEY (but especially in the early years of practice) it is necessary to recognize and trust our inner knowing, and to distinguish our feelings and thoughts from those of other people. As discussed in Chapter 4 (Simplicity), much of what we assume to be our thoughts and feelings, frequently are not. In fact, the body-mind-spirit complex is like a tuning fork, picking up and absorbing feelings and energies around it. While we each have an intuitive grasp of the unspoken or hidden dimensions in social relations, learning to be aware of these nuances and actively sorting them is critical to maintaining a free and open heart.

Nonverbal information coming from the aura, chakras, and thought-forms is received and processed so quickly by the higher vibrational energy of the spiritual faculties that we often do not know how to read their signs. In other words, our conscious awareness is slower than our intuitive or mystical awareness, which is the unity of knowledge and love. It is a knowing that arises from being empathetic, one, with others. Regardless of our mental acuity, our energy fields are in a state of contemplative awareness with all other energy fields.

Part of the development of spiritual strength is trust in our inner, mystical perceptions, in an environment of humility, honoring the inviolable space of others. Each of the following practices helps to foster and stabilize the still center.

PRACTICE 1: Non-Invasion of Space

We tend to be sloppy with our energy. We don't stay in our own space. We forget to honor the sacredness of every other being. We believe that love or commitment gives us the right to intrude upon another's personal space and vitality. Often this extension of energies occurs because we are empathic with—or we seek to control—the feelings of others. Visualize a conversation or other interaction with a friend, spouse, child, etc. Are you in your space? That is, is your energy within your body and aura or is it invasive of the other person? Visualize pulling yourself in to your center. Now, practice daily in varied situations. Observe when and how you cross the boundary into someone else's universe. When or how are you most susceptible to your personal space being invaded?

PRACTICE 2: Honoring Solitude

Imagine an inner hermitage in your heart. Center your energies within the heart. Feel the solitude of being with the Holy within. Are your energies centered within your physical body? What would it mean for your energy to *not* be centered? Where would it be, and can you sense where it is, right now? Cherish your solitude. Embrace your solitude. Imagine being in solitude while in loving relationships. Practice daily.

PRACTICE 3: Tracking Emotions

Below is a two-part meditation to help us observe how different emotions affect our mind and our actions. You can do this meditation at all times of the day and it can help you to recognize emotional tones and energies that are not your own, as well as restoring inner peace and keeping your heart and spirit clear and open.

To begin, place your feet on the floor and take some deep breaths. Imagine that a very pale, pink light is washing your entire body and energy system. It is a very soothing, translucent energy. Onto this palette of pale, pink light imagine areas in the body or auric field of colors that represent the emotions of someone in your life. For example, assign the color purple to your mother's emotions, the color blue to siblings, the color red to your father, the color green to partner or spouse, etc. On the palette of your energy, see what colors come up, where they are located, how much space they take up, and to whom they belong. When you get a fairly clear sense of this palette, open your eyes and, remaining in a meditative state, write what you remember, and/or sketch the colors on a piece of paper.

Next, imagine you are in your favorite place in nature. Experience the peace of being nourished by the natural environment. Feel the water, air, soil, grass, snow, fog, wind, rain, sun. Rest in this serenity. Now, simply invite a positive feeling to enter your awareness—love, tenderness, joy, compassion, etc. Allow these feelings to fill your aura, gently restoring, replenishing, and nourishing your entire being. Let excessive happiness be yours. Practice daily.

THE EXERCISES in this chapter are just a few of the sophisticated energetic practices employed in the world's religious traditions. Nonetheless, they can be helpful to the new monk who is learning to live in and integrate the spiritual and physical realms, uniting in themselves the divisions of the world, and developing whole-aura integrity, and a gentle, nonviolent manner of being.

TWENTY-FIVE

Spiritual Practices

To prepare for these exercises, begin with a meditation, prayer, nature walk, or period of silence. Then spend time in personal reflection, followed by writing about and/or sharing your insights in dialogue with others.

The Action of the Divine in Your Life

Review your life's journey. Begin as a child, recalling moments of insight and spiritual experience. Imagine your journey as a path through a vast field and see where the path turned or took a new direction. At those points, consider whether the shift was motivated by a spiritual intention, bringing you closer to your true direction in life. Or, perhaps, the choice was based on other, less healthy considerations, taking you away from the Spirit. In this way, take time to write vignettes, imagine scenes, and view your life as if "from above." Where is your life leading now?

During this process of reflection, notice how your true self struggled to remain innocent or untouched in the midst of the vagaries of personality, material pressures, and social obligation. Can you trace the work of God in your life? Do you recall instances when you received an insight or message from spirit, nature, or the Holy? Did you follow the call? Devote time and prayer to the process. You may return to this again and again.

Voluntary Simplicity

Practicing voluntary simplicity is an essential monastic exercise. Assess your life through the lens of these questions:

How can I make my life happier, more innocent, easier, and less complex?
Am I living simply?
What concrete changes can I make to bring about a change?
Is my lifestyle in alignment with my deepest intentions?
Is this what the Divine wants for me?
What can I do to transform myself from complexity to simplicity?

The Power of Passion

If you have never had an experience of your passion as belonging to yourself, and not as necessarily connected to, or instigated by, someone else, this is an important place to start. Perhaps you have had the experience of meeting someone who exudes great passion. If you reflect, you will realize the tremendous energy they have available for life, for the things that matter most. This person has found the creative source that is both spiritual and physical.

List all the expressions of passion that you can think of that are not sexual. Imagine when you were a young child and had an enormous curiosity about life. Where did that passion come from? Where did it go?

Imagine the passionate longing to know God, your own soul, and the nature of your true path in life. How does that passion feel? Write about it. Perhaps make a drawing, build with wood or clay, create a song, or express your passion in dance. What would you have to do to reclaim this intensity of desire?

Fidelity to the Divine

Have you ever been faithful to another person, animal, natural environment? Have you ever been faithful to yourself or to God? Has anyone been faithful to you? What does fidelity mean to you, and in your life? To live in a contemplative way is to be faithful to the Divine at the center of your being and action. Find a quiet spot or a time alone, and think back on your relationships, and on your feelings. How have you been affected by unfaithful relations? What kind of life do you want to have? As these questions appear, allow your whole being to experience the response of your heart, mind, emotions, and soul. Meditate on faithfulness. Think of ways you can be more committed to your path.

Love of God Alone

Begin the day with a prayer of remembrance of your devotion to the Holy. You might say: "Divine One, please help me remember my love of you as I go through the day." Or you may want to create your own prayer. As you repeat this prayer in the morning before you start your day, allow your longing for the Divine to well up.

Stay with the longing. Find something—a ribbon or prayer beads looped around the wrist—that can serve as a reminder of your commitment to love God. In your encounters with people, animals, or nature, remember to love the Divine in and through others. Perhaps you will sit outside for lunch. Allow yourself to feel the Spirit's presence in the trees, in the squirrel jumping from limb to limb, in the mother pushing a baby carriage. Repeat your prayer over and over, silently and slowly.

As this practice becomes a part of your daily ritual, you naturally will become more attentive to the yearning for God in others, and you will see more clearly the authentic reality behind appearances. If you start to forget, gently bring back your prayer and remind yourself to remain attentive to the sacred in all things.

Practicing Emptiness

Emptying the self is arduous, but it has many benefits, including opening the heart and freeing oneself from opinion and excess. The process becomes self-reflective and more manageable when you see it as part of your daily work. Choose one aspect of your identity that you feel is unhealthy or unspiritual and would like to "let go" or empty. Perhaps you feel that you are selfish; or you have a possessive streak. Sometimes you may feel callous to the suffering of others.

Use your creative imagination to visualize a scene that depicts this aspect of your personality. The scene could be from your personal life, a passage from Scripture, a movie, art, etc. Some people enjoy visualizing a scene from the life of a saint or religious figure. Perhaps the story of Siddhartha Gautama, a Hindu prince, is a good one. As he ventures outside the palace walls, the future Buddha encounters suffering for the first time. He sees an old man and realizes that everyone has to grow old. On his next trip, he sees a sick man, and knows that everyone could become ill at any time. On his third excursion, he sees a dead body, and realizes that everyone would die someday. The cessation of suffering is what he longs to discover. Thus, his compassion for all beings causes him to leave his princely home, become a monk, and help others find peace.

Put yourself in the story. What happens? Who appears in the story? How does turning away from suffering feel to you? How does selfishness feel? Experience the causes of this suffering. Pour out your wound, pain, or grief. Now visualize the compassion and love of Buddha (or another holy presence) for suffering and for our avoidance. Offer your wound to the Divine. In the silence, pray for understanding and release.

Discerning Our Path

In the contemplative traditions, discernment means to sift through and distinguish Spirit's involvement in your life from egoistic desires and inordinate attachments. This movement is experienced as consolation when it is aligned with God's life; and it is felt as desolation when it is dissonant from God's life. This is the discernment of spirits or the discernment of signs that guides you on the contemplative journey. The founder of the Jesuits, St. Ignatius of Loyola, is credited with developing the first systematic method of discernment in Christianity (See Chapter 10). Discernment does not depend on external aids, such as the throwing of the I Ching, or the reading of Tarot cards (although many people find such practices to be helpful), but instead reaches into the interior life to listen for and receive Divine guidance.

Ignatius writes in *The Spiritual Exercises*, Introduction #15:

During these Spiritual Exercises when a person is seeking God's will, it is more appropriate and far better that the Creator-God alone should communicate to the devout soul, embracing it in love and praise, and disposing it for the way which will enable the soul to serve God better in the future.

A good way to begin is by writing in a journal. Divide the page into two halves. On one side write "Consolation" and on the other, "Desolation." Under each category list the words and feelings that apply. Start by recording your present responses. Reflect on the way indecision or confusion affects your choice. Later you may want to track these same categories at different periods of your life, say during your twenties, in mid-life, or retirement. Note what brings consolation in your spiritual life, and what brings desolation. Where is the spirit calling you? As you review your life, pay particular attention to the interior desire for silence, solitude, rest, and freedom from social roles.

Prayerful Imagination

Spirit speaks through the imaginative, visual, and auditory qualities of your being. When you open yourself to the eye of spirit, you will tap into creative resources that will bring new wisdom about self and the world.

Imagine yourself as a disciple at the feet of a saint or a holy person you admire. In your mind or on paper, draw a visual rendition of qualities associated with this person's life. Notice the ones that attract you, and those that are repellant or cause fear. Allow yourself time to explore imaginatively the images, feelings, and thoughts that arise when you look at your drawing. Experience how it feels to embody these characteristics.

Befriending Silence

Contemplation is not something we *do,* but we can discern some of its signs and foster its growth in our hearts. What is the still voice inside calling you toward? Is there an interior intention for a different quality of being, and for a more simple, holy life? Try to listen to that quiet voice that enters like an old friend coming by for tea. Give yourself time each day for a period of silence. Let the silence fill your being and overflow into your mind and your heart. No matter how little time you have to devote to silence, keep up the practice.

Wherever Your Heart is, is an Altar

Create a sacred place or altar in your home, at work, and/or in nature. Make the space your own and sanctify it with objects that have meaning for you: a picture of a family member, holy person, or Divine figure; add prayer beads, a crucifix, holy water, candles, a sacred book or passage. During prayer or meditation, return to this place, and it will become a living source of peace and energy in your spiritual life.

Sanctifying Each Day

Monastic orders, in their wisdom, know that much of our spiritual growth depends upon allowing for sacred time. In traditional monasteries, the monks maintain a ritual of pray or meditation many hours during the day. The repetition of prayer, sitting in silent meditation, and the coming together in community, transcends ordinary time and space, creating an atmosphere of elevated consciousness. You probably do not live in a monastery and follow monastic rules. But this does not mean that you do not have your own interior spiritual cycle that orders your day. It is important to discover this spiritual rhythm and to formalize it through creating your own schedule.

Begin the process by reflecting on this: if you had no timetables, work schedules, or outside social demands, how would you spend your time spiritually? Would you read for a period of time when you arose in the morning? Would you get up at 3 a.m. to pray? Would you set aside twenty minutes or an hour for meditation? Perhaps you might take a meditative walk as the sun is breaking over the horizon and all creation is moist and full of dew. Allow yourself the time to really feel what would make you happy, without worrying about your busy life or your family or other responsibilities. Write down your ideas. Or draw, paint, dance, or sing.

Instead of seeing the difficulties that impede establishing daily order as obstacles, see them as invitations to potential creativity. Find innovative ways to integrate your ideal spiritual time with the practicalities of your present situation. Reconsider how you use time. For example, if you leave for work at 8:00 a.m., set your alarm for 5:00 a.m., and go to bed an hour earlier than you used to. During the extra hour or two you have in the morning, use the solitary quiet for the greatest benefit.

Or during a busy workday, make an appointment with yourself (time that you actually reserve in your calendar) for ten minutes or more of silence—it could be sitting quietly in a chapel, closing the door to your office, or lighting a candle and breathing in and out slowly. You might want to pray over your meals or find a time to be with others in meditation.

The essential element is remembering that your spiritual life is important. It is so easy to dismiss your soul's nourishment and to be distracted by the demands of every-day existence. But if you sincerely want to change your life, you have to work toward making things different. Creating a spiritual rule for your day will change your unconscious habituations and guide you to a new way of being.

Most helpful in your journey is paying constant attention to every aspect of your day. What was drowsy in the heart, or inattentive in the mind now becomes the material source of a heightened sensitivity: What did John at the grocery store say to make me feel sad? I woke up this morning in a place of solitude and openness, and now at 2:00 p.m. I feel fragmented and alone. What happened during the day to change my mood? What is the source of loneliness? Who is the "I" that is lonely? When you are mindful of your actions and see awareness as a natural response to the interior life, you polish the conscience of the soul. The light reflected in the mirror of your awakening illuminates all things anew.

Contemplative Vocation

This exercise assists in activating the contemplative core at the base of your outer actions. Begin with a meditative posture (you will find exercises in Chapter 24). Imagine a peaceful person whom you admire. Visualize yourself in a similar contemplative posture. Have you ever felt the desire to be mystically united with God, or infused with the Divine Presence?

Give meditative attention to your interior life. In what way is the inner voice calling you? Reflect on the movement of the spirit. Has there been a call for many years, drawing you more toward silence, devotion to God, or toward aloneness and solitude of spirit? Allow prayerful reflection on these thoughts.

You may need to do this exercise over a period of several hours, days, or weeks. Become attentive to your inner rhythm. Keep a detached spiritual eye on the secret and hidden workings of your heart, not judging what is revealed as either good or bad. You may discover that a part of you is in constant internal dialogue; that you may be already speaking its needs, even though you have not been listening.

When you have become more aware of your feelings, visions, dreams, or thoughts, try to describe to how the Divine calls you. Many spiritual exercises can assist you during these times. Attentive study to sacred writings and prayer are helpful. Daily practice of meditation orients your being toward deeper states of consciousness. Silence and solitude are spiritual vehicles that take you through the dark nights of the spirit. Being attuned to the rhythm of life is vital to contemplative stability. If there is a need to go on retreat for a weekend or week, do it. Get away from the phone, computer, books, television, and traffic. Find the rhythm of your interior life; without honoring its flow, our spirits are depleted.

Divine Feminine

Reflect on your relationship to the Divine Feminine figures (Mary, *Guanyin*), and to *via feminina*. What would that path be for you? Is it possible that you have been traveling with Hagia Sophia (or another goddess figure) all along without naming your spiritual orientation?

Consider ways in which culture has responded to the idea of God as Female. How has (if at all) the Divine Feminine and feminine energy been violated, shamed, abused, silenced, and/or ridiculed in you? As a female, as a male. Reflect on the ways that the feminine is celebrated in your culture (for example, sexual aspects versus the saintly or suffering mother).

Write a prayer or meditation to the Divine Mother or to any attribute of the divine nature that you find reflects the sacred feminine and ask (if you feel so called) to learn her way of compassion, mercy, and unconditional love.

Embedded in our collective consciousness are archetypal patterns of how the spiritual journey is supposed to look, which has spawned generations of desecration of the sacred feminine and often violence against her and women. This is not always or necessarily an intentional act of wounding, but nevertheless, has functioned as such in the collective consciousness. When you embark on the path of Sophia, you may discover hidden veins of shame and guilt associated with your choice, which are not solely personal feelings. This is the shame of not belonging to or fitting into a religious or cultural worldview, a reality that has been imbedded in human consciousness for many centuries. But you have chosen to follow a different path. Recognizing your volition helps to heal spiritual injury.

The Divine is far more comprehensive than any version that humanity speaks, writes, or embodies in a particular time. Give yourself permission to see that the path of the Divine Feminine you follow is an immense liberation. By praying or meditating on this gift, you will break out of imposed constrictions or oppressions, and be able to celebrate your free expression.

Sexuality Integrity

The dominant secular culture emphasizes sexuality. People are expected to perform according to cultural dictates, which is a form of oppression. Some cultures believe in arranged marriages. In others, if you had sex outside of marriage, you could be stoned or burned. When we really investigate how sexuality is controlled by the economy and materiality of a culture, we may be shocked and astonished. Also, we need to consider how or why a person exploits his or her own sexuality for materialistic and economic gain or cultural status. Every day, consensual agreements make demands on us as sexual and spiritual beings, expecting that we perform on the world's terms. We can choose to follow certain social norms, but unless our choice is an examined one, we are violating our integrity and dignity.

Monastic traditions are radical because monks choose to live countercultural lives. To have freedom in the contemplative life, we have to at least examine our cultural choices and ask if they benefit or thwart growth of self and of love. Choose for yourself what you need in order to maintain a cloistered space in the midst of the world. As Tessa Bielecki, a contemplative, once wrote: "Mysticism is not disguised sex. Sex is disguised mysticism."

Exercise 1: Look at your life in the context of the mutuality between the cloistered space—the space of freedom of person, of mind, of emotion, of your physical body—and relationship. How and in what ways (if at all) were those violated? For example, did you have a parent or relative who was physically, emotionally, sexually, and/or spiritually invasive? On the level of spirit, mind, or feeling, were you never really alone because this person's presence occupied an excessive or exaggerated space in your heart?

Exercise 2: Be aware of how sexual imagery is transmitted. When someone says, "Hello," is that "Hello" bringing sexual attraction, wanted or unwanted? When you think, *I'm getting vibes from this person,* do you mean you are detecting sexual energy? Is that sexual energy free and open? It is possessive? Possessive sexual energy is designed to make you an object, which invades the integrity of the body and the spirit.

Exercise 3: What did you experience in your first sexual encounter? What did you learn about yourself? What did you learn about your sexuality from these early experiences? How did they affect you?

Exercise 4: Maintain control over your sexual space and the integrity of your body. Know that you have the right to choose to spiritually relate to another human being. Know that sexuality is just one manifestation of intimacy, and of that spiritual relationship.

Practicing Celibacy

Irrespective of its implications as a lifestyle choice, celibacy is common to monastic culture. For this reason, and because there is wisdom in this choice, I strongly advocate a period of intentional abstinence as a way of reconnecting with the integrity of your body and your enclosure with the Divine. You may already be living a celibate life intentionally or unintentionally, but celibacy can be practiced in a marital or partner relationship as well.

Most important is to affirm a period of abstinence as a spiritual choice. If you are already without a sexual partner, then perhaps you want to discover the positive values in celibacy, which include personal freedom and time to re-connect with one's desire. If you are in a marital or partner relationship, you can claim a period of conscious abstinence once a week or once a month. Maybe you will be away from your spouse to a place of retreat, to be alone. Time apart will help to reestablish the integrity of body, mind, and spirit.

In either case, sanctify the period of celibacy as your vow. It is one thing to not have, or to avoid, sex. It is another to bless time apart from physical intimacy. Consider the following as a way to prepare yourself for abstinence. Choose a period of time (day, week, month, year) as your vowed celibacy. Anoint yourself with water or oil. Light a candle, or use the mark of another ritual action, as the beginning of your abstinence.

Prayer or meditation. Set aside a specific time for prayer or meditation. Try to give yourself enough time so you are not rushed (thirty minutes, an hour). The central aspect of celibacy is to rediscover the hermitage within, and your sanctuary in the Divine. Ask for purification and a cleansing of the enclosure. Ask for the release of pain, emotional and physical wounding. Pray for spiritual emptiness, and openness.

Journaling. Write about your experiences of and feelings about sexual relations. Allow yourself to see how sexuality has affected your life, sense of relationship, love, and self-esteem. Note the times when sexual relations were positive and when they were negative. Pay particular attention to subtle or overt sexual wounding you have experienced. Try to pour out your feelings about vulnerability, intimacy, and love. In addition to writing, you might want to "journal" with your body, by drawing, singing, walking, or dancing these feelings as a way of both releasing and claiming them.

Taking a Vow. Create a vow of health and integrity. Be faithful to your vow. For example, you may realize that sexual relations were always unequal and thus painful. Consider your orientation and role in the experience, as an effort to decontaminate the aspects of manipulation that some people couple with sex. You can vow to never have another sexual encounter until there is mutuality of giving and sharing. Vow to be honest and truthful to your deep intention. Be attentive to how you are drawn away from your vow by the demand of social norms or other people.

Embodiment

It is easy to forget that we inhabit a physical body, and all too often spiritually minded people neglect the integral relationship of body, mind, and spirit. Especially, in the pursuit of a new monastic way of life in the world, it is vitally important to honor the wisdom and the need of our bodies, which sustain our physical existence and our souls. You can begin this exercise by meditating on the health of your physical body and praying for guidance on how to turn away from destructive tendencies toward life-affirming ones. Remember not to judge, but instead use compassion to listen to what your body is telling you. Then perhaps it is helpful to engage with these spiritual exercises in meditation or prayer.

- Spiritually, how do you look upon your physical body? Is this a relationship of cooperation, mutuality, resistance, and/or neglect?
- How does your body feel in this moment? Does it have everything it needs?
- Is your physical body able to withstand your spiritual longings, or meditative intensity? Why or why not? What do you experience?
- Do you allow yourself to feel joy, happiness? What does this feel like in your body? How does that express itself physically? Is your body-spirit generally consumed by grief or sadness?
- Be aware and sensitive to the differences in physical ability and mental acuity as we age. When you were in (or are) in your twenties, what were your physical needs? What do you notice about your energy as you've grown older? Do you need more rest, more time alone? Are you able to accept the changes illness, aging, or disability bring?
- How can compassion for self and spiritual practice help?

Living in God's Time

The deep self is meant to live in God's time. By resting in the holiness of time, we make progress through inaction. When we follow the rhythm of what is eternal and immaterial, we enter an enchanted universe, a freedom of being and a sanctuary of rest.

The pursuit of a monastic commitment requires self-honesty and a receptive consciousness. It is most important to be aware of your deep desire, of what compels you to live each day, and what draws you to the vocation of monkhood. You might tell yourself, or maybe you already feel, *I want to be pure of heart. I want to be a mystic. I must know truth. I cannot abide without experiencing the Divine Presence!* Then it is worthwhile to reflect on your particular justification for or resistance to not fully giving yourself to the quest. Have you ever completely offered your life to someone or something? To the Holy One? It is also good to examine what impedes cognitive awareness of—and bringing into reality—the preciousness of life and the gifts of traveling a spiritual path. How would you go about healing your rationalizations?

Now respond to the following questions:

How do you use your time?

Do you know your natural rhythm, your spirit time?

What do you do when you get up in the morning? Before going to bed?

How can you create a space for sacred time and for blessing the day?

What is spiritually important for you to pursue now? Reflect on and document your spiritual need and desire for this next year.

TWENTY-SIX

Four Virtues of a Monastic Heart

XPLICIT TECHNIQUES of transformation are used to guide us
along the path of mystical union. At times, contemplative exercises
may consist solely of a singular prayer or meditation, visualization
exercise, or an extended process of discernment.

Another type of practice that I have found offers a real-life change of
attitudes and behaviors begins with the spiritual reading (*lectio divina*) of
a narrative passage from a wisdom text. This is followed by suggestions
on how to incorporate the soul's response to this text into one's life.

The four passages below, followed by practices, are directed specifically to the virtues found in Part One—Contemplations—of this book
but are applicable to any spiritual concern. That is, by considering the
meaning of humility, compassion, nonviolence, etc., in relation to these
exercises, you will help purify your heart and expand your soul's wisdom.
They also may generate journal reflections, be offered to prayer, encourage silence, and change the practical focus of daily life.

The Apostle

IN EMBRACING a spiritual or monastic way of life, we are guided to
become pilgrims, disciples, devotees, or apostles of the holy. The atti-

tude of the apostle is testament to a complete turn of heart, in which the seeker is dedicated to that which is "beyond personal accomplishment, beyond history, beyond even life itself, to some as yet unimagined end."[1] Apostles devote themselves to the transcendent—to the Cosmic Mystery. They give up their small will to surrender to and follow the Divine will. They are not concerned with the marks of success they leave, but rather with how to share God's voice and vision in the world.

Professor of English, Robert Inchausti, compares the worldly affirmation of the genius with the often-lowly social position assigned to the pilgrim or apostle. He writes:

Genius, in other words, is the fulfillment of a human potentiality. It expresses itself in works that are ends in themselves—masterpieces. And those masterpieces define what it means to be human. But apostles are not geniuses. They exist in a paradoxical relationship to the human enterprise. They are, if you will, contradictions to humanity as an end in itself. Apostles . . . are absolute dissidents and metaphysical rebels whose primary contribution to everyday life is to overcome its falsity and limitations by drowning them in the light of a higher truth."[2]

Most of us want to be recognized and accorded the appropriate status and reward for our contributions. We desire to fulfill our human potential, and there is nothing wrong with that. But the devotee has a different motivation. He or she pursues a divine mission, the *spiritual* potential that comes about with the total giving of oneself. This is a radically different orientation by which to live. It is a call to a deeper type of surrender, to recognizing the intense, personal action that the Divine exerts on our souls. It is awareness that a path of mystical solidarity with all of creation is imprinted in our beings and is working itself out through each person.

Practice

Reflect on what being a disciple means to you. Write your thoughts. Bring them into prayer or meditation. Is this where your heart is called?

If so, how can your life be more aligned with the posture of the apostle, in devotion to the Holy? What changes would you need to make to honor your life as a devotee?

Self-Responsibility

THE ESSENCE of the spiritual quest is the assumption of responsibility for turning one's life around and for pursuing the path of truth. In particular, is that the weight of transformation falls on the seeker—not the abbot, prioress or lama, for the disciple must be the one doing the hard work. It is of utmost importance to realize that you, alone, are responsible for seeking the Divine. This acceptance of responsibility propels us to search for answers, struggle toward holiness, ask for help, and find a reliable teacher.

The story that follows about a desert elder and his young acolyte illustrates the point. Recounted in "The Desert Fathers on Radical Self-Honesty" by Benedictine scholar and monk, Columba Stewart, I quote it at length. The story is instructive, as the speaker (a young monk) describes the practical issues that assailed him.

> "When I was young," he said, "I had this experience. I had a passion in my soul which mastered me. Having heard it said that Abba Zeno had healed many, I wanted to go find him and open myself to him. But the devil prevented me from doing so, saying, "Since you know what you must do, conduct yourself according to what you have read. Why go and scandalise the old man?" Each time that I was ready to go to him, the warfare in me abated a little, and I didn't go. . . . Often I would actually go to the old man in order to tell him everything, but the enemy would not let me speak by putting shame in my heart and saying to me, "Since you know how to heal yourself, what is the point of speaking about it? You're not giving yourself enough credit: you know what the fathers have taught." Such is what the adversary suggested to me so that I wouldn't reveal my sickness to the physician and be healed.

The old man knew very well that I was having these thoughts, but he didn't intervene, waiting for me to make them known to him myself. He said to me: "It is you who must say what is the matter with you." He taught me about the right path and sent me on my way.[3]

The story clarifies that by revealing our inner thoughts and hidden fears, we take ownership of our ability to act in accordance with what is most true. This is different than self-sufficiency, which often rejects or resists opening one's heart to another, bogged down in shame. We have to break from the illusion of self-sufficiency, the independence that is a refusal to be open, vulnerable, and honest.

Practice
Take time in silence and solitude to measure how responsible you have been to your spiritual growth. Do you expect your teacher or guide to do much of the work? Repeat the exercise reflecting on any resistance to help. As you falsely self-sufficient? Do you resist sharing inner thoughts and emotions that may reflect poorly on your self-image? Does your ability to take care of yourself sometimes mask the need to be responsible is an expanded manner, by bringing your concerns to another person, by opening your heart to its secrets? Meditate on the feelings that arise in you. Can you identify the ways in which you confuse responsibility with self-sufficiency? What actual steps can you take to act on and claim responsibility for your life?

Radical Honesty

THE DESERT ELDERS provide insight into how to conquer the hidden thoughts and emotions that assail the monks' progress, and the means by which they worked toward radical honesty. The principal element of that process was offering the secrets of one's heart to another person for discernment. This was typically done by a young, or (at any rate) novice monk to his or her monastic elder. This practice of self–revelation was both the means and the fruit of the monk's growth in singleness of heart.

From Columba Stewart:

The practice of manifesting the thoughts of the heart was simple. A monk would go to a trustworthy, usually older, monk and say, for example, "I am bothered by thoughts of envy towards someone. I wish I could see my parents. I think a lot about the happiness of the saints in heaven. I get distracted from my prayers. I wonder if I'll ever be a real monk." Sometimes the issue might be a particular sinful act, sometimes it might be something which wasn't sinful at all, but which was preoccupying.

The power of this simple, but difficult, practice lay in the fact that the monk was confident enough in God's mercy, working through the elder, to turn the soul inside out without cleaning it all up beforehand. This was spontaneous, not calculated, trust. . . .

Note that this is not obsessive introspection, or scrupulous self–analysis. The whole point was to prevent obsession. It is self–awareness rather than modern self–consciousness: no alienation, no wallowing in the self, rather a spontaneous freedom to lay it all out. And all of it had to be laid out, because one cannot see in the dark to tell what is good, what is evil, what is indifferent. . . .

For these people, then, humility, that key virtue, could be reduced in practice to this one indicator: the ability to speak honestly, overcoming embarrassment and shame, about the deepest stirrings of the heart. Abba Poemen said: "Teach your mouth to say that which you have in your heart." And they knew that this is the hardest thing anyone can ever do. . . .

[As in the case of Abba Zeno], this story touches on many key themes: the illusion of self-sufficiency and self-discernment; the power of embarrassment and shame; the patience and humility of the abba; the need to take the hard step of saying aloud the secrets of the heart; the pastoral sensitivity of the abba shown more in his overall strategy than in the actual advice he gave after the manifestation of conscience. . . . trapped in the confusion of sinful humanity.

Part of this confusion was an instinctive resistance to openness, a resistance to making real progress, owing to the human tendency to prefer familiar sickness to unfamiliar health. Monks in the desert, like modern people, fought to keep change at bay even while claiming to desire progress. This resistance appeared in many guises, and was often labelled self-will, about which there are hundreds of sayings, one of the most well-known being, "If you see a young man climbing toward heaven by his own will, grab his foot and pull him down, for it will be for his own good."[4]

Practice

Find a place to be quiet. Really consider whether you are honest with yourself, with others. Are you able to open the secrets of your heart, even attitudes that are painful or denied? Are you able to share these secrets with a spiritual companion? Please spend whatever time it takes to contemplate these important issues. It will lead to a new experience of wholeness.

Heal Worldly Ambition

I would suggest that the monastic archetype across cultures and religions pivots on the healing of worldly ambition. By "worldly ambition," I mean not only the actual striving to make something of oneself and achieve material goals without concern for the costs to self and others, but, also, the cynicism, despair, nihilism, deprivation, and loss that fuels worldly significance and its power in defining what constitutes the important or good life. It is this constellation of accepted social and cultural norms that contemplation and a monastic sensibility reform.

Society often fuels the desire to be successful, and to make "something" of ourselves, as if this is the entire goal of existence—even against the wellbeing of others, even opposed to habits of the heart. Humility and the other virtues remind us of the value in being unimportant in oneself, and to think well and highly of others. The virtue of humbleness, for example, is that it prunes the soul in a most beautiful way, helps it to grow toward the light, and produces much and better-quality fruit. When we practice being humble and simple of heart, in the most positive, spiritual sense, we belong to the circle of all beings living on the sacred vessel that is our Earth.

We also learn through the virtues of humility, nonviolence, compassion, etc. to leave behind a materialistic mindset and embrace the spirituality of generosity that is the foundation of all the great master teachings. This commitment includes the injunction to be concerned with the unity of all beings, to practice non-cooperation with violence and harm, and to work toward the universal principles of honesty, integrity, and good will.

It is this very concrete and tangible practice that resets the orientation of your life and the capacity of your love.

Practice

Consider the way your family and society have taught you to revere acquisitions. Did they ridicule you, the poor, or others who did not meet their expectations? How has (if it has) worldly ambition controlled the direction of your choice of profession, partner, or spiritual goals? Offer your questions in pray. Listen for guidance. How will you heal?

TWENTY-SEVEN

Writing Exercise

T HIS JOURNAL WRITING exercise was given to me over forty years
ago. It has proved to be immensely helpful in sorting through
emotions to undercover deeper sources of spiritual wounding,
and to free energy for the upwelling of grace, hope, and love.

These are the instructions:

Let's say you want to journal about an unpleasant or painful event
with a spouse or parent with the intention of discovering your deeper
emotional and spiritual wound or truth. The important action is to
pay attention to and concentrate on your feelings instead of justifying,
explaining, and/or rationalizing the other person's behavior.

For example, you decide to write about the time your spouse left you
for another person, and your inability to let go of suffering. The job is to
write what you *feel*. You might start out like this:

I am so angry that she left. I'm hurt in a place that I can't name,
but I don't believe she really meant to hurt me ... STOP WRIT-
ING ... right there you explained and justified and moved away
from feelings.

My heart hurts so much, I am devastated and lonely, although I must have done something to make this happen . . . STOP WRITING . . . now you are rationalizing why. It does not mean you did not contribute to the loss, but right now your goal is to access your pain, regret, etc., not think about and rationalize why it happened.

I don't understand why she left and not knowing is tearing me up. I feel abandoned, I feel lost. My world is upside down. Sometimes I hate her, but this is not a good way to be and I'm sure she didn't understand the effect this . . . STOP WRITING. . . . Stay with your feelings.

The point is, if you can stay with your feelings and catch every time you veer into explanations that take you away from feeling, you will dig deeper into the spiritual undercurrent, the most potent response of your soul to the event. What you are aiming for is what does your soul, the most sensitive and spiritual aspect of your being actually know and feel. Is it injustice, regret, fear, despair, loneliness, etc.?

When I did this exercise with respect to a decision that I was forced to make as a teenager by my parents, the result of the journaling led to a torrent of spiritual feelings, a soul and guttural explosion that I did not know were in me. Having lived for many years avoiding the pain of the drastic change that was imposed on my path in life, this response was the most honest and truthful, and resulted in a tremendous release and healing.

I hope you will experiment with the writing exercise!

TWENTY-EIGHT

Inner Monastery Meditation

To BEGIN the meditation, sit in a comfortable chair, with your back erect and feet on the floor (preferably with shoes removed).

Close your eyes and feel the warmth of the earth rising through your feet and the pure light of Spirit filling your mind from above.

With your breath draw in the common silence of Mother Earth and the great mercy of Holy Wisdom.

As you breathe in, may your body, mind, and spirit be filled with quiet and rest.

As you breathe out, let your breath carry away all your cares and your mind be stilled.

Feel the energies of heaven and earth, flowing through you.

Offer your body as a sanctuary for the uniting of spirit and matter.

May your entire physical presence become a shrine, your heart a birthplace, your soul a holy temple.

As you breathe in and out, use your breath to focus all your attention on your spiritual heart.

Here at the very center of yourself is an inner monastery, a holy hermitage that belongs to you alone. Find this sanctuary in your heart.

This is your sacred home, and it may be any place and it may look any way. It is where you and your Divine are One and have never been separate.

Breathe in and breathe out gently.

Only you can enter this holy sanctuary. No one can violate your spiritual bond. You are safe and at rest. There is only love.

Breathe in and breathe out gently.

Allow yourself to enter into the warm and inviting inner monastery, into the embrace of the Divine Presence.

Feel your whole being come to rest.

Slowly just sink down, letting everything go as you experience the freedom of being silent and still, vulnerable and intimate, open and receptive, alone with your Beloved.

Breathe in and breathe out gently.

Feel how nothing is needed here; how nurtured you are; how you are in a paradise, one to One, heart to Heart.

Rest in your inner monastery, allowing all your cares to be given away. Simply experience the wonder of never leaving your true home.

Feel your heart open to the whole world.

Breathe in and breathe out gently.

Pray now for the strength and courage to remember your inner monastery.

Breathe in and breathe out gently.

Now, make a vow or a commitment to be at peace and centered in your inner monastery.

Breathe in and breathe out gently.

Visualize that wherever you go and whatever you do, you will remain connected to the palace of rest in your heart.

Breathe in and breathe out gently.

In this way, each day will be a meditation, as the light of your holy hermitage illuminates and celebrates all your relationships and life itself.

Amen.

TWENTY-NINE

Selections From

A Feast of Prayers:
Universal Liturgy of Hours

MORNING PRAYER 1

Canticle of Praise
(this is a movement prayer)

Holy Earth, Holy Cosmos,
I bow before you
With my whole being.

Holy Creatures, Holy Nature,
I kneel upon the earth
In honor and thanksgiving
Of your blessed bounty.

Holy Waters, Holy Mountains,
I lay my body on your temple
In gratefulness for nurturing
My tender soul.

Holy Passion, Holy Longing,
I rise up before you
A devotee of truth,
Following wherever you lead me.

Holy Silence, Holy Solitude,
I place my hands over my heart
Breathing in serenity,
Breathing out your peace.

Holy Sorrow, Holy Suffering,
I close my hands in prayer
May I bear every wound
With compassion and nonharm.

Holy Humility, Holy Emptiness,
I bow my head before you
I have become nothing,
For your All to shine in my soul.

Holy Freedom, Holy Rejoicing,
I open my heart to the world
Offering myself to this day,
In joyfulness and gratitude.

Amen.

NOON PRAYER 1

Canticle of Desire

In the stillness of noon prayer,
    I long for you
Enflame my soul with love's desire
I am your disciple.

In the silence of meditation,
    I long for you
Take my life for your own
I am your disciple.

In the busyness of the day,
    I long for you
Harness my heart for your work
I am your disciple.

In the warmth of family and friends,
    I long for you
Use my joy for the world's awakening
I am your disciple.

You called and I said: "Take me!"
Now, I await your touch
Do not abandon me Great Silence
I am your disciple.

Amen.

EVENING PRAYER 1

Canticle of Healing

Light of Spirit, please hear my prayers:

For the dying and the ill,
send the light of solace.

For the violated and rejected,
send the angels of healing.

For the wounded and killed in war,
send the balm of peace.

For the poor and homeless,
send the heart of compassion.

For the betrayed and abandoned,
send the guardians of love.

For the earth and all our relations,
Let there be reconciliation.

For the mass of humanity
    without food,
    without parents,
    in poverty,
    alone and bereft
    May my heart break open,
    May I bear suffering in your name.

Make of my soul a home for the homeless
    and a refuge for the poor.
Grant me the strength to be a sign of peace.

Amen.

MORNING PRAYER 2

Canticle of Adoration

O Glorious One, form my heart into a
    bouquet of love:
May each breath be in praise of you
May each word announce your holy peace
May each action honor your hidden glory

I am a devotee of emptiness
neither seeking my own name nor will
but only your desire

I am devotee of humility
offering myself over to your wisdom
free of self-interest

I am a devotee of patience
listening for your voice
in every word and sigh

I am a devotee of peace
with a heart free from resentment
wide open to love

I am a devotee of compassion
nurturing every pain and sorrow
as my own

I am a devotee of gratitude
giving myself in service of love,
in daily wonder of life's gift

I am a devotee of gentleness
into the harsh world I vow to bring
happiness and tenderness

I am a devotee of prayer
whose heart is attuned to your rhythm,
my every breath whispering your name

May this day be filled with flowers and
    fragrances
in celebration of your mystery.

Shalom!

NOON PRAYER 2

Canticle of Creation

O Radiant Earth and Spirits of Nature!
    I call upon you!
Open my heart to love
in every action and in all of creation.

Mother Earth,
gestating in the womb of your red clay
consecrated by the family of matter
I am your offspring!

Sea water flows through my cells
clouds cast shadows over my heart,
blood of bison in my veins,
raven wind speaks me
Beauty fells my soul!

Thus comes morning, whispering
    Holy, Holy, Holy
then a chorus of voices,
Mother wakes up from slumber,
healing occurs nightly in the temple
    of dreams.

Come! Sky, Star, Planet
I am made of dust.
Where heaven kisses earth,
I am vastness and silence
Where souls are restored by
     drops of night,
I, too, am family.

Amen.

EVENING PRAYER 2

Canticle of Union

Holy Mystery, prepare me for your
    Night Vow:
In the beginning,
as it is now and ever shall be,
my life is yours.

I rest upon your verdant meadow,
sweet breezes adorn my soul
Your circle of saints surrounds me
placing flowered garlands upon my head.

Soothed by your Luminous Darkness,
A chorus of prayers liberates my sins
I am anointed with sweet oils
O Holy One, may I be worthy of your gift.

I surrender myself to you Beloved
our union consecrated by fire
Now your life lives in me
my nothingness is Your All.

Amen.

Appendix

Study Guide and Reflections

A REGULAR PROCESS of written journal reflection is a time-honored method of engaging with inner meaning and opening the soul to its true longing. What follows is a selection of study questions and reflections that I hope will assist you to "go deep" with your responses. The benefit of this dive into spiritual feelings and soul aspirations is that it brings clarity of heart and freedom of purpose.

The following journal reflections are organized around each of the book chapters (Preface to chapter 16). They are both a study guide and promptings for spiritual engagement with the text.

PREFACE: A New Silence

- Do you live between religious or secular worldviews? Does the idea of new traditions of contemplative wisdom speak to your experience?

- What does "a new silence" evoke?

- Explore the feelings that arise for you in reference to the words "monk" and "contemplative." Do you feel attraction, repulsion, conflict, yearning?

- What does being a "monk" mean to you?

- In what way is the inner voice calling you? Has there been an interior call for many years, drawing you more toward silence, devotion to God, or toward aloneness and solitude of spirit?

- Enter into the vision of a theology without walls. Do you feel this theology offers a way to reconcile or approach the variety of religions on Earth?

- Have you experienced any religion or spirituality in depth? Do you identify with the notion of an intercontemplative orientation?

CHAPTER 1: Humility

- Consider that humility is the "central work of the monk." What does this mean to you?

- Do these attributes of humility evoke a response: someone who is empty, less rather than more, lowly, or unpretentious?

- Rabbi Zlotshov holds that one attains humility by being in awe of the vastness of the Holy. Why is this so? Have you experienced the great blessing of awe, which is the state of nothingness, no independent self?

- Indigenous peoples revere the Earth and all relations as sacred. The circle of being is a living, holy entity, and to each we owe our respect, patience, and compassion. How has the natural world opened your heart to live together with others "like one being?"

- The Book of Sirach reminds us that the humble find favor with God. They recognize their limits and are attuned to how self-will and the need to be recognized subvert the heart's purity. Discuss this from your experience.

- Master Hui Neng says that we must cut off "me and mine" if we want to live with virtue. Do you recall a time when you showed reverence, perhaps bowing to your teacher, the ocean, or a tree in the forest? Or are you more like "the tall dry grasses that do no bend?"

- We are pierced by the world's suffering and experience divine intimacy. The Christian Bible holds that when we imitate Jesus' voluntary assumption of humility for our sake, we reciprocate God's generous self-offering. Let us contemplate.

- St. Francis advises us to "despise transitory praise, suppress bloated bragging, and reject pretense." Write about these in your own life.

- The *Bhagavad Gita* inspires devotion to and adoration of the Most High. It is out of love that we give away the false self. Reflect on being a devotee.

- Consider this passage from Rumi: "The I-less I fled from the I of the world." Write about if and how you are able to let go of the false self, or ego.

- *Dao dejing* holds a reverential attitude toward humility, specifically emphasizing the force of the gentle, flowing, and meek. Consider the power of the nonviolence of being.

CHAPTER 2: Compassion

- Compassion desires to alleviate the causes of anguish and injustice. Reflect on the importance of compassion in your desire to transform self and society.

- Contemplate the benefits of existence and gratitude for life. How does this remembrance ignite compassion in our hearts?

- Buddhists hold that remembrance of our mothers, who give us a body and suffer for our sake, are the clearest examples of compassion. What does a mother's compassion elicit in you?

- Compassion is inner strength and the courage to resist injustice. This is a power of the soul that each of us possesses. How have you resisted injustice, suffering, or despair?

- The author writes: "It is impossible to gauge the value of being a compassionate person of great feeling and care." Pray on this.

- With a compassionate heart we are able to mystically share in others' heartbreak and celebrate their fortune. Consider the ways that your heart experiences this sharing.

- How do you offer solidarity with and empathy for the lives of others and a world lacking faith?

- A compassionate person loves the world and is open to its pain. Are there times when you want others to suffer or refuse to forgive? Spend time with your heart, and work to break it open.

- Do you labor to liberate yourself and others from failure? Find the ways both small and large that you assist in healing human error and drawing us together as one.

- Have you ever experienced your own goodness—not from something you have done, but because you were created in the Divine image? Pray for this.

- Practice self-compassion. We all make mistakes, but often we do not forgive ourselves for them. Pray for self-forgiveness and repentance and outline concrete steps you can take to develop and practice self-compassion.

- Visualize the happiness of all beings. Meditate on this and on freeing all forms of suffering.

CHAPTER 3: Nonviolence

- What meaning do you derive from the idea of nonviolence as a central Divine attribute?

- How does a theology of nonviolence reform your understanding of spirituality and your path to God?

- If you truly believed in or realized Divine Nonviolence, what would you change in your life?

- Contemplate: Peace is God: absolute peace, peace in general, and peace in every instance.

- Nonviolence approaches reality from the perspective of the unity of all beings and the whole of creation. How have you experienced mystical unity in daily life?

- Spiritual nonviolence is never for social transformation without soul transformation. How are these two types of transformation connected in your life?

- List violent messages you have received from religion(s), culture, and/or family.

- The author describes spiritual violence as "any action that invades a person's sacred place, tramples truth, and/or degrades integrity." Have you experienced or inflicted spiritual violence? Meditate and write.

- What does the phrase "religious ego" mean to you?

- Do you find the dialogue and unity of religions to be important to you spiritually? Why or why not?

CHAPTER 4: Simplicity

- How can you simplify your daily life and focus on your passion for the monastic quest?

- Are you pure of heart—free from complexity, confusion, deceit? Write what is leading to a divided heart and reflect on ways to become simpler.

- The author emphasizes the importance of emotional simplicity in freeing the self. Describe simplicity of emotion, and the difference between a simple and a divisible or complex emotion.

- Write a list of complex emotions in yourself and in your family.

- How have emotional imbalances affected your well-being and relationship with others? Can you imagine ways to balance and simplify your emotional responses?

- Choose a complex emotion and try to uncover its nature. Is it a confused or oppressed emotion? Is it an emotion tied to negativity? Is it someone else's emotion?

- Contemplate the virtue of a simple heart—one that loves unconditionally, experiences suffering, knows peace, is without deceit or guile, is free of ego agendas, and confronts life openly.

- Imagine ways that you can devote yourself to the Divine, freeing your life from unwanted distractions and demands.

- Voluntary simplicity asks that we each be responsible for poverty and disparities in wealth. How can you practice and advance the spirit of simplicity?

- What kind of life would you lead if money were not an issue? Reflect on how to move your life in this direction even if a job is important now.

- What impact has your relationship to money or financial considerations had on your life choices and/or controlled your spiritual desire?

- Are your lifestyle and material possessions in alignment with your deepest intentions?

- What can be changed about your way of life, in order to move from complexity to simplicity? Be specific and write a concrete plan of action.

CHAPTER 5: Bearing Divinity

- Reflect on what intimacy, annihilation, or absorption into the Divine means to you. How do you relate to or experience this possibility?

- Reflect on your ability to be receptive and listen to spiritual advice.

- Are you comfortable with surrendering to God or Spirit? Why or why not?

- How does your understanding of faith affect your life choices?

- Is the Divine present to you? Daily, frequently, seldom, or never?

- What is Spirit calling you to at this time?

- The author introduces the idea of "bearing" divinity, using nine descriptions of how divinity is carried into the world. These are birth, natural, support, sustain, suffer, gifts, heart, sow, quality of being. Meditate on each of the ways we bear the Holy and record your responses.

- Write your own questions, hopes, and fears about drawing closer to the Divine.

CHAPTER 6: Mother of Contemplation

- What do the various metaphors ascribed to the holy rivers of India— purifying, sacred, erases sins, crossing from ignorance to rebirth, and compassion—evoke in you about the Divine Mother?

- Create an altar to the Divine Mother.

- Reflect on the meaning of *via feminina* and its value in your spiritual life.

- Numerous spiritual texts refer to Hagia Sophia, Holy Wisdom, as embodied and incarnated, the transfiguration of a new unity of male and female, spiritual and material, divine and earthly. Express your relationship to or experience of Sophia.

- Identify the beliefs, religions, or institutions that deny or denigrate the feminine, and prevent acknowledgment of women as prophets, founders of religion, and/or spiritual masters.

- How do these prohibitions impact on your spirituality, relationships, and ability to achieve freedom of self?

- What concrete steps can you take to reform oppressive elements in your life and heal the wounds of the feminine?

- Create a prayer or meditation to the Divine Mother or to any attribute of the divine nature that you find reflects the feminine divinity and ask to learn her path.

CHAPTER 7: Spiritual Formation

- Consider your soul—how it longs to share its wisdom and depth with others and for the world. Who speaks for its needs? Dialogue with your deep self.

- Reflect on any changes in your life's direction. Do you notice an interior, mystical process occurring in you? One that is calling you toward silence and solitude?

- Consider some attributes of formation and what you know about your progress, such as letting go of false habits and the mask of personality; relinquishing self-will for God's will in your life.

- How can you adjust or modify your daily existence to focus on a more spiritually attuned and sacred way of life?

- Formation is not only about self-realization; it is also about self-transcendence. What does this mean to you?

- Thomas Merton says the first thing you need to do, even before you think about contemplation, is to recover your natural unity, to reintegrate and learn to live as a unified human person. Do you feel that your heart is divided, fragmented? How can you heal inner division?

CHAPTER 8: Turning Life Around

Reflect on each of the elements that encourage a change of heart and a change of life. Write about which aspects appeal to you, which ones you need to develop, and where you are in the process. The elements:

Daily Ritual
Spiritual Companionship
Finding a Teacher
Study
Reflection
Contemplative Depth
Critical Engagement
Listening
Enclosure
Stability
Vows and Rules of Life

CHAPTER 9: Life in Relationship

- This chapter is especially important to the nontraditional monk in the world. Take time to contemplate and journal about how your call to silence and solitude and your soul's need to be close to the

Divine can be established in your relationships, especially in those of intimacy and sexuality. Consider the questions on page 117.

- Follow each of the six practices and write about them in your journal. Are you able to sustain in your relationships: nonattachment, emptying of ego, openness to others, faith in a spiritual direction, standing alone, and solitude?

- Consider the diagram on page 115. Trace how the Divine in your center is interacting with and enhancing everyone in your circle of relationships.

- If you are sexually active, is there room in your life to practice a period of abstinence from sex? If you are not having sexual relations, discover the positive values of celibacy.

- Consider living in community with partner, family, etc., as a way to expand the growth of the spirit and the maturing of love. What type of changes would you make?

- Adults have a duty to respect the world of children and to not lay a burden of dishonesty on their pure hearts. Meditate on how your childhood was or was not respected. Write about concrete changes you can make to heal your soul, and also to heal children.

- Make a promise to the next generation to stop violence against the innocent. Think about specific steps you can make.

- Consider your relationship to your parents. How can you let go of demand? Can you see your parents' role in the divine mystery?

- Is your work a means of spiritual growth for you? How can you instill a prayerful attitude into your workday?

- Meditate on this: We are children of the wind, of water, of air, of the earth, and of sun and moon.

CHAPTER 10: Spiritual Guidance

- Do you regularly consult with a spiritual guide? If not, consider setting up a companioning relationship.

- What does it mean to tread the *inner way*? Are you aware of your inner life, the movement of your spirit?

- Think about your relationship with God, Great Spirit. Can you write about it? What does this religious experience mean to you?

- Are you able to move away from solving psychological problems (even if temporarily) and sink into the sacred questions and the anxieties of your soul?

- Is your prayer life arid or unproductive? Or is it full?

- Do you feel unworthy and unable or afraid to love? How would you bring these issues to your spiritual friend?

- Thomas Merton claimed that the whole purpose of spiritual direction "is to penetrate beneath the surface of a [person's] life, to get behind the façade of conventional gestures and attitudes." Does Merton's insight resonate?

- Merton goes on to say that the process of revealing our façade of personality brings out inner spiritual freedom and truth. Do you find this to be a helpful description? Why or why not??

- Revealing thoughts and feelings is central to authentic spiritual sharing. Are you able to open yourself to your "spiritual physician" and heal your soul? Is there anything that you fear or resist in dialogue with a spiritual teacher or guide?

- Of the various types of spiritual relationships listed on pages 143–146, which appeal to your inner orientation? Explain why.

CHAPTER 11: Cultivation of Mindfulness

- Do you think you are only half aware most of the time? If so, why would that be?

- Do you currently practice techniques of mindfulness, in meditation or prayer, and in everyday activities?

- If spiritual awareness is our central vocation, how can you enhance its practice?

- Our daily norm is to be busy. Reflect on the many ways you are distracted and write about how to place the quest for peace and contemplation at the center of your attention.

- What would you need to change to be spiritually disciplined of mind and heart?

- The author states that the deepest state of mindfulness is pure contemplation, mystical consciousness. Have you experienced being absorbed or transfigured by the transcendent, by awe? Write about (or use any other creative process to express) the aftereffect that the presence of mystery has had on your life.

- Visualize seeing and approaching the world from a holy perspective. How does this alter your perception? Your relationship to others and the natural world?

- Does experiencing and knowing the sacredness of creation lead you to remorse or pain over any heedlessness in your past?

CHAPTER 12: Theology of Energy

- Reflect on the ways you have been attentive to yourself as a being of energy.

- List how and in what ways you have ignored the energetic system of body, mind, and spirit.

- How does knowing about your energetic field help you to be spiritually centered?

- How does your body and its energies respond to the vibration of positive and negative thoughts or situations?

- Consider a correlation between states of energy and your perception of sin, disease, health, enlightenment.

- Write and/or draw the weak and strong energetic points in your body.

- Describe "positive energy" or "positivity." How does positivity physically manifest in your body, mind, feelings, spirit, and health?

- Describe "negative energy" or "negativity." How does negativity physically manifest in your body, mind, feelings, spirit, and health?

- Reflect on ways to mitigate and heal negative influences and on ways to enhance positive energy through all areas of awareness.

- Meditate on the positive patterns in your life. Follow by expressing what you discover by creating a collage, drawing a picture, dancing, writing in your journal, working with clay, or any other creative process.

- Have you experienced mystical effects on your body, for example, light, fire, or love? How have these experiences affected your body and spiritual understanding?

- Explain and describe visions. Have you experienced spiritual visions, or locutions (hearing with the inner voice)?

CHAPTER 13: Spiritual Practice: Obstacles and Solutions

- What did you learn about yourself and your behavior from this chapter?

- Are you frustrated or dissatisfied with your spiritual practice and development?

- How do you think you avoid unpleasant or wounded feelings?

- Consider and meditate on each of the obstacles that impede growth. Afterward, list the strategies you use to avoid deeper spiritual issues.

Inertia
Discouragement
Confusion
Avoidance
Addiction
Willfulness
Resistance

Follow this imaginative exercise by bringing in the beneficial effects of gentleness, self-compassion, the role of faith, and the call of the Divine in releasing fear and opening the heart.

CHAPTER 14: Freeing the Spiritual Imaginary

- List the religious thinking that frames your spiritual attitudes, behaviors, customs, prejudices, symbols, and divine figures.
- How do you understand yourself with respect to an inherited religious or spiritual worldview?
- How would you describe "spiritual genetics"?
- Identify patterns of spiritual genetics in your family and in yourself.
- What elements of spiritual genetics have you "inherited" from your culture, religion?
- Does the notion of spiritual miasms resonate with you? Why or why not?
- Identify one or more major miasms in your life.
- How would you work to heal a spiritual miasm?

CHAPTER 15: The Wound of the Soul

- Explore the suffering you have experienced from your religion or lack thereof. Does it involve segregation, rejection, shaming, violence, misogyny, racism, sexual orientation?
- How has this suffering affected your spiritual growth and soul?
- Does your religious background or practice oppress and/or sustain you? Explain in what way?
- What deep beliefs do you harbor about yourself?
- What do you hide from self, others, God?
- Is there a pain, shame, guilt, or wound that remains unhealed?
- Explain your understanding of the soul and its dimensions.

- Does knowing about the higher and lower soul help you? In what way?
- Contemplate: The higher soul is always one with the Divine and pure. Write about how this transforms self-understanding and your spirituality.
- What types of prayer or other spiritual practices will help your soul grow?

CHAPTER 16: The Mysticism of Healing

- Trace your spiritual autobiography. Can you locate places of healing or of injury?
- How do you relate to the idea that there is an archetype of transformation already imprinted within you?
- Describe an experience you or someone else had in which a spiritual state resulted in a physical manifestation. Or, when a physical injury became a soul injury.
- Do you identify with and/or understand how mystical dying is a form of healing? Describe why or why not.
- Often the initial stage of spiritual transformation is a type of purification, in which we are awakened to our ego, and give up attachment to the false self. Reflect on one or more instances of purification you have experienced.
- To be illumined, is to wake up from a limited consciousness and to peer into the realm of the holy. Write about or draw an illuminative awakening you have had. In what way did it change your life focus?
- Most of us can relate to Augustine's lament: "From day to day, I deferred to live in you, but on no day did I defer to die in myself." In silence, consider how your will may be obstructing the path ahead.
- Consider the dark night of the soul. It is an important and blessed stage of spiritual growth. Take time to reflect on periods of dark night, in the past or present.
- Pray to give all of yourself to the Divine. Pray for the great gift of healing.

Notes

PREFACE

1. Raimon Panikkar, "Nine Ways Not to Talk about God." *Cross Currents,* Summer 1997, Vol. 47 Issue 2. http://www.crosscurrents.org/panikkar.htm.

2. Beverly J. Lanzetta, *The Other Side of Nothingness: Toward a Theology of Radical Openness* (Albany: State University of New York Press, 2001).

3. See Jerry L. Martin, ed. *Theology without Walls: The Transreligious Imperative* (New York: Routledge, 2019).

4. Raimundo Panikkar, *The Intrareligious Dialogue* (New York: Paulist Press, 1978), 12.

CHAPTER 1 • Contemplation on Humility

1. *St. Benedict's Rule: A New Translation for Today,* Patrick Marry, OSB (York, UK: Ampleforth Abbey Press, 1997), 21.

2. Issachar Ber of Zlotshov, *Mevasser Zedek,* quoted in Daniel C. Matt, "*Ayin*: The Concept of Nothingness in Jewish Mysticism," *Tikkun,* Vol. 3, No. 3, 2015: 46.

3. Nottawaseppi Huron Band of the Potawatomi Nation, "Seven Grandfather Teachings," https://www.nhbpi.org/seven-grandfather-teachings. Neshnabék is a name the Potawatomi people use for themselves in their language.

4. *Black Elk Speaks: Being the Life Story of a Holy Man of the Oglala Sioux,* as told through John G. Neihardt (Lincoln, NE: University of Nebraska Press, 1972), 43.

5. *The HarperCollins Study Bible,* New Revised Standard Version, 1993.

6. *The Sixth Patriarch's Dharma Jewel Platform Sutra,* with the commentary of Tripitaka Master Hua (Burlingame, CA: Buddhist Text Translation Society, Third Edition 2001), 175-77.

7. Thich Nhat Hahn, *Joyfully Together: The Art of Building a Harmonious Community* (Berkeley: Parallax Press, 2005), 40.

8. See Raoul Birnbaum, *The Healing Buddha* (Boston: Shambhala, 1989), 43.

9. *The HarperCollins Study Bible*, New Revised Standard Version, 1993.

10. *Kenosis* is a term in Christian biblical theology that expresses Christ's self-emptying in the Incarnation, in his positive obedience to the Father, in his conscious acceptance of death.

11. *The Life of St. Francis*, in *Bonaventure: The Soul's Journey into God, The Tree of Life, and the Life of St. Francis*, translation and introduction by Ewert Cousins (New York: Paulist Press, 1978), 228.

12. Ibid.

13. Ibid. 230.

14. *Bhagavad Gita: The Song of God*, commentary by Swami Mukundananda. https://www.holy-bhagavad-gita.org/chapter/11, verses 36-42.

15. Thomas Merton, *New Seeds of Contemplation* (New York: New Directions, 1972), 181.

16. Cited in William C. Chittick, *The Sufi Path of Love: The Spiritual Teachings of Rumi* (Albany: State University of New York Press, 1983), 191-193.

17. Franklin D. Lewis, *The Life, Teachings and Poetry of Jalal al-Din Rumi* (London: Oneworld Publications, 2016), 385.

18. *Dao dejing*, selections translated by Louis Komjathy, some of which appear in his *Handbooks for Daoist Practice*, Handbook 2, (Hong Kong: Yuen Yuen Institute, 2008; 10 vols.), chapters 24, 8, 29. Komjathy clarifies: *Adeptness translates as *shan* 善, which may mean "goodness" and "to be good at." In my way of reading the text, which emphasizes the central importance of silent meditation, this character relates to aptitude with practice.

CHAPTER 2 • Contemplation on Compassion

1. William C. Chittick, *The Sufi Path of Love: The Spiritual Teachings of Rumi* (Albany: State University of New York Press, 1983), 47.

2. This is one of the most-often quoted passages in the Qur'an.

3. Wendy Farley, *Tragic Vision and Divine Compassion: A Contemporary Theodicy* (Louisville, KY: Westminster/John Knox Press, 1990), 119.

4. Chen Chien Ming, "Why all Beings are our Benefactors," http://www.yogichen.org/cw/cw38/bk103.html

CHAPTER 3 • Contemplation on Nonviolence

1. Mohandas K. Gandhi, *Vows and Observances*, edited by John Strobmeier (Berkeley, CA: Berkeley Hills Books, 1999), 15.

2. *Catherine of Siena: The Dialogue*, translation by Suzanne Noffke, O.P. (New York: Paulist Press, 1980), 30, 35.

3. Martin Luther King, Jr., "Beyond Vietnam: A Time to Break Silence," in *The Radical King*, edited by Cornel West (Boston: Beacon Press, 2015), 216.

4. Pseudo-Dionysius, *Pseudo-Dionysius: The Complete Works*, translation by Colm Luibheid and Paul Rorem (New York: Paulist Press, 1987), 122.

Notes

CHAPTER 4 • Contemplation on Simplicity

1. Patanjali, *How to Know God: The Yoga Aphorisms of Patanjali*, translated with a new commentary by Swami Prabhavananda and Christopher Isherwood (New York: New American Library, 1953), 55.
2. Ibid. 56.
3. Cited in Thomas Merton, *The Way of Chuang Tzu* (New York: New Directions, 1965), 52–53.

CHAPTER 5 • Bearing the Divinity of the World

1. Jean-Luc Marion, *God without Being*, translated by Thomas A. Carlson (Chicago: University of Chicago Press, 1991), 1.
2. Previous two paragraphs are excerpts adapted from Beverly J. Lanzetta, *The Other Side of Nothingness: A Theology of Radical Openness* (Albany: State University of New York Press, 2001), 115-116.
3. Excerpt adapted, Ibid. 119-120.

CHAPTER 6 • Our Mother of Contemplation

1. Shiva—the third divinity in the Hindu trinity of Brahma, Vishnu, and Shiva. Literally in Sanskrit "the kind one, the friendly one," Shiva functions as the God of creation and dissolution who destroys ignorance and grants wisdom, and who is the embodiment of renunciation and compassion.
2. Although the Ganges is a notoriously polluted waterway, pilgrims continue to seek her mystical presence, and citizens depend on her for bathing, carrying the dead, and ablution. It is also telling how this embodiment of the Mother on Earth has had to bear the violence of pollution and has been taken for granted and desecrated. The Ganges reminds us how humanity's treatment of the Ganges often correlates to our treatment of the Divine Feminine on Earth.
3. Christopher Pramuk, *Sophia: The Hidden Christ of Thomas Merton* (Collegeville, MN: Liturgical Press, 2009), 109.
4. Ibid. 110.
5. Judith Deutsch Kornblatt, *The Wisdom Writings of Vladimir Solovyov* (Ithaca, NY: Cornell University Press, 2009), 82.

CHAPTER 7 • Spiritual Formation

1. W.Y. Evans-Wentz, ed. *Tibet's Great Yogi Milarepa* (New York: Oxford University Press, 1951), xiii-xiv.
2. Thomas Merton, *The Inner Experience: Notes on Contemplation*, edited by William H. Shannon (NY: Harper Collins, 2003), 3.

CHAPTER 8 • Turning One's Life Around

1. Columba Stewart, "The Desert Fathers on Radical Self-Honesty," in *Vox Benedictina: A Journal of Translations from Monastic Sources* (Saskatoon, Canada:

Peregrina Publishers, 1984). 8/1 (1991): 7–54.

2. Gail Fitzpatrick, OSCO, "Enclosure: The Heart of the Matter," in *A Monastic Vision for the 21st Century: Where Do We Go from Here?* Edited by Patrick Hart, OSCO (Kalamazoo, MI: Cistercian Publications, 2006), 150–151.

CHAPTER 9 · The Monk's Life in Relationship

1. Rainer Maria Rilke, *Letters to a Young Poet*, translated by Stephen Mitchell (NY: Vintage Books, 1987), 35–36.

2. Ibid. 39–40.

CHAPTER 10 · Spiritual Guidance: The Inner Way

1. *Russian Letters of Direction, 1834–1860*, translated by Iulia de Beausobre (Crestwood, NY: St. Vladimir's Seminary Press, 1975), 28.

2. Thomas Merton, *Spiritual Direction and Meditation* (Collegeville, MN: The Liturgical Press, 1960), 16.

3. Walpola Rahula, *What the Buddha Taught* (New York: Grove Press, 2007), chapter VII.

4. Joseph J. Allen, *Inner Way: Toward a Rebirth of Eastern Christian Spiritual Direction* (Grand Rapids, MI: Wm. B. Eerdmans, 1994), 4–5.

5. Dom Augustine Baker, cited in *Spiritual Direction and Meditation*, 20–21.

6. St. Anthony of Egypt, cited in *The Desert Fathers*, Helen Waddell, ed. (London: Collins, 1972), 147.

7. For a study of the spiritual physician, see *Inner Way*, 1–6.

8. Ibid. 5.

9. Kallistos Ware, *The Inner Kingdom* (Crestwood, NY: St. Vladimir's Seminary Press, 2001), 137.

10. Ignatius of Loyola, *The Autobiography of St. Ignatius of Loyola*, translated by Joseph F. O'Callaghan (New York: Fordham University Press, 1992), 24.

11. Ibid. 1.

12. John Cassian, *Conferences* II.4, translation and preface by Colm Luibheid (New York: Paulist Press, 1985), 64.

13. Dogen, quoted in Heinrich Dumoulin, *A History of Zen Buddhism* (New York: Faber & Faber, 1963), 163–164.

14. Hakuin, Ibid. 37.

15. Sharafuddin Maneri, *The Hundred Letters*, Paul Jackson, ed. (New York: Paulist Press, 1980), 26.

16. Cited in John A. Grim, *The Shaman: Patterns of Religious Healing Among the Ojibway Indians* (Norman, OK: University of Oklahoma Press, 1983), 199.

CHAPTER 11 · Cultivation of Mindfulness

1. Cited in Louis Komjathy, *Daoism: A Guide for the Perplexed* (New York: Bloomsbury Academic, 2014), 134.

2. Anonymous, *The Cloud of Unknowing and the Book of Privy Counseling*, William

Johnston, ed. (New York: Doubleday, 1973), 95.

CHAPTER 12 • Theology of Energy

1. John of the Cross, *The Living Flame of Love*, in *The Collected Works of St. John of the Cross*, translated by Kieran Kavanaugh and Otilio Rodriguez (Washington, DC: Institute of Carmelite Studies, 1991), 2.13, 662.

2. Ibid.

3. *The Unborn: The Life and Teachings of Zen Master Bankei 1622–1693*, translated by Norman Waddell (San Francisco: North Point Press, 1984), 10–11.

4. Hakuin Zenji, *The Embossed Tea Kettle and Other Works of Hakuin Zenji*, translated by R. Shaw (London: 1963), 33. Cited in William Johnston, *Mystical Theology: The Science of Love* (Maryknoll, NY: Orbis Books, 1995), 102.

5. Teresa of Avila, *The Interior Castle*, *The Collected Works of St. Teresa of Avila, Volume Two*, translated by Kieran Kavanaugh and Otilio Rodriguez (Washington, DC: Institute of Carmelite Studies, 1980), 4.1.10, 320.

6. Teresa of Avila, *The Story of My Life*, *The Collected Works of St. Teresa of Avila, Volume One*, translated by Kieran Kavanaugh and Otilio Rodriguez (Washington, DC: Institute of Carmelite Studies, 1976), 20.12, 177.

7. *The Interior Castle*, 4.1.10, 321.

8. Abu al-Hasan al-Shushtari, "O, Perplexed Heart!" in *Abu al-Hasan al-Shushtari: Songs of Love and Devotion*, translated by Lourdes Maria Alvarez (New York: Paulist Press, 2009), 48.

9. Teresa of Avila, *The Story of My Life*.

10. Thomas Merton, *A Thomas Merton Reader*, edited by Thomas P. McDonnell (New York: Image Books, 1974), 83.

11. Ibid.

12. Kenneth K. Tanka, "Mahayana Buddhist Visualization," in *Contemplative Literature: A Comparative Sourcebook on Meditation and Contemplative Prayer*, edited by Louis Komjathy (Albany, NY: State University of New York Press, 2015), 444, 446.

13. Robert Thurman, *The Tibetan Book of the Dead: Liberation Through Understanding in the Between* (New York: Bantam Books, 2011), 251.

14. St. Augustine, *The Confessions of St. Augustine*, translated by John K. Ryan (New York: Image Books, 1960), 7.10.16, 170.

15. William Johnston, *Mystical Theology: The Science of Love* (Maryknoll, NY: Orbis Books, 1995), 58.

16. Ibid. 57.

17. John of the Cross, *The Spiritual Canticle*, in *The Collected Works of St. John of the Cross*, translated by Kieran Kavanaugh and Otilio Rodriguez (Washington, DC: Institute of Carmelite Studies, 1991), 13.4, 521.

CHAPTER 13 • Spiritual Practice: Obstacles & Solutions

1. Kallistos Ware, *The Inner Kingdom* (Crestwood, NY: St. Vladimir Seminary Press, 2000), 45.

CHAPTER 14 • Freeing the Spiritual Imaginary

1. The French psychoanalyst Pierre Bordieu first advanced the term "moral imaginary." See Grace M. Jantzen, "Flourishing: Towards an Ethic of Natality," *Feminist Theory*, 2 (2001): 219–232.

2. Nanci Hogan, "The Implications of a Politics of Natality for Transnational Feminist Advocacy: Transforming the Human Rights Moral Imaginary," in *Grace Jantzen: Redeeming the Present*, edited by Elaine L. Graham (Surrey, England: Ashgate Publishing Limited, 2009), 228–229.

CHAPTER 15 • The Wound of the Soul

1. Teresa of Avila, *The Interior Castle, The Collected Works of St. Teresa of Avila*, vols. 1–3, translated by Kieran Kavanaugh and Otilio Rodriguez (Washington, DC: ICS Publications, 1987) 6.11.2, 422. All citations from Teresa of Avila that follow are from *The Collected Works*.

2. Teresa of Avila, *Spiritual Testimonies*, 430–431.

3. Julian of Norwich, *Showings*, translated by Edmund Colledge and James Walsh (New York: Paulist Press, 1979), Long Text (hereafter LT), 186.

4. Ibid. 204–5.

5. Ibid. 242.

6. Stewart Burns, *To the Mountaintop: Martin Luther King Jr.'s Mission to Save America 1955–1968* (San Francisco: HarperSanFrancisco, 2004), 110.

7. Martin Luther King, Jr., *A Testament of Hope: The Essential Writings of Martin Luther King, Jr.*, edited by James M. Washington (New York: Harper Collins, 1986), 85.

8. McGinn, "The Language of Inner Experience in Christian Mysticism," *Spiritus* 1(2001), The John Hopkins University Press, 159.

9. Ibid.

10. Teresa of Avila, *The Book of Her Life*, 29.13, 252.

11. Ibid. 12.11, 251.

12. Teresa of Avila, *The Interior Castle*, 6.1.8, 363.

13. Ibid. 4.2.5–6, 324–325.

14. Ibid. 6.2.2, 367.

15. Ibid. 6.11.1–2, 421–422.

16. Ibid. 6.2.8, 370.

17. Ibid. 6.6.5, 393.

18. Ibid. 7.2.6, 435; 7.2.9, 436.

19. Grace Jantzen, *Julian of Norwich: Mystic and Theologian* (New York: Paulist Press, 2000), 171.

CHAPTER 16 • The Mysticism of Healing

1. Purusa-Sukta 10.90 (*The Hymn of Man*), Rigveda. Translated by Wendy O'Flaherty and cited in Kenneth Kramer, *World Scriptures: An Introduction to Comparative Religions* (Mahwah, NJ: Paulist Press, 1986), 35.

2. Cited in John A. Grim, *The Shaman: Patterns of Religious Healing Among the*

Ojibway Indians (Norman: University of Oklahoma Press, 1987), 45-46.

3. William C. Chittick, *The Sufi Path of Love: The Spiritual Teachings of Rumi* (Albany: State University of New York Press, 1983), 215.

4. Ewert H. Cousins, *Global Spirituality: Toward the Meeting of Mystical Paths* (Madras, India: Radhakrishnan Institute for Advanced Study in Philosophy, 1985), 41.

5. Cited in Ewert H. Cousins, *Christ of the 21st Century* (Rockport, MA: Element Books, 1992), 143-44.

6. A few stanzas of the Canticle serve to express Francis' profound sentiment of love and hope: "Most high, all-powerful, good Lord, all praise be yours, all glory, all honor and all blessing. To you alone, Most High, do they belong. No mortal lips are worthy to pronounce your name. All praise be yours, my Lord, in all your creatures, especially Sir Brother Sun who brings the day; and light you give us through him. How beautiful he is, how radiant in his splendor! Of you, Most High, he is the token." Citation taken from *The Prayers of Saint Francis*, edited by W. Bader (New York: New City Press, 1988), 42.

7. The term *epectasis* is taken from Philippians 3.13, "forgetting what lies behind and straining forward to what lies ahead." See Gregory of Nyssa, *Commentary on the Song of Songs*, translated by Casimir McCambley (Brookline, MA: Hellenic College Press, 1987).

8. Ibid. 62.

9. Raoul Birnbaum, *The Healing Buddha* (Boston: Shambhala, 1989), 15.

10. Ibid. 16.

11. Ibid. 13.

12. Ibid. 14.

13. Julian of Norwich, *Showings*, translated by Edmund Colledge and James Walsh (New York: Paulist Press, 1978), 178-80.

14. *The Healing Buddha*, 31.

15. *The Cloud of Unknowing and the Book of Privy Counseling*, edited by William Johnston (New York: Image Books, 1973), 103.

16. See *Pseudo-Dionysius: The Complete Works*, translated by Colm Luibheid and Paul Rorem (New York: Paulist Press, 1987). Dionysius makes numerous references to the threefold way in the *Celestial Hierarchy*. A particularly pointed passage is found in the *Ecclesiastical Hierarchy*: "With regard to the initiates, their first power is that of being purified. Their middle power is, after purification, the illumination which makes it possible for them to contemplate certain sacred things. Finally, they have the power, more divine than others, of being enlightened in the perfect understanding of the sacred illuminations which they have been permitted to contemplate." *Pseudo-Dionysius: The Complete Works*, 235.

17. See Teresa of Avila, *The Collected Works of St. Teresa of Avila*, translated by Kieran Kavanaugh and Otilio Rodriquez (Washington, DC: ICS Publications, 1985) and John of the Cross, *The Collected Works of St. John of the Cross*, translated by Kieran Kavanaugh and Otilio Rodriquez (Washington, DC: ICS Publications, 1979) for further insight into the stages of mystical growth in Christian mysticism. Also of interest in the Christian context is St. Bonaventure's *Itinerarium mentis in deum* (The Soul's

Journey into God), which depicts the soul's healing as a progression of six stages of ascent into union with the divine. In Sufism, consult Farid ud-Din Attar, *The Conference of the Birds* (London: Routledge & Kegan Paul Ltd., 1969). In Hinduism, the *Bhagavad Gita* sheds light on the process of purification, illumination, and release-ment of I-hood. While employing different imagery, Buddhism seeks to undercut the illusion of the self's attachment to identity through a process of deconstruction and purification, followed by periods of illumination and final *satori* or *nirvana*.

18. Evelyn Underhill, *Mysticism: A Study in the Nature and Development of Man's Spiritual Consciousness* (New York: New American Library, 1974). Underhill lists the following states: awakening, purgation, illumination, dark night, and union. See especially Section II: The Mystic Way.

19. *The Confessions of St. Augustine*, translated by John K. Ryan (New York: Image Books, 1960), 150.

CHAPTER 18 • Lectio Divina: Spiritual Reading

1. Kathryn and Ewert Cousins, *How to Read a Spiritual Book* (New York: Paulist Press, 1981), 7.

2. Ibid. 8.

3. Ibid. 15. Gregory of Nyssa, *The Life of Moses*, translated by Abraham J. Malherbe (New York: Paulist Press, 1978), 83.

4. *How to Read a Spiritual Book*, 19.

CHAPTER 20 • Preparing for Vows

1. See Nass Cannon, "Stand on Your Own Feet! Thomas Merton and the Monk without Vows or Walls," *The Merton Annual* 25 (2012): 154-68.

2. Thomas Merton, *Witness to Freedom: Letters in Times of Crisis*, edited by William H. Shannon (New York: Harcourt Brace & Company, 1995), 255.

3. Ibid.

4. Nass Cannon, 164-65.

CHAPTER 21 • Diksha and the Sannyasin

1. Swami Sivamurti Saraswati, "Training the Disciple, Yoga Magazine July 2005. http://www.yogamag.net/archives/2000s/2005/gjuly05/trandis.html

2. "On Guru and Disciple: From the Teachings of Swami Sivananda Saraswati," *Yoga Magazine* July 2005. http://www.yogamag.net/archives/2000s/2005/gjuly05/gudisiv.html. Namaskara is a traditional greeting of respect, made by bringing the palms together before the face or chest and bowing.

3. Swami Sivamurti Saraswati, "Training the Disciple," *Yoga Magazine* July 2005. http://www.yogamag.net/archives/2000s/2005/gjuly05/gudisiv.html

CHAPTER 22 • Rule of Life

1. These introductory paragraphs are quoted from, Beverly Lanzetta, *The Monk Within: Embracing a Sacred Way of Life* (Sebastopol: Blue Sapphire Books, 2018), 337-38.

CHAPTER 24 · Meditation Exercises

1. This practice is similar to many the world over, especially that of Centering Prayer as taught by Frs. Thomas Keating and Basil Pennington (reference in bibliography).

CHAPTER 26 · Four Virtues of a Monastic Heart

1. Robert Inchausti, *Thomas Merton's American Prophecy* (Albany NY: The State University of New York Press, 1998), 1.

2. Ibid.

3. Columba Stewart, "The Desert Fathers on Radical Self-Honesty," in *Vox Benedictina: A Journal of Translations from Monastic Sources* (Saskatoon: Peregrina Publishers, 1984). 8/1 (1991): 7-54.

4. Ibid.

Monastic Bibliography

Abhishiktananda. *Ascent to the Depth of the Heart: The Spiritual Diary of Swami Abhi-shiktananda.* Translated by David Fleming. Delhi: ISPCK, 1993.

———. *The Secret of Arunachala: A Christian Hermit on Shiva's Holy Mountain.* Delhi: ISPCK, 1998.

———. *Witness to the Fullness of Light: The Vision and Relevance of the Benedictine Monk Swami Abhishiktananda.* Edited by William Skudlarek. New York: Lantern Books, 2011.

Aiken, Robert. *Taking the Path of Zen.* San Francisco: North Point Press, 1982.

Ali Shomali, Mohammad, and William Skudlarek, eds. *Monks and Muslims: Monastic and Shi'a Spirituality in Dialogue.* Collegeville, MN: Liturgical Press, 1989.

Anonymous. *Silence: A Series of Conferences Given by a Camaldolese Hermit.* Bloomingdale, OH: Ercam Editions, 2011.

Anonymous. *The Cloud of Unknowing and The Book of Privy Counseling.* Edited by William Johnston. New York: Image Books, 1996.

Baldwin, Lewis V., and Victor Anderson, eds. *Revives My Soul Again: The Spirituality of Martin Luther King Jr.* Minneapolis: Fortress Press, 2018.

Bankei, Yotaku. *The Unborn: The Life and Teachings of Zen Master Bankei 1622–1693.* Norman Waddell, trans. San Francisco: North Point Press, 1982.

Barnhart, Bruno, and Joseph Wong. *Purity of Heart and Contemplation: A Monastic Dialogue between Christian and Asian Traditions.* New York: Continuum, 2001.

Barrows, Anita, and Joanna Macy, trans. and eds. *In Praise of Mortality (Selections from Rilke's Duin Elegies & Sonnets to Orpheus).* New York: Riverhead Books, 2005.

——— *Rilke's Book of Hours: Love Poems to God.* New York: Riverhead Books, 1996, 2005.

——— *A Year with Rilke: Daily Readings from the Best of Rainer Maria Rilke.* New York: Harpers, 2009.

Benedict, Saint, Abbot of Monte Cassino. *The Rule of Saint Benedict*. Edited by Timothy Fry. New York: Vintage Books, 1998.

Bernard of Clairvaux. *The Step of Humility and Pride*. Kalamazoo, MI: Cistercian Publications, 1989.

Bielecki, Tessa. *Holy Daring: An Outrageous Gift to Modern Spirituality from Saint Teresa, the Grand Wild Woman of Avila*. Rockport, MA: Element, 1994.

_____ *Wild at Heart: Radical Teachings of the Christian Mystics*. Louisville, CO: Sounds True (Audiobook), 2006.

_____ *Teresa of Avila: Mystical Writings*. New York: Crossroads, 1994.

Bodo, Murray. *Francis: The Journey and the Dream*. Cincinnati, OH: St. Anthony Messenger Press, 1988.

Bourgeault, Cynthia. *Centering Prayer and Inner Awakening*. New York: Cowley Publications, 2004.

_____ *Mystical Hope: Trusting in the Mercy of God*. New York: Cowley Publications, 2001.

Brussat, Frederic, and Mary Ann Brussat. *Spiritual Literacy: Reading the Sacred in Everyday Life*. New York: Scribner, 1996.

Cameron, Averil et al. *Desert Mothers: Women Ascetics in Early Christian Egypt*. New York: Edwin Mellen Press, 1993.

Caplow, Florence, and Susan Moon, eds. *The Hidden Lamp: Stories from Twenty-five Centuries of Awakened Women*. Summerville, MA: Wisdom Publications, 2013.

Carney, Eido Frances, ed. *Receiving the Marrow: Teachings on Dogen by Soto Zen Women Priests*. Olympia, WA: Temple Ground Press, 2012.

Carretto, Carlo. *I, Francis*. Translated by Robert R. Barr. New York: Orbis Books, 1982.

Casey, Michael. *Sacred Reading: The Ancient Art of Lectio Divina*. Ligouri, MO: Ligouri Publications, 1996.

_____ *The Undivided Heart: The Western Monastic Approach to Contemplation*. Petersham, MA: St. Bede's Publications, 1994.

Cattoi, Thomas, and June McDaniel. *Perceiving the Divine Through the Human Body: Mystical Sensuality*. New York: Palgrave Macmillan, 2011.

Chittister, Joan. *Called to Question: A Spiritual Memoir*. New York: Sheed and Ward, 2004.

_____ *Illuminated Life: Monastic Wisdom for Seekers of Light*. New York: Orbis Books, 2000.

_____ *Wisdom Distilled from the Daily: Living the Rule of St. Benedict Today*. San Francisco: HarperOne,1991.

_____ *The Rule of Benedict: A Spirituality for the 21st Century*. New York: Crossroad Books, 1992.

_____ *The Time Is Now: A Call to Uncommon Courage*. New York: Convergent Books, 2019.

Chodron, Pema. *When Things Fall Apart: Hard Advice for Difficult Times*. Boston: Shambhala, 1997.

_____ *The Places that Scare You: A Guide to Fearlessness in Difficult Times.* Boston: Shambhala, 2001.

_____ *Comfortable with Uncertainty: 108 Teachings.* Boston: Shambhala, 2002.

_____ *Taking the Leap: Freeing Ourselves from Old Habits and Fears.* Boston: Shambhala, 2009.

Cleary, William. *Prayers to She Who Is.* New York: Crossroad Books, 1995.

_____ *In God's Presence: Centering Experiences for Circles and Solitudes.* Mystic, CT: Twenty-Third Publications, 1994.

_____ *How the Wild Things Pray.* Leavenworth, KS: Forest of Peace Publishing, 1999.

_____ *Prayers to an Evolutionary God.* Woodstock, VT: Skylight Paths Publishing, 2004.

Corbin, Henry. *Alone with the Alone: Creative Imagination in the Sufism of Ibn 'Arabi.* Princeton: Princeton University Press, 1969.

Cummings, Charles. *Monastic Practices.* Kalamazoo, MI: Cistercian Publications, 1986.

Day, Dorothy. *The Long Loneliness: The Autobiography of the Legendary Catholic Social Activist.* New York: Harper One, 2017.

Dear, John. *The Nonviolent Life.* Corvallis, OR: Pace e Bene Press, 2013.

de Bethune, Pierre-François. *By Faith and Hospitality: The Monastic Tradition as a Model for Interreligious Encounter.* Translated by Dame Mary Groves. Herefordshire, England: Gracewing, 2002.

de Caussade, Jean-Pierre. *The Fire of Divine Love: Readings from Jean-Pierre de Caussade.* Liguori, MO: Triumph Books, 1995.

de Dreuille, Mayeul. *From East to West: A History of Monasticism.* Herefordshire, England: Gracewing, 1999.

_____ *The Rule of St. Benedict: A Commentary in Light of World Ascetic Traditions.* England: Gracewing, 2000.

de Mello, Anthony. *One Minute Wisdom.* New York: Doubleday, 1985.

_____ *The Way to Love: The Last Meditations of Anthony de Mello.* New York: Doubleday, 1991.

Dekar, Paul R. *Community of the Transfiguration: The Journey of a New Monastic Community.* Eugene, OR: Cascade Books, 2008.

Despeux, Catherine, and Livia Kohn. *Women in Daoism.* Cambridge, MA: Three Pines Press, 2003.

Dogen, Eihei. *Moon in a Dewdrop: Writings of Zen Master Dogen.* Kazuaki Tanahashi, ed. San Francisco: North Point Press, 1985.

Du Boulay, Shirley. *Beyond the Darkness: A Biography of Bede Griffiths.* New York: Doubleday, 1998.

_____ *Teresa of Avila: An Extraordinary Life.* New York: Bluebridge, 1991, 2004.

_____ *The Cave of the Heart: The Life of Swami Abhishiktananda.* New York: Orbis Books, 2005.

Earle, Mary C. *The Desert Mothers: Spiritual Practices from the Women of the Wilderness.* New York: Moorhouse Publishing, 2007.

Easwaran, Eknath. *Love Never Faileth.* Tomales, CA: Nilgiri Press, 1984, 1996.

———— *Gandhi The Man: The Story of His Transformation*. Tomales, CA: Nilgiri Press, 1972, 1997.

———— *Original Goodness: Strategies for Uncovering Your Hidden Spiritual Resources*. Tomales, CA: Nilgiri Press, 1972 and 1997.

Ellsberg, Robert. *All Saints: Daily Reflections on Saints Prophets and Witnesses for Our Time*. New York: A Crossroad Book, 2005.

———— *Blessed Among All Women: Women Saints, Prophets, and Witnesses for Our Time*. New York: A Crossroad Book, 2005.

———— *The Saints' Guide to Happiness: Practical Lessons in the Life of the Spirit*. New York: Doubleday, 2003.

Evagrius Ponticus. *The Praktikos and Chapters on Prayer*. Translated by John Eudes Bamberger. Kalamazoo, MI: Cistercian Publications, 1981.

Evans-Wentz, W.Y., ed. *Tibet's Great Yogi Milarepa: A Biography from the Tibetan*. New York: Oxford University Press, 1969.

Ferrer, Jorge. *Participation and the Mystery: Transpersonal Essays in Psychology, Education, and Religion*. Albany: State University of New York Press, 2017.

Finley, James. *Merton's Palace of Nowhere: A Search for God through Awareness of the True Self*. Notre Dame, IN: Ave Maria Press, 1978.

————. *The Contemplative Heart*. Notre Dame: IN: Sorin Books, 2000.

Flanagan, Bernadette. *Embracing Solitude: Women and New Monasticism*. Eugene, OR: Cascade Books, 2014.

Flinders, Carol Lee. *At the Roots of this Longing: Reconciling a Spiritual Hunger and a Feminist Thirst*. San Francisco: HarperCollins, 1998.

———— *Enduring Grace: Living Portraits of Seven Women Mystics*. San Francisco: HarperCollins, 1993.

———— *Enduring Lives: Portraits of Women and Faith in Action*. New York: Jeremy P. Tarcher/Penguin, 2006.

Fischer, Kathleen. *Women at the Well: Feminist Perspectives on Spiritual Direction*. New York: Paulist Press, 1988.

Fox, Matthew. *Hildegard of Bingen: A Saint for Our Times: Unleasing Her Power in the 21st Century*. Vancouver: Namaste, 2012.

———— *Meister Eckhart: A Mystic-Warrior for Our Times*. Novato, CA: New World Library, 2014.

———— *Christian Mystics: 365 Readings and Meditations*. Novato, CA: New World Library, 2011.

Gandhi, Mohandas K. *Book of Prayers*. Edited by John Strohmeier. Berkeley: Berkeley Hills Books, 1999.

———— *The Way to God*. Edited by M. S. Desphande. Berkeley: Berkeley Hills Books, 1999.

———— *The Words of Gandhi*. Edited by Richard Attenborough. New York: Newmarket Press, 1982, 1996.

———— *Vows and Observances*. Edited by John Strohmeier. Berkeley: Berkeley Hills Books, 1999.

Garling, Wendy. *Stars at Dawn: Forgotten Stories of Women in the Buddha's Life.* Boulder: Shambhala, 2016.

Glassman, Bernie. *Bearing Witness: A Zen Master's Lessons in Making Peace.* New York: Bell Tower, 1998.

_____ and Rick Fields. *Instructions to the Cook: A Zen Master's Lessons in Living a Life that Matters.* New York: Bell Tower, 1996.

Griffiths, Bede. *The Golden String: An Autobiography.* Springfield, IL: Templegate Publishers, 1954, 1980.

_____ *The Marriage of East and West: A Sequel to the Golden String.* Springfield, IL: Templegate Publishers, 1982.

_____ *Bede Griffiths: Selections from His Writings.* Edited by Peter Spink. The Modern Spirituality Series. Springfield, IL: Templegate Publishers, 1992.

Gyaltsen, Khenpo Konchog. *The Great Kagyu Masters.* Ithaca, NY: Snow Lion Publications, 1990.

Gyatso, Palden. *The Autobiography of a Tibetan Monk.* New York: Grove Press, 1997.

Hallisey, Charles, trans. *Therigatha: Poems of the First Buddhist Women.* London: Murty Classical Library of India, 2015.

Hanh, Thich Nhat. *Chanting from the Heart: Buddhist Ceremonies and Daily Practices.* Berkeley: Parallax Press, 2007.

_____ *The Miracle of Mindfulness: An Introduction to the Practice of Meditation.* Boston: Beacon Press, 1975.

_____ *Peace Is Every Step: The Path of Mindfulness in Everyday Life.* New York: Bantam Books, 1991.

_____ *Love in Action: Writings on Nonviolent Social Change.* Berkeley: Parallax Press, 1993.

_____ et al. *For a Future to Be Possible: Commentaries on the Five Mindfulness Trainings.* Berkeley: Parallax Press, 1993.

_____ *Stepping into Freedom: An Introduction to Buddhist Monastic Training.* Berkeley: Parallax Press, 1997.

_____ *The Heart of the Buddha's Teaching: Transforming Suffering into Peace, Joy and Liberation.* Berkeley: Parallax Press, 1998.

Hart, Patrick. *A Monastic Vision for the 21st Century: Where Do We Go From Here?* Kalamazoo, MI: Cistercian Publications, 2006.

Hays, Edward. *Prayers for a Planetary Pilgrim: A Personal Manual for Prayer and Ritual.* Notre Dame, IN: Forest of Peace, 1989.

_____ *The Gospel of Gabriel: A Life of Jesus The Christ.* Notre Dame, IN: Forest of Peace, 1996.

_____ *The Passionate Troubadour: A Medieval Novel about St. Francis of Assisi.* Notre Dame, IN: Forest of Peace, 2004.

Henry, Patrick, ed. *Benedict's Dharma: Buddhists Reflect on the Rule of Saint Benedict.* New York: Riverhead Books, 2001.

Henry, Patrick G., and Donald K. Swearer. *For the Sake of the World: The Spirit of Buddhist and Christian Monasticism.* Minneapolis: Fortress Press, 1989.

Herrou, Adeline. *A World of Their Own: Daoist Monks and Their Community in Contemporary China*. St. Petersburg, FL: Three Pines Press, 2013.

Heschel, Abraham Joshua. *The Sabbath: Its Meaning for Modern Man*. New York: Farrar, Straus and Giroux, 1951, 2005.

———. *The Prophets*. New York: HarperCollins, 1962, 2001.

———. *I Asked for Wonder: A Spiritual Anthology*. Edited by Samuel H. Dresner. New York: Crossroad Books, 1983, 2000.

Hildegard of Bingen. *Mystical Writings*. Translated by Robert Carver. Edited by Fiona Bowie and Oliver Davies. New York: Crossroad Books, 1990.

Hillesum, Etty. *An Interrupted Life: The Diaries of Etty Hillesum 1941-1943*. Translated by Arno Pomerans. New York: Pantheon Books, 1983.

Huston, Paula. *The Holy Way: Practices for a Simple Life*. Chicago: Loyola Press, 2003.

Isaac of Nineveh, St. *Daily Readings with St. Isaac of Syria*. Translated by Sebastian Brock. Springfield, IL: Templegate Publishers, 1989.

———. *On Ascetical Life*. Translated by Mary Hansbury. Crestwood, NY: St. Vladimir's Seminary Press, 1989.

———. *The Wisdom of St. Isaac of Nineveh*. Translated by Sebastian Brock. Piscataway, NJ: Gorgias Press, 2006.

Jager, Willigis. *Contemplation: A Christian Path*. Ligouri, MO: Triumph Books, 1994.

———. *Mysticism for Modern Times: Conversations With Willigis Jager*. Translated by Paul Sheppard. Edited by Christoph Quarch. Ligouri, MO: Ligouri Publications, 2006.

———. *Search for the Meaning of Life: Essays and Reflections on the Mystical Experience*. Ligouri, MO: Triumph Books, 1995.

Jantzen, Grace M. *Julian of Norwich: Mystic and Theologian*. New York: Paulist Press, 1988.

Johnson, Elizabeth. *She Who Is: The Mystery of God in Feminist Theological Discourse*. New York: Crossroad Books, 1992.

Johnston, William. *Mystical Theology: The Science of Love*. New York: Orbis Books, 1995.

Kaplan, Aryeh. *Meditation and Kabbalah*. San Francisco: Weiser Books, 1985.

Katagiri, Dainin. *Returning to Silence: Zen Practice in Daily Life*. Boston: Shambhala Publications, 1988.

Keating, Thomas. *Open Heart, Open Mind: The Contemplative Dimension of the Gospel*. New York: Continuum, 1995.

———. *The Heart of the World: An Introduction to Contemplative Christianity*. New York: The Crossroad Publishing Company, 1999.

Khan, Hazrat Inayat. *The Inner Life*. Boston: Shambhala, 1997.

———. *The Art of Being and Becoming*. New Lebanon, NY: Omega Publications, 1982, 2009.

King, Martin Luther, Jr. *Strength to Love*. Philadelphia: Fortress Press, 1963.

———. *The Autobiography of Martin Luther King, Jr.* Edited by Clayborne Carson. New York: Grand Central Publishing, 1998.

_____ . *Where Do We Go From Here: Chaos or Community?* Boston: Beacon Press, 1967.

King, Ursula. *Spirit of Fire: The Life and Vision of Teilhard de Chardin.* New York: Orbis Books, 1996.

Komjathy, Louis. *Daoism: A Guide for the Perplexed.* New York: Bloomsbury Academic, 2014.

_____ . *Taming the Wild Horse: An Annotated Translation and Study of the Daoist Horse Taming Pictures.* New York: Columbia University Press, 2017.

_____ "The Daoist Mystical Body." In *Perceiving the Divine through the Human Body: Mystical Sensuality.* Edited by Thomas Cottai and June McDaniel. New York: Palgrave Macmillan, 2011, 67–103.

_____ *The Daoist Tradition: An Introduction.* London and New York: Bloomsbury Academic, 2013.

Kownacki, Mary Lou. *A Monk in the Inner City: The ABC's of a Spiritual Journey.* New York: Orbis Books, 2008.

_____ *Between Two Souls: Conversations with Ryokan.* Grand Rapids, MI: William B. Eerdmans, 2004.

_____ *The Nonviolent Moment: Spirituality for the 21ˢᵗ Century.* Erie, PA: Pax Christi USA, 2002.

_____ *Peace is Our Calling: Contemporary Monasticism and the Peace Movement.* Erie, PA: Benet Press, 1981.

Lane, Belden. *The Solace of Fierce Landscapes: Exploring Desert and Mountain Spirituality.* New York: Oxford University Press, 1998.

Lanzetta, Beverly. *The Monk Within: Embracing a Sacred Way of Life.* Sebastopol, CA: Blue Sapphire Books, 2018.

_____ *Foundations in Spiritual Direction: Sharing the Sacred Across Traditions.* Sebastopol, CA: Blue Sapphire Books, 2018.

_____ *Nine Jewels of Night: One Soul's Journey into God.* Sebastopol, CA: Blue Sapphire Books, 2014.

_____ *Path of the Heart: A Spiritual Guide to Divine Union.* Expanded with Commentary. Sebastopol, CA: Blue Sapphire Books, 2014.

_____ *Emerging Heart: Global Spirituality and the Sacred.* Minneapolis: Fortress Press, 2007.

_____ *Radical Wisdom: A Feminist Mystical Theology.* Minneapolis: Fortress Press, 2005.

_____ *The Other Side of Nothingness: Toward a Theology of Radical Openness.* Albany: State University of New York Press, 2001.

Luibheid, Colin, trans. *John Cassian: Conferences.* New York: Paulist Press, 1985.

McEntee, Rory, and Adam Bucko. *The New Monasticism: An Interspiritual Manifesto for Contemplative Living.* Maryknoll, NY: Orbis Books, 2015.

McGinn, Bernard, ed. *The Essential Writings of Christian Mysticism.* New York: The Modern Library, 2006.

Medwick, Cathleen. *Teresa of Avila: The Progress of a Soul.* New York: Doubleday, 1999.

Merkle, Judith A. *A Different Touch: A Study of Vows in Religious Life*. Collegeville, MN: Liturgical Press, 1998.

Merton, Thomas. *Contemplation in a World of Action*. Notre Dame, IN: University of Notre Dame Press, 1998.

_____ *New Seeds of Contemplation*. New York: New Directions, 1972.

_____ *The Asian Journal of Thomas Merton*. Edited by Brother Patrick Hart. New York: New Directions, 1975.

_____ *Dialogues with Silence: Prayers and Drawings*. Edited by Jonathon Montaldo. San Francisco: HarperCollins, 2001.

_____ *Choosing to Love the World: On Contemplation*. Edited by Jonathon Montaldo. Louisville, CO: Sounds True, 2008.

_____ *Entering the Silence: Becoming a Monk and Writer*. The Journals of Thomas Merton, Vol. 2 1941-1952. Edited by Jonathon Montaldo. San Francisco: HarperCollins, 1996.

_____ *A Year with Thomas Merton: Daily Meditations from His Journals*. Edited by Jonathon Montaldo. San Francisco: HarperCollins, 2004.

_____ Ed. and Introduction. *Gandhi on Non-Violence*. New York: New Directions, 1964.

_____ *The Inner Experience: Notes on Contemplation*. Edited by William H. Shannon. San Francisco: HarperCollins, 2003.

_____ *The Monastic Journey*. Edited by Patrick Hart. Kansas City, MO: Sheed Andrews and McMeel, Inc., 1977.

_____ *The Way of Chuang Tzu*. New York: New Directions, 1965.

_____ *Thoughts in Solitude*. New York: Farrar, Straus and Giroux, 1956.

_____ Trans. *The Wisdom of the Desert: Sayings from the Desert Fathers of the Fourth Century*. New York: New Directions, 1960.

Mitchell, Donald W., and James Wiseman, eds. *The Gethsemani Encounter: A Dialogue on the Spiritual Life by Buddhist and Christian Monastics*. New York: Continuum, 1999.

Muller, Wayne. *How Then Shall We Live? Four Simple Questions That Reveal the Beauty and Meaning of Our Lives*. New York: Bantam, 1996.

_____ *Legacy of the Heart: The Spiritual Advantages of a Painful Childhood*. New York: Fireside, 1992.

_____ *Sabbath: Restoring the Sacred Rhythm of Rest*. New York: Bantam Books, 1999.

Murcott, Susan. *The First Buddhist Women: Translation and Commentary on the Therigatha*. Berkeley: Parallax Press, 1991.

Murk-Jansen, Saskia. *Brides in the Desert: The Spirituality of the Beguines*. New York: Orbis Books, 1998.

Newman, Barbara, ed. *Voice of the Living Light: Hildegard of Bingen and Her World*. Berkeley: University of California Press, 1998.

Norris, Kathleen. *Acedia and Me: A Marriage, Monks, and A Writer's Life*. New York: Riverhead Books, 2008.

_____ *The Cloister Walk*. New York: Riverhead Books, 1997.

Nouwen, Henri J. M. *The Inner Voice of Love: A Journey Through Anguish to Freedom*. New York: Doubleday, 1996.

———— *The Genesee Diary: Report from a Trappist Monastery*. New York: Image Books, 1981.

———— *The Road to Daybreak: A Spiritual Journey*. New York: Image Books, 1990.

O'Donohue, John. *Anam Cara: A Book of Celtic Wisdom*. New York: HarperCollins, 1997.

———— *Eternal Echoes: Explaining our Yearning to Belong*. New York: HarperCollins, 1999.

———— *Beauty: The Invisible Embrace*. New York: HarperCollins, 2004.

———— *To Bless the Space Between Us: A Book of Blessings*. New York: HarperCollins, 2008.

O'Halloran, Maura. *Pure Heart, Enlightened Mind: The Zen Journals and Letters of Maura "Soshin" O'Halloran*. Boston: Charles E. Tuttle Co., Inc., 1994.

O'Murchu, Diarmuid. *Poverty, Celibacy and Obedience: A Radical Option for Life*. New York: A Crossroad Book, 1999.

———— *Quantum Theology: Spiritual Implications of the New Physics*. New York: A Crossroad Book, 1997.

———— *Reclaiming Spirituality*. New York: A Crossroad Book, 1997.

———— *Religious Life in the 21st Century: The Prospect of Refounding*. New York: Orbis Books, 2017.

Palden, Gyatso. *The Autobiography of a Tibetan Monk*. New York: Grove Press, 1997.

Panikkar, Raimon. *Blessed Simplicity: The Monk as Universal Archetype*. New York: The Seabury Press, 1982.

———— *Mysticism and Spirituality. Part One: Mysticism, Fullness of Life*. Edited by Milena Carrara Pavan. Maryknoll, NY: Orbis Books, 2014.

———— *Mysticism and Spirituality. Part Two: Spirituality: The Way of Life*. Edited by Milena Carrara Pavan. Maryknoll, NY: Orbis Books, 2014.

———— *The Intra-religious Dialogue*. New York: Paulist Press, 1999.

———— *The Unknown Christ of Hinduism*. Maryknoll, NY: Orbis, 1981.

Pennington, Basil M. *A Place Apart: Monastic Prayer and Practice for Everyone*. New York: Doubleday, 1983.

———— *Centering Prayer: Renewing an Ancient Christian Prayer Form*. New York: Image Books, 1980.

Perron, Gregory. "Dwelling in the Heart of the Desert: On the Dialogue of Religious Experience and Monastic Interreligious Dialogue." In *Dilatato Corde*, Vol. 2:1 (January–June, 2012); see www.dimmid.org/index.asp?Type=B_BASIC&SEC={89DEEC0D-25FA-49DE-BBA4-14B6F11C5886}.

———— "Entering the Heart of Our Heart: A Reflection on the Why of Catholic Monastic Celibacy." *Bulletin of Monastic Interreligious Dialogue*, No: 78 (October 2006); see www.monasticdialogue.org.

———— "The Significance of the Gethsemani Encounters and Monastic Interreligious Dialogue." *Bulletin of Monastic Interreligious Dialogue*, No: 78 (January 2007); see www.monasticdialogue.org.

Peters, Greg. *The Story of Monasticism: Retrieving an Ancient Tradition for Contemporary Spirituality*. Grand Rapids, MI: Baker Academic, 2015.

Poor Clares. *Rule and Testament of St. Clare and Constitutions of the Poor Clares*. Cincinnati, OH: Franciscan Institute Press, 1987.

Porter, Bill. *Road to Heaven: Encounters with Chinese Hermits*. San Francisco: Mercury House, 1993.

Prabhu, Joseph, ed. *The Intercultural Challenge of Raimon Panikkar*. Maryknoll, NY: Orbis Books, 1996.

Pramuk, Christopher. *Sophia: The Hidden Christ of Thomas Merton*. Collegeville, MN: Liturgical Press, 2009.

Raasch, Joanna, and Harriet Luckman. *Purity of Heart in Early Ascetic and Monastic Literature: Essays in Honor of Juana Raasch, O.S.B.* Collegeville, MN: Liturgical Press, 1999.

Regnault, Lucien. *The Day-to-Day Life of the Desert Fathers in Fourth-Century Egypt*. Petersham, MA: St. Bede's Publications, 1999.

Roberts, Elizabeth, and Elias Amidon. *Earth Prayers from Around the World: 365 Prayers, Poems and Invocations for Honoring the Earth*. San Francisco: Harper Collins, 1991.

_____ *Life Prayers from Around the World: 365 Prayers, Blessings and Affirmations to Celebrate the Human Journey*. San Francisco: Harper Collins, 1996.

Saint Isaac of Ninevah. *On Ascetical Life*. Crestwood, NY: St. Vladimir's Seminary Press, 1989.

Saint John of the Cross. *The Collected Works of St. John of the Cross*. Translated by Kieran Kavanaugh and Otilio Rodriguez. Washington, DC: ICS Publications, 1991.

_____ *Dark Night of the Soul*. Translated by Mirabai Starr. New York: Riverhead Books, 2002.

Saint Teresa of Avila. *Collected Works, 3 Vols.* Translated by Kieran Kavanaugh and Otilio Rodriguez. Washington, DC: ICS Publications, 1980.

_____. *The Interior Castle*. Translated by Mirabai Starr. New York: Riverhead Books, 2003.

_____ *The Interior Castle*. Translated by Benedictines of Stanbrook. Introduction by Beverly Lanzetta. New York: Barnes & Noble Books, 2005.

Sardello, Robert. *Silence: The Mystery of Wholeness*. Berkeley: North Atlantic Books, 2006.

_____ fer, Kurtis R. *Himalayan Hermitess: The Life of a Tibetan Buddhist Nun*. New York: Oxford University Press, 2004.

Schmitt, Miriam, and Linda Kulzer, eds. *Medieval Women Monastics: Wisdom's Wellsprings*. Collegeville, MN: Liturgical Press, 1996.

Schneiders, Sandra M. *Buying the Field: Catholic Religious Life in Mission to the World*. New York: Paulist Press, 2013.

_____ *Finding the Treasure: Locating Catholic Religious Life in a New Ecclesial and Cultural Context*. New York: Paulist Press, 2000.

_____ *Selling All: Commitment, Consecrated Celibacy, and Community in Catholic Religious Life.* New York: Paulist Press, 2001.

Sellner, Edward C. *Finding the Monk Within: Great Monastic Values for Today.* Mahwah, NJ: HiddenSpring, 2008.

Shapiro, Rabbi Rami H. *Minyan: Ten Principles for Living a Life of Integrity.* New York: Bell Tower, 1997.

Sinetar, Marsha. *Ordinary People as Monks and Mystics: Lifestyles for Self-discovery.* New York/Mahwah, NJ: Paulist Press, 1986.

Skudlarek, William. *Demythologizing Celibacy: Practical Wisdom from Christian and Buddhist Monasticism.* Collegeville, MN: Liturgical Press, 2008.

_____ ed. *God's Harp String: The Life and Legacy of the Benedictine Monk Swami Abhishiktananda.* Brooklyn: Lantern Books, 2010.

_____ and Bettina Baumer, eds. *Witness to the Fullness of the Light: The Vision and Relevance of the Benedictine Monk Swami Abhishiktananda.* Brooklyn: Lantern Books, 2011.

Soelle, Dorothee. *Suffering.* New York: Fortress Press, 1984.

_____ *The Silent Cry: Mysticism and Resistance.* New York: Fortress Press, 2001.

Stewart, Columba. *Cassian the Monk.* New York: Oxford University Press, 1998.

_____ "Evagrius Ponticus on Prayer and Anger." In *Religions of Late Antiquity in Practice*, Richard Valantasis, ed. Princeton: Princeton University Press, 2000: 65–83.

_____ *Prayer and Community: The Benedictine Tradition.* Maryknoll, NY: Orbis Books, 1998.

_____ "The Desert Fathers on Radical Self-Honesty." In *Vox Benedictina: A Journal of Translations from Monastic Sources.* Saskatoon, Canada: Peregrina Publishers, 8/1 (1991): 7–54.

_____ "The Origins and Fate of Monasticism." In *Spiritus: The Journal of Christian Spirituality.* Baltimore: The Johns Hopkins University Press, 10 (2010): 257–264.

Swan, Laura. *The Forgotten Desert Mothers: Sayings, Lives, and Stories of Early Christian Women.* New York: Paulist Press, 2001.

_____ *Engaging Benedict: What the Rule Can Teach Us Today.* Notre Dame, IN: Ave Maria Press, 2005.

_____ *The Wisdom of the Beguines: The Forgotten Story of a Medieval Women's Movement.* Katonah, NY: BlueBridge, 2014.

Sweeney, Jon M., ed. *What I Am Living For: Lessons from the Life of Thomas Merton.* Notre Dame, IN: Ave Maria Press, 2018.

Teasdale, Wayne. *A Monk in the World: Cultivating a Spiritual Life.* Novato, CA: New World Library, 2002.

_____ *The Mystic Heart: Discovering a Universal Spirituality in the World's Religions.* Novato, CA: New World Library, 1999.

_____ *Bede Griffiths: An Introduction to His Interspiritual Thought.* Woodstock, VT: Skylight Paths, 2003.

_____ *The Mystic Hours: A Daybook of Interspiritual Wisdom and Devotion.* Novato, CA: New World Library, 2004.

Thurman, Howard. *Jesus and the Disinherited.* Boston: Beacon Press, 1976.

_____ *Howard Thurman: Essential Writings.* Edited by Luther E. Smith, Jr. Maryknoll, NY: Orbis Books, 2006.

Tisdale, Sallie. *Women of the Way: Discovering 2,500 Years of Buddhist Wisdom.* San Francisco: HarperCollins, 2006.

Tiso, Francis. "Raimundo Panikkar on the Monk as 'Archetype,'" *Dilatato Corde* 1:2; July-December 2011 https://dimmid.org/index.asp?type=B_BASIC&SEC=%7B383FB138-0B7E-4BB4-9629-665574E6B40C%7D

Trapnell, Judson B. *Bede Griffiths: A Life in Dialogue.* Albany: State University of New York Press, 2001.

Trungpa, Chogyam. *Training the Mind and Cultivating Loving-Kindness.* Edited by Judith L. Lief. Boston: Shambhala, 1993.

_____ *Cutting Through Spiritual Materialism.* Boston: Shambhala, 1973.

Tzu, Lao. *Tao Te Ching: A New English Version.* Translated by Stephen Mitchell. New York: Harper Perennial Classics, 2006.

Underhill, Evelyn. *Mysticism: A Study in the Nature and Development of Man's Spiritual Consciousness.* New York: E. P. Dutton, 1961.

Valters, Paintner. *The Artist's Rule: Nurturing Your Creative Soul with Monastic Wisdom.* Notre Dame, IN: Ave Maria Press, 2011.

_____ *Desert Fathers and Mothers: Early Christian Wisdom Sayings—Annotated & Explained.* Woodstock, VT: Skylight Paths, 2012.

_____ *Illuminating the Way: Embracing the Wisdom of Monks and Mystics.* Notre Dame, IN: Ave Maria Press, 2016.

Waddell, Helen. *The Desert Fathers.* New York: Vintage Books, 1998.

Waddell, Norman, trans. *The Unborn: The Life and Teaching of Zen Master Bankei 1622-1693.* San Francisco: North Point Press, 1984.

Ward, Benedicta. *The Lives of the Desert Fathers.* Kalamazoo, MI: Cistercian Publications, 1981.

Weingast, Matty. *The First Free Women: Poems of the Early Buddhist Nuns.* Boulder: Shambhala, 2020.

Wilson-Hartgrove, Jonathan. *New Monasticism: What It Has To Say To Today's Church.* Grand Rapids, MI: Brazos Press, 2008.

Zangano, Phyllis. *Woman to Woman: An Anthology of Women's Spiritualities.* Collegeville, MN: The Liturgical Press, 1993.

Selection of Publishers of Primary Texts of Mystics and Monks

Cistercian Publications [Christian Monasticism]
https://cistercianpublications.org

Fons Vitae [Sufi Mysticism]
https://fonsvitae.com/

Liturgical Press [Christian Spirituality, Prayer, Monasticism]
https://litpress.org/

Paulist Press, The Classics of Western Spirituality [Jewish, Christian, Islamic]
https://www.paulistpress.com/Products/CategoryCenter/COWS/all-titles.
aspx?categoryId=COWS

Shambhala Publications [Buddhism]
https://www.shambhala.com/

SVS Press [Monastic Wisdom]
https://svspress.com/

Spiritual Direction Reading List

Addison, Howard. *Show Me Your Way: The Complete Guide to Exploring Interfaith Spiritual Direction.* Woodstock, VT: Skylight Paths Publishing, 2000.

Allen, Joseph J. *Inner Way: Toward a Rebirth of Eastern Christian Spiritual Direction.* Grand Rapids, MI: William B. Eerdmans, 1994.

Barry, William, and William J. Connelly. *The Practice of Spiritual Direction.* San Francisco: Harper, 1952.

Billy, Dennis. *With Open Heart: Spiritual Direction in the Alphonsian Tradition.* Liguori, MO: Liguori Press, 1989.

Burckhardt, Titus, trans. *Letters of a Sufi Master: The Shaykh ad-Darqawi.* Louisville, KY: Fons Vitae, 1998.

Byrne, Lavinia, ed. *Traditions of Spiritual Guidance.* Collegeville, MN: The Liturgical Press, 1990.

Casey, Michael. *Sacred Reading: The Ancient Art of Lectio Divina.* Liguori, MO: Liguori Publications, 1996.

Conroy, Maureen. *Looking Into the Well: Supervision of Spiritual Directors.* Chicago: Loyola University Press, 1995.

_____ . *The Discerning Heart: Discovering a Personal God.* Chicago: Loyola Press, 1993.

Dougherty, Mary Rose. *Group Spiritual Direction: Community for Discernment.* New York: Paulist Press, 1995.

Dyckman, Katherine Marie, and L. Patrick Carroll. *Inviting the Mystic, Supporting the Prophet: An Introduction to Spiritual Direction.* New York: Paulist Press, 1981.

Edwards, Tilden. *Spiritual Director, Spiritual Companion: Guide to Tending the Soul.* New York: Paulist Press, 2001.

Empereur, James L. *Spiritual Direction and the Gay Person.* New York: Continuum, 2002.

Fischer, Kathleen. *Women at the Well: Feminist Perspectives on Spiritual Direction*. New York: Paulist Press, 1988.

Fortunato, John E. *Embracing the Exile: Healing Journeys of Gay Christians*. New York: The Seabury Press, 1983.

Gandhi, Mohandas K. *Prayer*. Berkeley: Berkeley Hill Books, 2000.

Gratton, Carolyn. *The Art of Spiritual Guidance: A Contemporary Approach to Growing in the Spirit*. New York: Crossroad, 1992.

Hall, Thelma. *Too Deep for Words: Rediscovering Lectio Divina*. New York: Paulist Press, 1988.

Hart, Thomas N. *The Art of Christian Listening*. New York: Paulist Press, 1980.

_____. *Spiritual Quest: A Guide to the Changing Landscape*. New York: Paulist Press, 1999.

Holmes, Barbara A. *Joy Unspeakable: Contemplative Practices of the Black Church*. Minneapolis: Fortress Press, 2017.

Houdek, Frank J., S.J. *Guided by the Spirit: A Jesuit Perspective on Spiritual Direction*. Chicago: Loyola Press, 1996.

Lanzetta, Beverly. *Foundations in Spiritual Direction: Sharing the Sacred Across Traditions*. Sebastopol, CA: Blue Sapphire Books, 2018.

Larkin, Ernest O.Carm. *Silent Presence: Discernment as Process and Problem*. Denville, NJ: Dimension Books, 1981.

McGreal, Wilfred. *At the Fountain of Elijah: The Carmelite Tradition*. New York: Orbis Books, 1999.

Merton, Thomas. *Spiritual Direction & Meditation*. Collegeville, MN: The Liturgical Press, 1960.

Merton, Thomas, trans. *The Wisdom of the Desert: Sayings from the Desert Fathers of the Fourth Century*. New York: New Directions, 1970.

Nemeck, Francis Kelly, and Marie Theresa Coombs. *O Blessed Night: Recovering from Addiction, Codependency and Attachment based on the insights of St. John of the Cross and Pierre Teilhard de Chardin*. New York: Alba House, 1991.

_____. *The Way of Spiritual Direction*. Collegeville, MN: The Liturgical Press, 1985.

Neufelder, Jerome M., and Mary C. Coelho, eds. *Writings on Spiritual Direction By Great Christian Masters*. New York: The Seabury Press, 1982.

Ochs, Carol, and Kerry Olitzky. *Jewish Spiritual Guidance: Finding Our Way to God*. New York: Jossey-Bass, 1997.

Palmer, G.E.H., Philip Sherrard, and Kallistos Ware, eds. *Philokalia*, vols. 1-5. Boston: Farber & Farber, 1979.

Rakoczy, Susan, ed. *Common Journey, Different Paths: Spiritual Direction in Cross-Cultural Perspective*. Maryknoll, NY: Orbis Books, 1992.

Ranft, Patricia. *A Woman's Way: The Forgotten History of Women Spiritual Directors*. New York: Palgrave Macmillan, 2001. Ruffing, Janet. *Spiritual Direction: Beyond the Beginnings*. New York: Paulist Press, 2000.

Russell, Norma, and Benedicta Ward, trans. *The Lives of the Desert Fathers*. London: Mowbray and Kalamazoo, MI: Cistercian Publications, 1980.

Schachter-Shalomi, Zalman. *Spiritual Intimacy: A Study of Counseling in Hasidism.* Northvale, NJ: Jason Aronson, 1996.

Shapiro, Rami, and Aaron Shapiro. *Writing, the Sacred Art: Beyond the Page to Spiritual Practice.* Nashville, TN: Skylight Paths Publishing, 2012.

Swan, Laura. *The Forgotten Desert Mothers: Sayings, Lives, and Stories of Early Christian Women.* New York: Paulist Press, 2001.

Vest, Norene, ed. *Tending the Holy: Spiritual Direction Across Traditions.* New York: Morehouse Publishing, 2003.

Waddell, Helen, trans. *The Desert Fathers.* New York: Vintage Books, 1998.

Ward, Benedicta, trans. *The Desert Fathers: Sayings of the Early Christian Monks.* New York: Penguin Classics, 2003.

Welch, John O.Carm. *The Carmelite Way: An Ancient Path for Today's Pilgrim.* New York: Paulist Press, 1996.

Wilson, H.S., Judo Poerwowidagdo, Takatso Mofokeng, Robert Evans, and Alice Evans. *Pastoral Theology from a Global Perspective: A Case Method Approach.* New York: Orbis Books, 1996.

Acknowledgements

I AM GRATEFUL for the work of the scholars and monastics I have cited in this text and for the encouragement of the many participants and students who gather year after year to share in a journey of the heart.

I am thankful for the members of the Community of a New Monastic Way for their devotion to the divine journey and support of my work during more than forty years. Their commitment to a monastic life in the world and to transcribing my audio recordings has been singularly important in bringing this book to print.

I thank Laurie Gibson who has guided the text into its present form through her generous and always enlightening copy-editing of each chapter, and to Tessa Avila for the creation of the index.

For my friend and assistant, Vania Kent, who has done so much to help this book be birthed—creating and maintaining my two websites, posting weekly meditations, as well as transcribing audio talks and editing text—I am filled with gratitude.

I am forever indebted to my friend and fellow monk in the world, Nelson Kane, who has patiently guided this book into print. Without his steady wisdom, none of my writings would be published! A gifted graphic designer, it is Nelson's exceptional appreciation of the relationship between visual text and spiritual meaning that enriches the book's content and fosters a contemplative reading environment.

And, as always, I am eternally grateful for my family of children and grandchildren who are the source of unending love, strength, and support.

Index

A

abbas and *ammas* (desert fathers and mothers), 132–134

Abulafia, Abraham, 149

addiction, as obstacle to spiritual practice, 186–187

alchemy, as metaphor for integration of self and divine, 224–226

Allen, Joseph J., 130

al-Shushtari, Abu al-Hasan, 174

B

Baker, Dom Augustine, 131

Bankei (Zen Master)

    The Unborn, 170–171

"bearing," meditations on, 63–66

beliefs and values, reorienting, 91–93

Ber, Issachar of Zlotshov, 17

Bhagavad Gita, 25–26

Birnbaum, Raoul, *The Healing Buddha*, 226–227

Black Elk, 19

body (human)

    embodiment in spiritual practice, 320–321

    mystical effects on, 169–170

    spiritual energy and, 167–172

Book of Her Life, The (Teresa of Avila), 174–175, 215

Buddha, Gautama

    enlightenment of, 194–195

    on healing, 226–227

Buddhism

Rule of Benedict
  on complaining, 151
  on humility, 16
  monk's vow of *conversatio morum*, 89
Rule of Life (code of conduct), 285–287
rules of life in monastic formation, 106–107
Rumi, Jalal al-Din
  on the alchemy of healing, 224
  "Attributes of Acts," 33–34
  "Naughting the Self," 26–28

S
samadhi
  defined, 54
  as the focus of spiritual guidance, 127
  types of, 54–55
Saraswati, Swami Gyanbhikshu, 278
Saraswati, Swami Satyananda
  on *diksha*, 273–275
Saraswati, Swami Sivananda, 277–278
satyagraha ("soul-force"), 43
Sayings of the Desert Fathers, 137
scheduling (monastic), 237–245
Schumacher, Sr. Theresa, on vows, 255–261
Scripta Leonis, Rufini et Angeli, 224–225
senses, spiritual, 301–302
Sermon on the Mount (Jesus), 65
  nonviolence and, 41–42
Seven Grandfather Teachings (Potawatomi Nation), 18
sexuality/celibacy
  Rilke on, 118
  spiritual exercises, 318–319
simplicity
  of emotion, 53–58
  of life, 58–59
  meditations on, 60–62
Sirach 3:17-24, 19–20
Sivaraman, Krishna, 130
skandhas (aggregates of personality), 54
social injustice, as wound of the soul, 211–212
solitude, as relationship practice in monastic life, 113–115
Solovyov, Vladimir, 74
Soto Zen Master Dogan, 141
soul

turning one's life around. *see* conversion of life

U

Unborn: The Life and Teachings of Zen Master Bankei, The, 171

V

via feminina, 73–79
  defined, 3
  spiritual practices, 317
Vimalakirti, on healing, 227
vows in monastic formation, 106–107
  example ceremony for, 266–271
  preparing for, 262–271
  Sr. Theresa Schumacher on, 255–261

W

Ware, Kallistos, 190
Whirling Dervishes (Sufism), 149
world, divinity of, 68–69
wound of divine love, 213–214
  four effects, 216–218
wounds of the soul, 206–220
  divine love, 213–214
  personal injury, 210
  social injury, 211
  social injustice, 211–212
writing
  during conversion of life, 101–102
  exercise, 330–331

Y

Yakut, shamanic journey of, 223–224
Yoga sutras (Patanjali), 54
  Swami Prabhavananda on, 54–55
Yong, Shao, 146

Z

Zen Masters
  Bankei, 170–171
  Hakuin Ekaku, 141–142, 172
Zhuang Zhou, 61–62
Zhuangzi, The, 149
Zlotshov, Issachar Ber of, 17

Books by Beverly Lanzetta

The Monk Within:
Embracing a Sacred Way of Life
ISBN 978-0-9840616-5-5

Foundations in Spiritual Direction:
Sharing the Sacred Across Traditions
ISBN 978-0-9840616-0-0

Path of the Heart:
A Spiritual Guide to Divine Union
ISBN 978-0-9840616-2-4

Nine Jewels of Night:
One Soul's Journey into God
ISBN 978-0-9840616-1-7

Emerging Heart:
Global Spirituality and the Sacred
ISBN 978-0-8006-3893-1

40 Day Journey with Joan Chittister
ISBN 978-0-8066-8031-6

Radical Wisdom:
A Feminist Mystical Theology
ISBN 0-8006-3698-8

The Other Side of Nothingness:
Toward a Theology of Radical Openness
ISBN 0-7914-4950-5

BEVERLY LANZETTA, Ph.D. is a theologian, spiritual teacher, and the author of many groundbreaking books on emerging global spirituality and new monasticism, including *The Monk Within: Embracing a Sacred Way of Life*, *Radical Wisdom: A Feminist Mystical Theology*, *Emerging Heart: Global Spirituality And the Sacred*, and *Nine Jewels of Night: One Soul's Journey into God*. Dedicated to a vision of theological openness and spiritual nonviolence, her work has won praise for its wisdom, eloquence, and mystical insight and is considered to be a major contribution to what theologian Ursula King called "a feminine mystical way for the 21st century". Beverly has taught theology at Villanova University, Prescott College, and Grinnell College and has started a number of religious and monastic initiatives including the Desert Interfaith Church, Interfaith Theological Seminary, Hesychia School of Spiritual Direction, and the Community of a New Monastic Way. She is a much-sought-after mentor for the new generation, including the "spiritual but not religious" and new monastics alike, as she brings with her forty years of experience as a guide to answering the universal call to contemplation.